MW00633125

SAP PRESS e-books

Print or e-book, Kindle or iPad, workplace or airplane: Choose where and how to read your SAP PRESS books! You can now get all our titles as e-books, too:

- By download and online access
- For all popular devices
- And, of course, DRM-free

Convinced? Then go to www.sap-press.com and get your e-book today.

SAP° Analytics Cloud: Predictive Analytics

PRESS

SAP PRESS is a joint initiative of SAP and Rheinwerk Publishing. The know-how offered by SAP specialists combined with the expertise of Rheinwerk Publishing offers the reader expert books in the field. SAP PRESS features first-hand information and expert advice, and provides useful skills for professional decision-making.

SAP PRESS offers a variety of books on technical and business-related topics for the SAP user. For further information, please visit our website: *www.sap-press.com*.

Abassin Sidiq
SAP Analytics Cloud (3rd Edition)
2024, 422 pages, hardcover and e-book
www.sap-press.com/5753

Bertram, Dannenhauer, Holzapfel, Loop, Range
SAP Analytics Cloud Performance Optimization Guide
2023, 344 pages, hardcover and e-book
www.sap-press.com/5669

Das, Berner, Shahani, Harish
SAP Analytics Cloud: Financial Planning and Analysis
2022, 468 pages, hardcover and e-book
www.sap-press.com/5486

Bertram, Charlton, Hollender, Holzapfel, Licht, Paduraru
Designing Dashboards with SAP Analytics Cloud
2021, 344 pages, hardcover and e-book
www.sap-press.com/5235

Butsmann, Fleckenstein, Kundu
SAP S/4HANA Embedded Analytics: The Comprehensive Guide (2nd Edition)
2021, 432 pages, hardcover and e-book
www.sap-press.com/5226

Antoine Chabert, David Serre

SAP® Analytics Cloud: Predictive Analytics

Rheinwerk
Publishing

Editor Megan Fuerst
Acquisitions Editor Hareem Shafi
Copyeditor Julie McNamee
Cover Design Graham Geary
Photo Credit Shutterstock.com: 114374821/© ESB Professional
Layout Design Vera Brauner
Production Kyrsten Coleman
Typesetting SatzPro, Germany
Printed and bound in the United States of America, on paper from sustainable sources

ISBN 978-1-4932-2478-4

© 2024 by Rheinwerk Publishing, Inc., Boston (MA)
1st edition 2024

Library of Congress Cataloging-in-Publication Control Data
Names: Chabert, Antoine, author. | Serre, David, author.
Title: SAP analytics cloud : predictive analytics / by Antoine Chabert and
    David Serre.
Description: 1st edition. | Bonn ; Boston : Rheinwerk Publishing, [2024] |
    Includes index.
Identifiers: LCCN 2024001796 | ISBN 9781493224784 (hardcover) | ISBN
    9781493224791 (ebook)
Subjects: LCSH: SAP ERP. | SAP cloud platform. | Data mining. | Predictive
    analytics. | Forecasting--Data processing. | Strategic planning.
Classification: LCC QA76.9.D343 C4449 2024 | DDC
    004.67/82--dc23/eng/20240207
LC record available at https://lccn.loc.gov/2024001796

All rights reserved. Neither this publication nor any part of it may be copied or reproduced in any form or by any means or translated into another language, without the prior consent of Rheinwerk Publishing, 2 Heritage Drive, Suite 305, Quincy, MA 02171.

Rheinwerk Publishing makes no warranties or representations with respect to the content hereof and specifically disclaims any implied warranties of merchantability or fitness for any particular purpose. Rheinwerk Publishing assumes no responsibility for any errors that may appear in this publication.

"Rheinwerk Publishing" and the Rheinwerk Publishing logo are registered trademarks of Rheinwerk Verlag GmbH, Bonn, Germany. SAP PRESS is an imprint of Rheinwerk Verlag GmbH and Rheinwerk Publishing, Inc.

All of the screenshots and graphics reproduced in this book are subject to copyright © SAP SE, Dietmar-Hopp-Allee 16, 69190 Walldorf, Germany.

SAP, ABAP, ASAP, Concur Hipmunk, Duet, Duet Enterprise, Expenselt, SAP ActiveAttention, SAP Adaptive Server Enterprise, SAP Advantage Database Server, SAP ArchiveLink, SAP Ariba, SAP Business ByDesign, SAP Business Explorer (SAP BEx), SAP BusinessObjects, SAP BusinessObjects Explorer, SAP BusinessObjects Web Intelligence, SAP Business One, SAP Business Workflow, SAP BW/4HANA, SAP C/4HANA, SAP Concur, SAP Crystal Reports, SAP EarlyWatch, SAP Fieldglass, SAP Fiori, SAP Global Trade Services (SAP GTS), SAP GoingLive, SAP HANA, SAP Jam, SAP Leonardo, SAP Lumira, SAP MaxDB, SAP NetWeaver, SAP PartnerEdge, SAPPHIRE NOW, SAP PowerBuilder, SAP PowerDesigner, SAP R/2, SAP R/3, SAP Replication Server, SAP Roambi, SAP S/4HANA, SAP S/4HANA Cloud, SAP SQL Anywhere, SAP Strategic Enterprise Management (SAP SEM), SAP SuccessFactors, SAP Vora, TripIt, and Qualtrics are registered or unregistered trademarks of SAP SE, Walldorf, Germany.

All other products mentioned in this book are registered or unregistered trademarks of their respective companies.

Contents at a Glance

Contents

7 Time Series Forecasting Models Using Datasets 143

8 Best Practices and Tips for Time Series Forecasting Models 169

9 The Data Science behind Time Series Forecasting Models

12   Creating Regression Insights to Enrich Stories   261

Preface

Predictive analytics is a branch of data analytics that uses historical data to make predictions about future outcomes. It uses various statistical methods and machine learning algorithms to empower organizations to anticipate trends, identify patterns, and make accurate forecasts.

Organizations now have access to vast amounts of data, and predictive analytics helps them make sense of this data to inform strategic decisions. By analyzing historical data, companies can predict future trends, customer behaviors, market dynamics, and potential risks. Businesses that effectively leverage predictive analytics can gain a competitive edge by anticipating customer needs, optimizing operations, and identifying new market opportunities before their competitors do.

SAP Analytics Cloud blends predictive analytics with business intelligence and enterprise planning capabilities to help you get predictions where you need them and make better business decisions.

Objective of This Book

This comprehensive guide enables you to implement predictive projects in SAP Analytics Cloud. It's designed as a reference book for users of all levels who want to enhance their skills and understanding—from beginners to advanced users.

Throughout each section, we'll illustrate the predictive concepts using real-world examples. We'll also provide you with tips and tricks so that you can get the most out of SAP Analytics Cloud predictive capabilities.

SAP Analytics Cloud is a cloud application evolving at a fast pace. It's not possible to be exhaustive and final in this book on the predictive capabilities of SAP Analytics Cloud. Our main goal is that you understand the predictive logic of the application and that you become familiar with the key features so you can autonomously discover more advanced features. We hope that when you're done reading, you'll have gained sufficient skills and knowledge to successfully implement your predictive projects in SAP Analytics Cloud.

> **An Important Note on Terminology**
>
> We'll follow these naming conventions throughout the book:
>
> - *Smart predict* relates to the overall capabilities offered by predictive scenarios in SAP Analytics Cloud, regardless of the data context.

- *Predictive scenarios* are the main objects used to create predictive models and deliver predictions. There are three distinct types of predictive scenarios: time series forecasting, classification, and regression.
- *Predictive planning* specifically refers to the intersection of predictive analytics and enterprise planning capabilities. Only time series forecasting scenarios are integrated with enterprise planning. Predictive planning enables users to run time series forecasting scenarios in the context of planning models.

Target Audience

This book is targeted toward anyone interested in implementing predictive projects in SAP Analytics Cloud. However, in some sections, we'll assume that you're familiar with basic SAP Analytics Cloud concepts. Having an elementary understanding of SAP Analytics Cloud data models and stories, while not strictly necessary, will help you make the best use of this book. Data models and stories are introduced in Chapter 2.

Advanced mathematical or statistical skills aren't required to read this book. Some chapters explain the data science concepts powering the different types of predictive models. However, we made our best effort to use mathematical notations sparingly and always to formalize concepts that are first explained with understandable language. If you're versed in data science, you can read these chapters to learn how smart predict techniques work.

This book has been designed with different readers in mind:

- **Financial planners**
  Financial planners can learn how to generate and automate large scale predictive forecasts.
- **Data analysts**
  Data analysts can learn how to enhance their stories with predictions, without data science or advanced mathematical knowledge.
- **Data scientists**
  Data scientists can understand how to leverage the automated predictive capabilities of SAP Analytics Cloud to spend less time on low added-value tasks. Data scientists can also use this book to relate the automated smart predict approach to the predictive techniques they know.

Structure of This Book

This book is divided into 13 chapters grouped into 3 parts. We'll provide an overview of each in the following sections.

Part I: Getting Started

In Part I, you'll learn fundamental information about predictive analytics in general and everything you need to know to start using the predictive features of SAP Analytics Cloud. Here is an overview of the key topics, organized by chapter:

- **Chapter 1**
  We'll introduce predictive analytics, explain its importance and how it's integrated into SAP Analytics Cloud.

- **Chapter 2**
  We'll introduce the different types of SAP Analytics Cloud objects, focusing on the predictive scenario, which is the object that makes it possible to create predictions in SAP Analytics Cloud.

- **Chapter 3**
  We'll explain how to make a predictive project successful, and we'll describe the typical stakeholders involved in such a project.

Part II: Time Series Forecasting Models

In Part II, you'll learn everything you need to know to create and use time series forecasting models. Here is an overview of the key topics, organized by chapter:

- **Chapter 4**
  We'll introduce the fundamental time series forecasting concepts and how they surface in SAP Analytics Cloud.

- **Chapter 5**
  You'll follow a step-by-step workflow explaining how to include predictive forecasts into the enterprise planning process.

- **Chapter 6**
  You'll learn how to automate the delivery of predictive forecasts in the context of your planning process.

- **Chapter 7**
  You'll follow a step-by-step workflow that shows how to create predictive forecasts on top of datasets.

- **Chapter 8**
  You'll discover best practices, hints, and tips to improve your time series forecasting models and avoid common pitfalls.

- **Chapter 9**
  We'll unveil the automated predictive techniques used to create time series forecasting models.

Part III: Classification Models and Regression Models

In Part III, you'll learn everything you need to know to create and use classification and regression models in SAP Analytics Cloud. Here is an overview of the key topics, organized by chapter:

- **Chapter 10**
  We'll introduce the fundamental classification and regression concepts and how they surface in SAP Analytics Cloud.

- **Chapter 11**
  You'll follow a step-by-step workflow showing how to train, evaluate, improve, and finally use a classification model to enrich a story with predictions.

- **Chapter 12**
  You'll follow a step-by-step workflow showing how to train, evaluate, improve, and finally use a regression model to enrich a story with predictions.

- **Chapter 13**
  We'll unveil the automated predictive techniques used to generate classification and regression models.

Acknowledgments

We would like to extend our individual thanks to those who made this book possible.

I would like to thank my marvelous family: my wife Nadège and my three daughters Salomé, Anatolie, and Lila, who are the fireflies that illuminate my life. Everything is possible! I am so grateful to my parents Anne and Guy, and to my sister Noémie. This book would not have been possible without my partner in crime, David Serre, who paved the way in the early days of the writing process; the continuous support of my manager, Eric Fenollosa; and the trust of my predictive mentor, Erik Marcade; in addition to so many SAP colleagues; in particular, kudos to the entire predictive product development team led by Glen Barton, who brought the predictive scenarios to life and continues to develop them—you know who you are.

—*Antoine Chabert*

I would like to express my gratitude to those who have supported me throughout the journey of writing this book. First and foremost, I would like to thank my wife, whose patience and support were essential to this project. Many thanks go to my manager, Glen Barton, whose flexibility and encouragement allowed me to balance my professional responsibilities with the demands of authoring a book. This endeavor would have been significantly more difficult without such an accommodating work environment. I must also acknowledge my colleague, Antoine Chabert, with whom I shared the task of writing this book. His invaluable feedback has been pivotal in bringing this work to fruition. Lastly, I must thank my colleagues of the predictive development team, who patiently answered my numerous questions about the internal mechanics of smart predict. I hope this book honors their dedication to predictive excellence.

—David Serre

Finally, a note of special thanks from both of us. We would like to thank the team at SAP PRESS, especially our book project manager, Megan Fuerst, for guiding us through deadlines and shaping the book to its current form, and to Hareem Shafi for the original book idea.

Conclusion

This book aims to provide you with concrete information so that you can be confident using the SAP Analytics Cloud predictive capabilities. We've tried to make this book as accessible and comprehensive as possible, ensuring you get the best out of the predictive capabilities of SAP Analytics Cloud. Whether you're a first-time user or an experienced enthusiast, we made sure that you'll be able to follow along and gain a deeper understanding. Now, let's dive in.

Happy reading!

PART I

Getting Started

Chapter 1

An Introduction to Predictive Analytics in SAP Analytics Cloud

Let's start with the basics: What is predictive analytics? Where does it come into play in SAP Analytics Cloud, and what role can it serve for your organization?

This chapter will introduce you to predictive analytics and why predictive analytics capabilities have been included in SAP Analytics Cloud. We'll first explain the importance of considering predictive analytics in your analytical projects in Section 1.1. In Section 1.2, we'll describe how predictive analytics is currently integrated in SAP Analytics Cloud and the possibilities this integration brings. We'll finish by mentioning typical customer use cases in Section 1.3 to further inspire you for your own projects.

1.1 The Importance of Predictive Analytics

Our first section will briefly introduce predictive analytics and the importance of considering it in your analytics projects. The following subsections will first concentrate on a brief history of predictive analytics, and then we'll concentrate on specific business use.

1.1.1 A Brief History of Predictive Analytics

Predictive analytics is part of the broader field of artificial intelligence (AI) and is a subset of machine learning, as represented in Figure 1.1. Despite the ongoing AI hype, predictive analytics isn't new. Throughout history, human beings have always tried to project possible or plausible futures to better control their destiny. No wonder a famous modern software company is called Oracle.

One of the first modern uses of predictive analytics dates from 1689. Predictive analytics was then used by the British insurance and reinsurance market Lloyd's to underwrite insurance for sea voyages. Using data, the company would accept the risk of sea trips in return for a premium price. Lloyd's used past trip datasets to evaluate the risk of these trips and predict liability patterns. Lloyd's continues to use predictive models nowadays, and the idea has become general practice in the insurance industry.

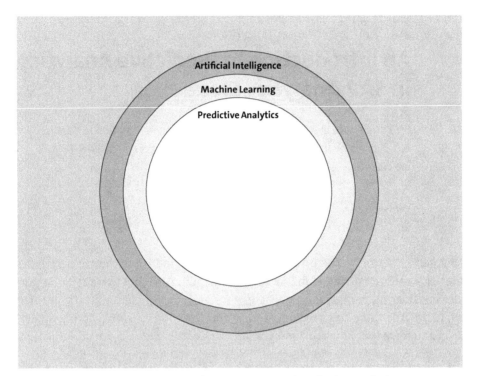

Figure 1.1 Artificial Intelligence, Machine Learning, and Predictive Analytics

Fast-forward to the recent past decades where we've experienced an exponential development of AI technologies. In 2024, databases, predictive algorithms, and analytics are an integral part of our technological environment as company workers and information consumers. Without us even noticing, we're surrounded by predictive analytics, whether this relates to the next Netflix movie we might want to watch, the forecast of a company stock, or the potential winner of the next sports match.

Whether we like it or not, predictive analytics has now become infused in our day-to-day lives. It's therefore key that we can gain knowledge about the concepts and ideas supporting it. Or to reword Pericles a bit, just because you don't take an interest in predictive analytics doesn't mean that predictive analytics won't take an interest in you.

1.1.2   The Role of Predictive Analytics in Business

Predictive analytics helps uncover relationships and patterns within large volumes of data that can be used to predict future behaviors and events. Unlike traditional analytics, predictive analytics is forward-looking, using past events to anticipate the future.

Through the evolution of technology and the maturation of analytical practices, many organizations crossed the chasm and moved from the classical yet important questions of "What happened?" and "Why did it happen?" to the more future-looking question of "What will happen?" (see Figure 1.2).

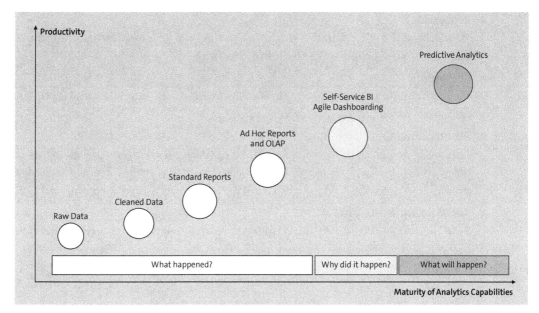

Figure 1.2 Analytics Capabilities and Productivity Gains

If we consider recent analytic revolutions, we evolved from a world where standard reporting set up by information technology (IT) was the de facto corporate view of the reality, to the self-service analytics revolution where every company worker can explore corporate data on their own.

Traditional analytics are nicely complemented by the ability to make use of past data to project future events, values, or forecasts. Every time we ask ourselves "What will happen," predictive analytics is there to help. Predictions are of premium value, as they make it possible to project the future course of business and give the possibility to end users to influence this probable future.

Eric Siegel, a recognized predictive expert, titled one of his books *Predictive Analytics: The Power to Predict Who Will Click, Buy, Lie, or Die*. This reflects the importance and the extent of insights that predictive analytics can provide us with.

There are six major types of techniques that we can relate to predictive analytics (clustering and social network analysis can also be considered descriptive analytics). Each technique helps in the context of different business use cases:

- **Time series forecasting**
  This technique can help us forecast the future evolution of a given indicator, for example: What will the evolution of SAP stock look like in the coming 10 days?
- **Classification**
  This technique can help predict the probability of future events, for example: What is the probability that the San Antonio Spurs will win the next basketball game?

- **Regression**
  This technique can help predict the future values for a given indicator, for example: What is the price I could sell a secondhand car for?

- **Clustering**
  This technique can help us group similar observations, for example: Can I group my customers based on their commercial value?

- **Recommendation**
  This technique provides us with the ability to recommend interesting elements or products to customers, for example: If you liked reading this book, seeing this movie, or listening to this song, you might also like the next element we recommend.

- **Social network analysis**
  This technique consists of analyzing graphs and relationships across different objects from which we can derive target actions, for example: Customers of a telecommunications company are related by the ways they call each other.

1.2 Predictive Analytics in SAP Analytics Cloud

In this section, we'll cover the specific integration of predictive analytics in SAP Analytics Cloud. You'll first learn more on the history of predictive analytics integration in SAP Analytics Cloud. We'll also explain how business intelligence, enterprise planning, and predictive analytics complement each other.

1.2.1 A Brief History of Predictive Analytics in SAP Analytics Cloud

SAP Analytics Cloud is a software as a service (SaaS) product combining business intelligence and enterprise planning capabilities. With SAP Analytics Cloud, you can bring together analytics and planning with unique integration to SAP applications and smooth access to heterogeneous data sources. Here are the major milestones that led to the integration of predictive analytics in SAP Analytics Cloud:

- **2013**
  SAP acquires KXEN. KXEN is a French-American software company that developed expertise in automated predictive analytics for 15 years prior to the SAP acquisition. The integration of the KXEN technology into the SAP product portfolio leads to the creation of the on-premise product SAP Predictive Analytics and the Automated Predictive Library (APL) as part of SAP HANA. Both SAP Predictive Analytics and APL are still supported by SAP as of 2024.

- **2015**
  SAP Analytics Cloud is brought to the market for the first time. SAP Analytics Cloud is an SaaS product combining business intelligence and enterprise planning capabilities.

- **2018**

  Smart predict capabilities are delivered as part of SAP Analytics Cloud. From day one, smart predict includes three major types of predictive techniques: time series forecasting, classification, and regression. Smart predict is initially focused on augmenting business intelligence dashboards with predictions. Predictive analytics and enterprise planning capabilities aren't strongly connected at the time.

- **2020**

  Predictive planning is delivered as part of SAP Analytics Cloud. Predictive planning puts time series forecasting into the hands of enterprise planners and is tightly integrated with planning models.

- **2024**

  Hundreds of customers and partners are taking advantage of smart predict capabilities to augment their business intelligence and enterprise planning use cases with predictions.

1.2.2   Business Intelligence, Enterprise Planning, and Augmented Analytics

Now that we understand the background, let's explore how the three major pillars of modern analytics platforms—business intelligence, enterprise planning, and augmented analytics—complement each other. To begin, here's a quick definition of each:

- **Business intelligence**

  This provides the ability to explore data, create powerful dashboards (known as stories in SAP Analytics Cloud), and perform enterprise reporting.

- **Enterprise planning**

  This provides planners with the ability to plan and forecast, collaborate, follow specific workflows, and use predictive forecasting to support human-based forecasting activities.

- **Augmented analytics**

  This is the magic pillar that makes business intelligence and enterprise planning conversational and smarter, as well as enabling predictions to be integrated in the context of business intelligence and enterprise planning workflows.

Augmented Analytics and Predictive Analytics

Augmented analytics includes several capabilities, including conversational, automated, and predictive analytics. Conversational analytics helps generate ad hoc analytics while having a conversation in natural language with the product. Conversational analytics includes capabilities such as the just ask feature. Automated analytics is generated automatically to help the end user. Automated analytics includes capabilities such as smart insights and smart discovery. In this book, we're focused strictly on predictive analytics capabilities.

SAP Analytics Cloud uniquely combines and provides these three pillars together as you can see in Figure 1.3. The interactions between these pillars create mutual benefits when augmenting business intelligence and enterprise planning with predictions:

- Business intelligence stories aren't exclusively focused on past data review and analysis. They can combine past-data and forward-looking predictions.
- Enterprise planning benefits from predictive forecasts being delivered directly in the context of planning processes. Planners can base their forecasting activities on data-driven forecasts.
- Predictive analytics also benefit from the story visualization layer as predictions are much simpler to understand when they are provided in a visual format in the preferred interaction area.

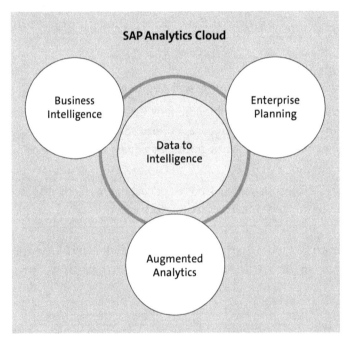

Figure 1.3 The Three Pillars of SAP Analytics Cloud

Having all these analytical pillars as part of a single analytics offering is what you'd legitimately expect. However, not all analytics products on the market live up to such expectations. They might offer business intelligence capabilities, enterprise planning capabilities, or predictive analytics capabilities but not necessarily all these capabilities bundled together.

Figure 1.4 provides an overview of the capabilities within these analytical pillars, placing our subject of focus, predictive analytics, in the context of the broader SAP Analytics Cloud feature set.

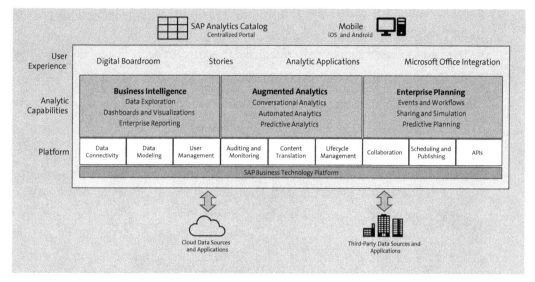

Figure 1.4 SAP Analytics Cloud Capabilities

To close this section, let's consider the benefits that predictive analytics brings to business intelligence and enterprise planning scenarios.

Combine Business Intelligence and Predictive Analytics

The first use case for which smart predict was initially created consists of delivering predictions to business users in the context of their dashboards. Business users can then determine what happened, why it happened, and what will happen in a single place to make business decisions. More specifically, it's possible to have access to probabilities of specific events, predicted values, or predictive forecasts combined with actual data. In other words, business intelligence gets enhanced to augmented business intelligence thanks to the addition of predictive analytics to expand the ways that business users can be answered.

Combine Enterprise Planning and Predictive Analytics

The addition of predictive forecasting to enterprise planning makes it possible to transform traditional planning activities into a data-driven and forward-looking process, that is, augmented planning.

Let's take the example of a company forecasting expenses regularly to ensure that they stay within budget. This company will have to carry the following activities to refresh the forecast:

- New actual expenses will need to be considered.
- Data must be prepared accordingly.
- Predictive forecasts will need to be refreshed.

- Stories will help visualize the data, whether it's the actuals, the budget, the plan, or the predictive forecasts.
- The new forecast will need to be established and finalized.
- All of this is done in a collaborative manner.

The high-level planning process is represented in Figure 1.5. Predictive analytics can be fully integrated as part of the planning process.

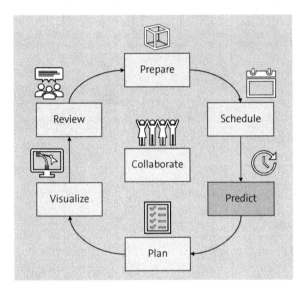

Figure 1.5 Augmented Planning Process

1.3   Customer Use Cases

In the next section, we'll discuss various use cases in which customers are applying predictive analytics to solve real-world problems. We'll start with time series forecasting and then move on to classification and regression.

1.3.1   Time Series Forecasting

There is a great diversity of use cases when it comes to time series forecasting. Whether you're willing to forecast expenses, sales, revenue, or workforce evolution, you'll be able to take advantage of the out-of-the-box time series forecasting capabilities. On top of the few examples we'll be highlighting next, consider that SAP Analytics Cloud is a generic analytics tool and flexible enough to be applied to additional time series forecasting use cases. If you have access to a long enough data history and want to make your forecasting more accurate, you'll be able to take advantage of predictive planning.

We'll review a few use cases in the following sections. For detailed information on time series forecasting, see Part II.

Expense Forecasting

Expense forecasting is one of the low-hanging fruits you can think of when using predictive planning. In most cases, expenses tend to steadily evolve over time as companies develop and grow. This makes the expense forecasting activity a great fit for predictive planning. The assumption that expenses will evolve in a comparable way in the future, like they have been doing in the past, holds true here. One notable exception was the recent COVID-19 pandemic and its effect on reducing global business travel expenses. Companies had to adapt their forecasting activities to the new normal of travel expenses.

There are public, documented examples of companies using the predictive planning capabilities in the context of expense forecasting scenarios:

- F. Hoffmann-La Roche AG (also known as Roche) is a major Swiss pharmaceutical company. Leveraging the predictive planning capabilities, Roche has streamlined its financial forecast process to generate a $4.2 billion forecast. It now takes Roche just two hours instead of several weeks to generate a new financial forecast. Roche successfully shifted the focus of their R&D finance organization from traditional bottom-up financial forecasting to an automated predictive forecasting approach by automating 14,000 out of 20,000 forecast data entry points. You can read more here: *http://s-prs.co/v577100*.

- SAP Corporate Controlling governs SAP's financial activities. Twice every quarter, the controlling team handles a total year projection of the profit and loss (P&L) statement of the entire SAP Group to provide an accurate outlook and to help the company strategize confidentially into the future. SAP Corporate Controlling uses predictive planning capabilities to create an accurate total year projection of the P&L statement. The controlling team uses predictive analytics through time series forecasting scenarios to look at historical patterns in data and project into the future. You can read more here: *http://s-prs.co/v577101*.

Revenue, Sales, and Demand Planning

When we think of company financials, expenses and revenues are two sides of the same coin as part of P&L. It's only logical that some popular use cases relate to revenue and sales forecasting.

In the context of certain businesses, revenue or sales can be harder to predict compared to expenses. The reason for this lies in the possible irregularities that might occur in the evolution of revenue or sales over time. It requires thorough data analysis to generate accurate predictive forecasts. That said, it's worth it for you to use smart predict in such cases.

When it specifically comes to sales planning (also called demand planning), the data volumes that are in play can be huge. Imagine a major retailer having to forecast product demand across many product references and supermarkets. There are some limits to implementing such massive time series forecasting with smart predict that we'll detail in the next chapters. Other products in the SAP portfolio can help with such massive time series forecasting use cases, for instance SAP HANA in general or SAP Integrated Business Planning for Supply Chain (SAP IBP) for sales and operations planning (S&OP) use cases.

Following are a couple of examples:

- A major US-based company is using the predictive planning capabilities to forecast the evolution of revenue across its major product divisions. The work traditionally handled by planners is now eased and accelerated through predictive planning. The data-driven forecasting approach has already proven more accurate compared to human-based forecasting. Both activities nicely complement each other to lead to a better visibility of future revenue evolution.

- Similarly, a South African company is using predictive planning to forecast the income they are likely to receive from their customers monthly. The number of divisions and the number of income line items they are dealing with would make it challenging to plan if the planning activities weren't supported by predictive planning.

Workforce Planning

The two use cases we just mentioned are very financial by nature. Human resources (HR) can also benefit from the use of time series forecasting in the context of workforce planning. For instance, you might be asking yourself about the future evolution of your overall workforce and want to project the evolution of employee numbers. Predictive planning can help you do this. As another example, employees are constantly raising questions to HR. To cope with the flow of incoming questions, it's important to ensure the right number of HR employees are being staffed to answer them.

Following are a couple examples:

- A major European telecommunications company wants to define a strategic plan to evolve their workforce in the coming years. They used predictive planning to project the evolution of the number of employees per business division in upcoming years, compare this to their strategic needs, and make sure they measure the employees they will need to hire to cope with their strategic direction.

- SAP internally developed an application to forecast the number of HR inquiries that are raised by employees over several topics (vacation, pay, etc.). Predictive planning helps forecast the volume of daily incoming tickets to ensure that HR resources are staffed accordingly to cope with the incoming questions.

Liquidity Planning

Liquidity planning (also known as cash flow forecasting) is another significant use case that predictive planning can support. Companies need reliable liquidity planning, as they want to avoid liquidity bottlenecks and insolvency. Predictive planning can help forecast the incoming and outgoing cash flows and help liquidity planners with a data-driven approach to cash flow forecasting. SAP Analytics Cloud includes predefined business content that presents how predictive planning can be integrated in an end-to-end liquidity planning approach. You can refer to "Liquidity Planning for SAP S/4HANA Cloud (SAP Best Practices)" here: *http://s-prs.co/v577102*.

The following example applies: Especially during the COVID-19 pandemic but also since then due to world geopolitical uncertainties, cash flow is a big focus topic for companies across the world. Typically, liquidity planners want to ensure that companies aren't falling short of cash, so that they can accomplish their development projects. We've already been in touch with several companies, US-based and Europe-based, looking for a more data-driven way to approach cash forecasting activities.

1.3.2   Classification and Regression

The use of classification and regression is also beneficial for a variety of business use cases. We'll just detail a few examples. Keep in mind that if you need to predict event probabilities (who is likely to perform a given action?) or predict values (how much/how many of these are likely to be?), you can take advantage of classification and regression capabilities.

We'll review a few use cases in the following sections. Detailed information on classification and regression will be provided in Part III.

Employee Turnover

An interesting area to apply classification is the prediction of employee turnover, that is, determining which employees are likely to leave my company in the near or mid-term. A typical example is wanting to predict the likeliness of a certain event—an employee will or won't be leaving. Many companies are using smart predict classification capabilities for such use cases to ensure that they can cope with their strategic needs in terms of the employee workforce.

Following are a couple of examples:

- A global US company, leader in the energy business, is looking to better understand and predict the reasons for employees retiring or leaving the company in an effort to anticipate leaves and make sure positions are staffed adequately to cope with the course of the business.

- A German administration is anticipating a wave of departures, looking at the current employee demographics, and getting help from predictive analytics to understand when departures might take place and how to mitigate them.

Sports Competitions

Sports competitions—soccer, rugby, equestrian sports, or esports—are by nature disputed and undecided. That said, it's possible to use past athlete performance to forecast game or competition outcomes. Collecting past performance of teams, generating classification or regression models, and applying these models to the upcoming games can help us predict game outcomes or athlete performance.

Following are a couple of examples:

- EquiRatings is a global equestrian technology company based in Ireland that provides data-driven solutions for Olympic teams. They are making use of classification and regression models to forecast the athlete performance throughout all major equestrian competitions. You can read more of their story here: *http://s-prs.co/v577103*.

- SAP is partnering with Team Liquid to make esports predictions. Team Liquid is a professional esports organization, and SAP helps them analyze their performance and create new strategies. You can read more about the use of predictive models here: *http://s-prs.co/v577104*.

Accounts Receivable Forecasting

Accounts receivables are typically the largest asset on any organization's financial statement. Using the results from a regression model, invoice payment predicted delays can be presented to enable collections managers to prioritize their time on high-value invoices and customers with poor predicted payment behavior. You can read more about this here: *http://s-prs.co/v577105*.

1.4   Summary

In this chapter, we first went over the importance of predictive analytics for business use. We explained how predictive analytics has been included as part of SAP Analytics Cloud core capabilities and the benefit it brings for enterprise planning and business intelligence use cases. Finally, we highlighted various use cases and customer examples.

In the next chapter, we'll explain a fundamental piece of predictive analytics: predictive scenarios.

Chapter 2
What Are Predictive Scenarios?

To use predictive analytics in SAP Analytics Cloud, it's essential to understand your building blocks within the broader predictive ecosystem, most importantly, the predictive scenario.

This chapter begins with an introduction to different SAP Analytics Cloud objects that relate to predictive analytics in Section 2.1. In Section 2.2, we'll detail the object that makes it possible to do predictive analytics in SAP Analytics Cloud: the predictive scenario. Then in Section 2.3 we'll discuss other SAP Analytics Cloud objects that can be used as part of a predictive workflow.

2.1 Introducing Predictive Scenarios

A *predictive scenario* is an SAP Analytics Cloud object that enables predictive capabilities. It's a workspace that enables you to create predictive models to address business questions requiring the creation and use of predictions. The capabilities provided by the predictive scenarios are also referred to as *smart predict*.

There are three distinct types of predictive scenarios, and each type corresponds to a specific predictive problem:

- Time series forecasting to predict the future values of a numerical quantity that depends on time
- Classification to predict the category an entity belongs to
- Regression to predict the value of a numeric attribute in a set of entities (e.g., estimated price of a set of cars)

Next, we'll cover the basics of using predictive scenarios.

2.1.1 Using and Securing Predictive Scenarios

You can access predictive scenarios by using the **Predictive Scenarios** icon [icon] in the main navigation toolbar. The main navigation, shown in Figure 2.1, allows you to navigate to the different functional areas of SAP Analytics Cloud. It's to the left of the screen and is always visible.

They are also available in the **Create** menu [icon] in the top toolbar of the **Files** area.

Figure 2.1 SAP Analytics Cloud Main Navigation Bar

The predictive scenarios are stored in the file system. They benefit from the usual capabilities of the file system (including security and sharing capabilities) with two exceptions:

- As of the time of writing, it's not possible to duplicate a predictive scenario in the file system. Predictive scenarios can only be moved.
- Import and export of predictive scenarios across SAP Analytics Cloud tenants currently isn't possible.

A Cloud Foundry tenant is required to use the predictive scenarios. You can refer to SAP Note 2661746 for more details.

To use predictive scenarios, you'll need to be granted specific privileges. These privileges are provided by two default roles:

- **Predictive content creator**
  Users with this role have all the privileges associated with the predictive scenarios (view, create, update, and delete).
- **Predictive admin**
  Users with this role have all the privileges associated with the predictive scenarios as well as a set of administrative privileges, including privileges for users, connections, and data repository management.

More details about these roles are available in the **Security Administration** section for predictive scenarios of the SAP Analytics Cloud online help: *http://s-prs.co/v577128*.

2.1.2 User Interface of Predictive Scenarios

Smart predict provides a consistent user interface (UI) independently of the type of predictive scenario you select. Whether you're working with time series forecasting, classification, or regression, you'll benefit from a consistent user experience (UX). Figure 2.2 shows the main parts of the UI of the predictive scenarios:

❶ Toolbar

❷ Modeling reports

❸ Settings panel and status panel

❹ Predictive model list

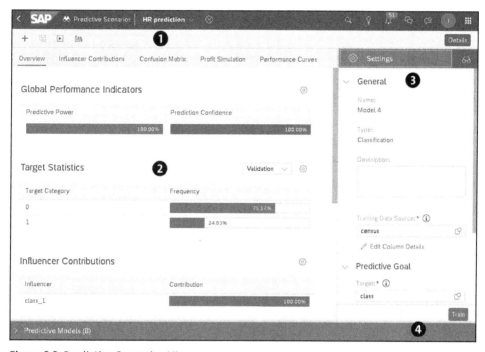

Figure 2.2 Predictive Scenarios UI

The following sections explain the main elements of the predictive scenario UI.

Settings Panel

The **Settings** panel is where you define the predictive model settings: the training dataset to be used, the target to be predicted, and so on. The **Settings** panel can be opened or closed using the **Details** button in the rightmost part of the toolbar. The **Train** button below the **Settings** panel enables the predictive model to be trained once the settings are defined.

Status Panel

The **Status** panel displays two types of messages that relate to predictive model training:

- **Error**

  This type of message is generated when an error prevents the predictive model from being trained. The message describes the nature of the error and provides hints to help you fix it.

- **Warning**

  This type of message is generated when a potential problem is detected, but it doesn't prevent training the predictive model. For instance, smart predict may warn you about data quality issues and provide advice to fix them.

The **Status** panel is found in the same place as the **Settings** panel and can be opened using the **Status** button 👓 at the top-right side of the **Settings** panel. If warning or error messages are available, the **Status** message is displayed automatically after the predictive model is trained or when you open it.

Toolbar

The toolbar provides the most important actions to work with the predictive models:

- **Create Predictive Model** ⊞

  Allows creating a new predictive model. The settings of the newly created predictive model are empty. If the predictive model you were previously editing has unsaved settings, you'll be prompted to save, discard the changes, or cancel.

- **Save Predictive Model** 💾

  Allows saving the predictive model setting changes. If the predictive model was already trained, you'll be warned that you're about to lose the existing training results. The goal is to guarantee that the displayed training results always correspond to the current predictive model settings.

- **Train Predictive Model** ▶

  Allows training a predictive model using the defined settings. The settings are automatically saved before training the predictive model. The **Train Predictive Model** button and the **Train** button below the **Settings** panel have the same effect, so you can use one or the other.

- **Apply Predictive Model** 🗒

  Allows generating predictions using the trained predictive model.

More actions are available in the context menu of the predictive model list.

Modeling Reports

The predictive model training generates a set of visualizations providing information about the following:

- The predictive model performance
- Explanations to help you understand the predictive model logic
- Insights

These visualizations are grouped into reports focused on specific topics, called modeling reports. You can browse the different reports using the various tabs at the top of the modeling report area. Within a given report, you may need to scroll down when all the visualizations can't be displayed on screen at the same time.

A configuration icon ⊗ is available for most of the visualizations, enabling you to further customize the displayed information. You can choose to visualize the data using a table rather than a bar chart, change the displayed series, sort the displayed data, and so on. Don't be afraid to play with the visualization settings, as you can reset the configuration to its default using the **Reset** button. You can get more details about using the visualization settings at *http://s-prs.co/v577106*.

Figure 2.3 shows the settings for a specific visualization named **Global Performance Indicators**. We can see the visualization is configured to be displayed as a form showing four properties.

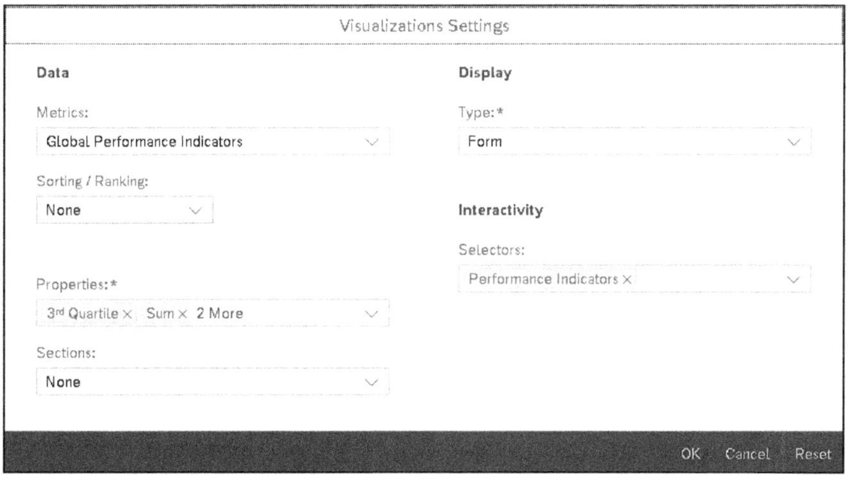

Figure 2.3 Visualization Settings

Predictive Model List

Building the best possible predictive model is by nature an iterative activity. You'll often have to experiment with different settings to get the best results for your specific business case. These experiments will translate as different predictive models as part of one predictive scenario. These predictive models are available in the predictive model list at the bottom of the UI.

By default, the **Predictive Models** list is collapsed so more space is available to display the predictive model settings and the modeling reports. You'll need to open the list whenever you need it. Figure 2.4 shows the predictive model list for a classification predictive scenario.

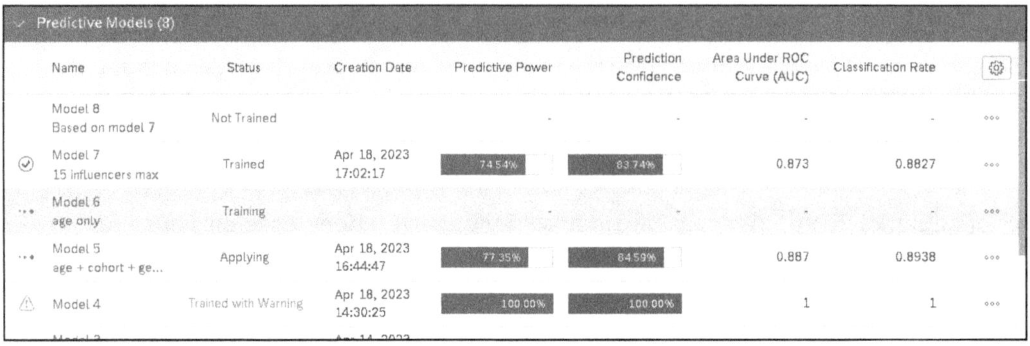

Figure 2.4 Predictive Model List

Each row in the list corresponds to a predictive model and displays mainly two types of information: the predictive model status and a set of performance metrics for the predictive model. The performance metrics allow comparing the performance of the models so you can easily find the one that best fits your needs. The **Select Columns** icon ⚙ makes it possible to configure the set of performance metrics to be displayed.

The **Status** column reflects the status of the predictive model and can take values falling into three categories:

- **Model training status**
  This is the main information displayed in the **Status** column. The different training statuses are **Not Trained**, **Trained**, **Trained with Warning**, or **Train Failed** if errors occurred during training. You can click the status of a specific predictive model to display the warning or error message if there is any.

- **Model application status**
  After a model application, the predictive model training status is replaced with the application status: **Applied** or **Apply Failed**. If the status is **Apply Failed**, you can click **Status** to display the associated error message. The application status is transient and is replaced with the training status after 10 minutes.

- **Action in progress**
  When the predictive model is training or applying, the **Status** column shows that an operation is in progress, replacing the training status with **Training** or **Applying**. Sometimes you may also see the **Train Pending** and **Apply Pending** statuses. In this case, the training or application operation can't be processed immediately because all resources on your SAP Analytics Cloud system are currently busy. Your request will start as soon as processing resources become available.

More actions are available through the context menu ⋯ , as follows:

- **Open**

  Opens the settings and modeling report for the predictive model. It has the same outcome as clicking the corresponding row in the list.

- **Duplicate**

  Creates a new predictive model in a **Not Trained** state with the same settings as the initial predictive model. When experimenting with the predictive model settings, this allows you to replicate your settings from an existing predictive model instead of reentering them from scratch.

- **Delete**

  Deletes the predictive model. The predictive model entry and associated settings and modeling reports are removed from the list.

2.2   The Different Types of Predictive Scenarios

As mentioned in the previous chapter, smart predict provides three types of predictive scenarios, allowing you to address different types of predictive questions. We'll provide a quick introduction to them here:

- **Time series forecasting**

  A time series forecasting predictive scenario allows predicting the future values of a numerical quantity based on the historical past values for this quantity. For instance, you would use a time series forecasting predictive scenario to predict the number of shoes you'll sell in the next 12 months based on the sales of the past years.

  If you sell other products beside shoes, or different types of shoes, the time series forecasting predictive scenarios provide the **Entity** field, which offers the ability to forecast per product.

  Using time series forecasting predictive scenarios is addressed in detail in Chapter 5.

- **Classification**

  A classification predictive scenario allows predicting the category an entity belongs to or the likelihood of occurrence of a future event. For instance, you would use a classification predictive scenario to predict which employees have the highest risk to leave the company or which the customers may be the most likely to upgrade their subscription plan.

  Using classification predictive scenarios is addressed in detail in Chapter 11.

- **Regression**

  A regression predictive scenario allows predicting the value of an entity's attribute. For instance, you would use a regression predictive scenario to predict the estimated payment time of invoices based on the payment time of similar invoices in the past. Regression could also be used to estimate the customer's lifetime value.

  Using regression predictive scenarios is addressed in detail in Chapter 12.

2.3   The Predictive Ecosystem

SAP Analytics Cloud provides several types of objects that you can use along with predictive scenarios to fulfill your predictive needs. The following sections describe the SAP Analytics Cloud objects that you're most likely to use when running a predictive project and basic instructions that provide a foundation for the rest of the book.

2.3.1   Datasets

A *dataset* is a structured collection of data relating to a specific topic of interest. In SAP Analytics Cloud, a dataset is a tabular representation of data. Datasets are organized with columns standing for attributes and rows standing for records of whatever the dataset is about. For instance, in a dataset about customers, each row would stand for a specific customer, and each cell of the row would contain the value of an attribute for this specific customer.

SAP Analytics Cloud datasets can be used as data sources for smart predict and stories. Datasets are the only data source that can be used for classification and regression models in smart predict. Time series forecasting models can use both datasets and planning models. Both datasets and planning models can be used in stories.

Datasets are simple data structures that don't require much configuration. You may want to use datasets when the sophistication of planning models isn't needed. For instance, datasets are recommended when you want to perform quick experiments without having to define a full-fledged planning model.

Predictive scenarios require datasets with a specific structure. Chapter 4, Section 4.2, describes the exact requirements for time series forecasting, and Chapter 10, Section 10.3, describes the exact requirements for classification and regression models.

There are two types of datasets in SAP Analytics Cloud:

- **Acquired datasets**
  These datasets are created by copying the data uploaded to SAP Analytics Cloud to the SAP Analytics Cloud underlying database. One typical use case for acquired datasets is importing data from a comma-separated values (CSV) file or Microsoft Excel file, yet data can be imported from many data sources, including SAP and third-party databases and applications.

- **Live datasets**
  These datasets allow accessing data from an on-premise SAP HANA system (called a *data repository* in SAP Analytics Cloud) without needing to replicate the data. Data isn't copied to SAP Analytics Cloud's underlying database, and changes made in SAP HANA are immediately available in SAP Analytics Cloud if the structure of the SQL view's underlying table isn't changed (no column is added or removed). Using smart predict with live datasets requires installing the Automated Predictive Library (APL),

a predictive library with the same predictive algorithms as smart predict. The data is processed by APL inside your SAP HANA system without having to transfer the data to SAP Analytics Cloud. Only the resulting predictive model is stored in SAP Analytics Cloud. You may want to use smart predict with live datasets if you're using an on-premise SAP HANA system and want to avoid replicating the data to SAP Analytics Cloud.

Let's walk through the basic steps to create an acquired dataset from a CSV or Microsoft Excel file:

1. Click the **Datasets** icon ![icon] in the SAP Analytics Cloud main navigation bar to navigate to the datasets area.
2. Click **Create New · From a CSV or Excel File**.
3. In the dialog box that opens, click **Select Source File**.
4. Select a file on your computer, and click **Open** to validate the selection.
5. Click **Import** to validate the import settings.
6. Select a folder in SAP Analytics Cloud where the dataset will be saved, and click **OK**.

The file is uploaded to SAP Analytics Cloud. The dataset is automatically created and opened in the dataset editor. The dataset editor allows you to perform some simple data transformations and edit the metadata of the dataset columns, as shown in Figure 2.5. Chapter 10, Section 10.3.2, shows some uses of the dataset editor in the context of creating predictive models.

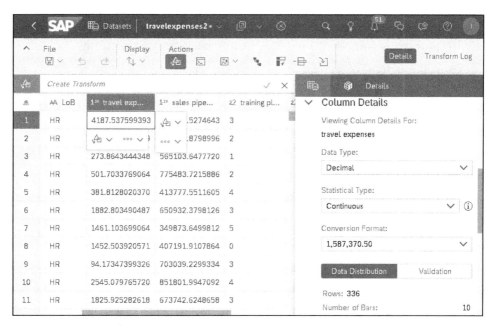

Figure 2.5 Dataset Editor

2.3.2   Planning Models

A planning model in SAP Analytics Cloud is a data source that allows enriching the data with metadata—currencies, hierarchies, aggregation type, and so on—that can be used for financial planning activities. This metadata enables you to create a richer representation of the data in line with your specific business.

Planning models are extended versions of analytic models with more capabilities. Both models can be used to create stories, but only the planning models can be used as data sources in predictive planning. Planning models provide a versioning capability allowing you to manage variations of the data, for instance, enabling the comparison of several projections of how financial key performance indicators (KPIs) might evolve in the future.

Planning models can be used both with the time series predictive scenarios and stories. We provide more details regarding the different aspects of the planning models in Chapter 5, Section 5.2.

It's possible to create planning models from scratch by defining their structure first. You must define the measures, the dimensions, and all the metadata of the model. The process of creating a planning model from scratch is explained in this video: *www.youtube.com/watch?v=PCqCXCsDiOg*. Once the structure of the planning model is defined, you can feed the model with data by entering values using a planning table in a story for instance. This is the recommended approach of creating a planning model if you're starting a new planning project and you don't have existing data yet.

However, if you already have data available, it may be more convenient to create your planning model by importing this data. This way, in a few steps you have a planning model ready to use without having to define its whole structure explicitly.

Let's walk through the basic steps to create a planning model from existing data:

1. Click the **Modeler** icon 🔷 in the main navigation bar to navigate to the **Modeler** area, shown in Figure 2.6.

2. In the **Modeler** area, under **Create New**, click **Model**.

3. You'll be prompted to choose how you want to create the planning model. Choose **Start with data** (default option), and click **Next**.

4. In the **Select a data source** dialog, select the type of data source you want to use to import the data. Select **File (Local File or File Server)**. For the purpose of this example, we're assuming you want to import a CSV or a Microsoft Excel file, but many more options are available.

5. Now in the **Create Model from File** dialog, click **Select Source File** to select the file to be imported.

6. Select the file to be imported from your computer file system, and click **Open**.

7. In the **Create Model from File** dialog, click **Import**.

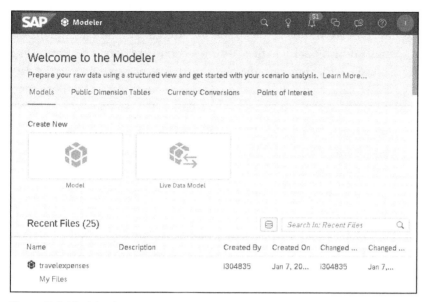

Figure 2.6 Modeler Area

8. The content of the file is imported to the newly created planning model. This model is opened in the modeler so you can edit it, as shown in Figure 2.7. Initially, it's not saved. Click the **Save** ![save icon] icon in the **General** area of the toolbar to save your planning model.

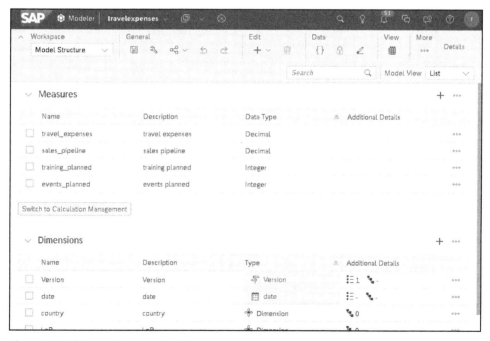

Figure 2.7 Editing a Planning Model

Once the model is created, it's usually worth checking and possibly fixing the metadata. With planning models, you need to pay specific attention to the date dimension. To create a proper planning model, you need a dimension with a **Date** type. Depending on the date format used in the imported file, the dimension corresponding to the date column may be created automatically with the **Generic** type instead of the **Date** type. So first, you should make sure to configure the date dimension, as follows:

1. In the model editor top toolbar, select **Workspace · Model Structure**.

2. Scroll to the **Dimensions** section and click the dimension corresponding to the date column of the imported file.

3. A panel named **Dimension** opens to the right, allowing you to edit the dimension's properties.

4. In the **Type** dropdown list, select **Date**. A **Change Dimension Type** dialog opens, as shown in Figure 2.8.

5. In the **Granularity** dropdown list, choose the time granularity for your date. Be careful to choose the right granularity as it can't be changed afterwards. In our example, the date granularity is **Month**.

6. In the **Conversion Format** field, enter the date format that should be used to parse the dates. Usually, the format that's automatically proposed is correct. In our example, the date values in the imported data are formatted using three digits for the month and two digits for the year, separated by a dash character.

7. Click **OK** to validate the configuration of the date dimension.

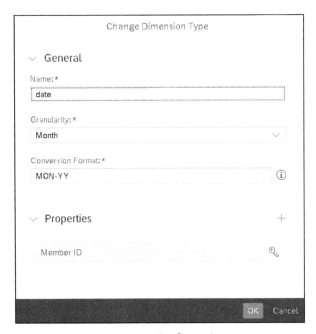

Figure 2.8 Date Dimension Configuration

If the dimension that includes the dates is initially created with the **Generic** type, the planning capabilities of the model are not enabled. To enable the planning capabilities, follow these steps:

1. Click the **Model Preferences** 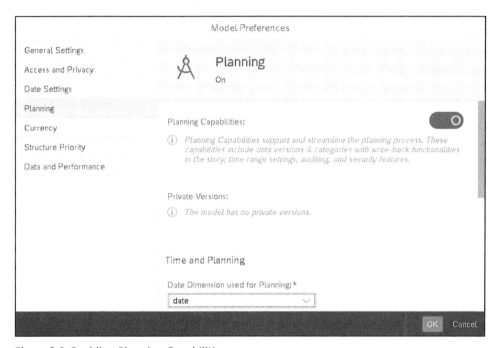 icon in the top toolbar.

2. In the **Model Preferences** dialog, click **Planning** in the navigation menu on the left.

3. Enable the **Planning Capabilities** using the toggle button, as shown in Figure 2.9.

4. Click **OK** to validate the settings.

Figure 2.9   Enabling Planning Capabilities

Finally, you need to configure the time range of your planning model, which defines the range of dates that can be used by the planning model. The time range is defined by a starting year and an ending year. By default, when the model is created, the time range corresponds to the range of the dates in the imported file. For instance, if the imported file contains dates from January 2022 to December 2023, the default time range starts in 2022 and ends in 2023. However, the imported dates correspond to the past, and you want to forecast the future, so the default time range must be extended to include future years. Here are the steps to extend the planning time range until the end of 2024:

1. Scroll to the **Dimensions** section and hover over the cell corresponding to the **Type** column for the date dimension.

2. Click the **Edit Dimension Table** icon. The **Dimension Table** panel opens to the right.

3. Scroll down to **From/To Year** in the **Date** section.

4. In the date selector corresponding to the ending year, select **2024**, as shown in Figure 2.10.

5. Save your planning model.

Figure 2.10 Planning Time Range

2.3.3   Stories

A story is a dashboard that you create to visualize data stored in analytic models, planning models, or datasets. It allows combining different types of visualizations (including charts, tables, geo maps, etc.) spread on multiple pages to build static reports that can be shared with other SAP Analytics Cloud users. Stories are the place where the predictions generated using smart predict are consumed.

Let's see how to create a new story to display visualizations next:

1. From the homepage, click the **Stories** icon [img] in the main navigation toolbar to navigate to the **Welcome to Stories** page as shown in Figure 2.11.

2. In the **Create New** section of the welcome page, you must choose the type of layout you want for the first page of your story. Click one of the three options: **Responsive**, **Canvas**, or **Grid**, as described here:

   – **Responsive**
   Use a **Responsive** layout if you want the page to automatically adapt to different display sizes. The visualizations are moved automatically to ensure that all page elements remain visible on the smallest screens.

   – **Canvas**
   Use a **Canvas** if you want to enforce absolute positioning of the elements in the page.

   – **Grid**
   Use **Grid** if you want to display the data in a spreadsheet like a grid.

3. You'll be prompted to choose a design mode: **Optimized Design Experience** or **Classic Design Experience**. The optimized design experience proposes an improved UX with better response time than the classic design experience, but a few capabilities

of the classic design experience aren't available in the optimized design experience yet. We recommend always choosing the optimized design experience, except if you need capabilities that are currently available only in the classic design experience.

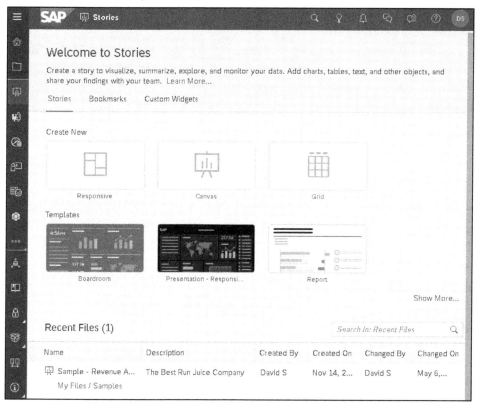

Figure 2.11 Welcome to Stories Page

You're now ready to design a story by adding visualizations, filters, or even more pages. You can learn more about using stories at *http://s-prs.co/v577107*.

2.3.4   Multi Actions

Multi actions allow orchestrating and automating operations on planning models. A multi action is composed of several simple operations called "steps" that are executed sequentially in a predefined order. A multi action can run the following operations:

- Run a data action.
- Train and apply a time series smart predict model.
- Publish a planning model version.
- Import data.
- Call an HTTP application programming interface (API).

There are two ways to run a multi action:

- **Manual execution**
  Allow the users of a story to run a multi action by adding a button, called a multi action trigger, in the story.

- **Scheduled execution**
  Schedule the execution of a multi action using the SAP Analytics Cloud calendar. The multi action is then executed automatically at a fixed date and time. It's possible to set up recurrent schedules, for instance, to run the multi action every Monday morning.

We'll explain how to set up multi actions in Chapter 6.

2.3.5   Data Actions

Data actions allow orchestrating and automating data operations on planning models. A data action is composed of several simple operations called "steps" that are executed sequentially in a specified order. A data action can run the following operations:

- Data copy, possibly between two distinct models
- Data allocation
- Currency conversion (if enabled in the planning model)
- Advanced calculations based on a script language

When it's created, a data action is associated with a specific planning model and can perform operations only on that model (except for the **Cross-Model Copy** operation that involves a second planning model). If you need to perform operations on several planning models, then you need several data actions.

Let's follow the steps to create a data action:

1. From the homepage, click the **Data Actions** icon ▤↓ in the main navigation toolbar to navigate to the data actions welcome page.

2. In the **Create New** section of the screen, click **Data Action**. The data action editor opens.

3. In the **Name** field, enter a name for the new data action. Optionally, you can provide a description in the **Description** field.

4. Using the **Default Model** selector in the **Default Settings** section, select the planning model associated with the data action.

5. In the top toolbar, click **General · Save · Save** to save the data action.

6. Select the folder where you want to save the data action, and click **OK**.

You're now ready to design the data action by adding and configuring different operations.

Figure 2.12 shows a data action with two operations.

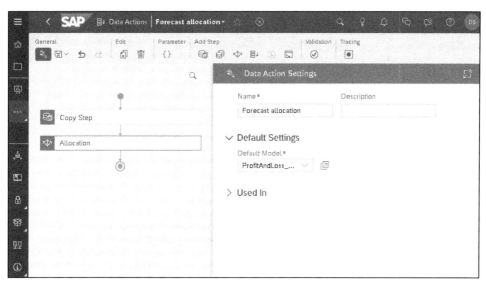

Figure 2.12 Data Action Editor

You can learn more about configuring data actions at *http://s-prs.co/v577108*.

2.4   Summary

In this chapter, we introduced predictive scenarios and the role they can play in a predictive project. We covered the different types of predictive scenarios and provided examples of use cases. Finally, we introduced other SAP Analytics Cloud objects that you may also want to use in your predictive projects.

Now that our building blocks are in order, we'll get started with our predictive project in the next chapter.

Chapter 3
Predictive Analytics Projects

It's time to plan and implement your predictive analytics project. To do so, you need to know two things: the who (the stakeholders) and the how (the method).

This chapter explains how a predictive analytics project can be implemented step-by-step and the most important aspects to consider. We first review the typical stakeholders for such a project in Section 3.1, and their respective roles and contributions. We then present an implementation method for predictive analytics projects and walk you through the different steps of the project in Section 3.2.

3.1 Predictive Analytics Project Stakeholders

A predictive analytics project is like any information technology (IT) project. It involves a team of people in charge of the required project tasks and committed to the project's final success. In the following sections, we'll walk you through typical stakeholders involved in such projects. We'll detail the roles and contributions that these stakeholders are expected to have as part of the project (note that we focus on generic stakeholder roles in this section). In practice, multiple individuals can fill in for a given role. One individual can also bring contributions for different project roles.

3.1.1 Business Owners

In most cases, business owners occupy management positions or represent different divisions of the business (finance, human resources [HR], production, etc.). They can be the sponsors; they are also the major stakeholders of the project.

Business owners, as their name hints, own the business side of the project. They are the ones expressing business needs. Every predictive analytics project starts with one or several business goals that need to be achieved. While business owners might or might not be predictive savvy, they are the ones defining tangible business expectations that will trigger the need for a predictive analytics project. Examples of such tangible expectations might include the following:

- Can we use predictive planning to replace some of our manual planning processes and gain further forecasting accuracy through this?

- Can we predict the outcome of specific events, for instance, if our employees might be leaving next year?
- Can we predict certain values, for instance, invoice payment delays?

An efficient communication channel needs to be established between the technical team in charge of the project and the business owners.

A critical part of the project definition is to establish a project plan, clarifying and detailing the business expectations from business owners. The project plan helps derive business goals into predictive analytics goals. In the initial stages of the project, it's important to evaluate whether business goals are achievable. If they aren't achievable, business owner expectations need to be reset accordingly.

Throughout the project's evolution, the team in charge of the project implementation must stay in regular touch with the business owners to present intermediate results and get their blessing that things are moving in the right direction. As the project ends, business owners review and validate the tangible outcomes delivered by the project. Stories are a great tool to help with this review and validation as they are the frontend for the business.

3.1.2   Data Engineers

Data engineers are typically part of IT teams. Sometimes called data architects, data engineers play a significant role in predictive analytics projects. No predictive analytics project can be completed without data, and the data needs to be of sufficient quality and quantity to achieve satisfactory predictive results.

In the early stage of the project, business goals will be declined as predictive analytics goals. To achieve the desired predictive goals, data must be identified, consolidated, and prepared so that prediction creators can create and run predictive scenarios on top of the source data.

The fundamental role of data engineers is to provide reliable data that forms the basis of accurate predictive models. Data can be modeled in different formats, such as datasets or planning models. Data engineers need to model the data assets to fulfill the needs of prediction creators.

When the predictive analytics project comes closer to completion, they also need to create stable data pipelines so that predictive models can be refreshed accordingly.

3.1.3   Prediction Creators

Prediction creators can be found as part of business divisions, as part of IT, or as part of internal data science teams. They create predictive scenarios and models using the data provided to them by the data engineers. They are the main end users for smart predict and predictive planning.

Prediction creators are responsible for providing accurate predictions to prediction consumers. To guarantee the desired prediction accuracy, they need to create different predictive models on the available data, typically trying to enrich the base data with additional variables or to make sure the data has enough observations, until they achieve a satisfactory state for predictive scenarios and predictive models. They also take care of predictive planning automation needs, designing the required multi action, to deliver predictive forecasts regularly.

Prediction creators need to stay in close touch with story designers and prediction consumers to make sure their predictions are reported in a way that is clearly understood by the final end users. They will also present their work outcomes to business owners.

Note that prediction creators don't necessarily need to be professional data scientists to operate the predictive analytics capabilities of SAP Analytics Cloud. The product capabilities have been designed so that they can be accessible to most end users with only basic statistical skills to interpret the predictive model performance. This book should turn you into a prediction creator too!

3.1.4   Story Designers

Story designers can be part of IT teams (professional IT story designers). They can also be part of business divisions to serve the specific needs of these divisions.

The predictive capabilities of SAP Analytics Cloud make it possible to deliver predictions as additional data in datasets and planning models. In most cases, predictions are consumed in the context of stories, as they are the preferred place for information consumers to interact with analytical and planning insights.

Story designers are responsible for relating existing analytical or planning data models with data models that contain predictions to create simple and straightforward stories. While story designers relate to data engineers and prediction creators as part of the core project team delivering reference SAP Analytics Cloud assets, their final customers are the information consumers and the business owners. Creating delightful stories is a process that requires knowing the end user expectations in detail, as well as mastering story features and design practices.

Learn More about Story Design

To learn more about story design, we recommend *Designing Dashboards with SAP Analytics Cloud* (SAP PRESS 2021), where you can learn to design dashboards for any use case.

3.1.5   Prediction Consumers

Prediction consumers typically come from the business side of the company. They are the end users consuming predictions to help them make decisions and improve the course of the business. Prediction consumers, in most cases, won't interact directly with predictive scenarios and predictive models. They will interact with analytics and predictions in the context of stories that have been designed specifically by story designers to serve their needs.

Prediction consumers are usually not familiar with the process of predictive analytics, so it's essential that the predictions delivered to them are presented in a straightforward way that they can make sense of, that they can relate to their business knowledge, and that they can trust. We'll see in the next chapters that providing trusted predictions is a key strength of predictive capabilities.

3.1.6   Information Technology

The IT team is a central team in each company that will be responsible for analytics projects. Team members are involved in the predictive analytics project to address diverse needs, such as data access and security needs. For instance, data engineers, prediction creators, story designers, and prediction consumers are granted different security rights in SAP Analytics Cloud and will access assets on a need-to-know basis. IT delivers the proper project technical environment for the distinct roles to cooperate and deliver the predictive analytics project. Some of the core project team will be part of the IT division of the company.

3.2   How to Implement a Predictive Analytics Project

Now that we've presented the typical stakeholders that form part of a predictive analytics project, we'll present an end-to-end implementation method. The most recognized method to implement predictive analytics projects is the cross-industry standard process for data mining, also known as CRISP-DM. You can read more about this method at *http://s-prs.co/v577109*. This process consists of six major phases as described in Figure 3.1:

1. **Business understanding**
   During the first phase, the business requirements and the business success criteria will be identified and assessed. The business requirements will be translated into a predictive analytics question, with corresponding goals and success criteria. A project plan will be created.

2. **Data understanding**
   In the second phase, the available data sources will be reviewed, and data will be

analyzed in detail to understand what it corresponds to and whether it's usable as such in the context of the ongoing project.

3. **Data preparation**
The third phase focuses on sourcing, cleansing, and formatting/integrating the data where required.

4. **Predictive modeling**
This fourth phase consists of selecting the proper modeling techniques (e.g., classification, regression, or time series forecasting) and generating predictive scenarios and predictive models.

5. **Predictive model evaluation**
In the fifth phase, predictive models are evaluated through analysis of training results and review of the overall process.

6. **Delivering predictions**
In the sixth phase, the trained predictive models will be used productively by delivering predictions available to SAP Analytics Cloud users and potentially to other systems through data export.

In the next subsections, we'll walk you through the step-by-step process and the detailed tasks required as part of each of the six project phases.

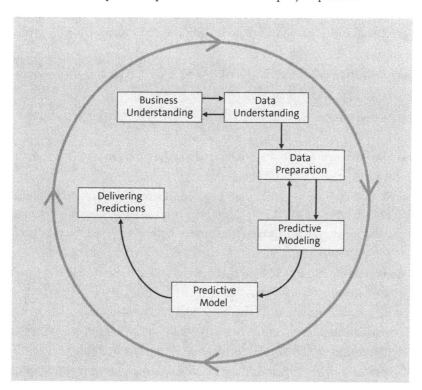

Figure 3.1 Predictive Analytics Project Method (Derived from CRISP-DM)

3.2.1   Business Understanding

The first phase of the predictive analytics project consists of determining the business expectations and the related implications; that is, what does the business owner want to accomplish? You need to spend the required time analyzing in depth the business objectives and what the business considers as project success criteria. This information will form the cornerstone of your project plan.

The business has high-level expectations that you must analyze and translate into a predictive analytics approach. Here are some examples of the high-level business requirements:

- Can we improve our planning accuracy? Can we do a better job in forecasting sales or expenses?
- Can we predict which employees might be leaving next year?
- Can we predict when customers will pay invoices?

The business objectives will be your North Star to propose a fit-for-purpose predictive analytics approach and a project plan to achieve these objectives on time. In certain cases, the business requirements can't be addressed with predictive analytics, and you'll have to make this clear from day one.

You should not rush or neglect the business understanding step. If you do, you might be wasting a great deal of time and effort producing the right answer to the wrong question.

You need to take time to fully assess the situation, and ask yourself and answer questions like these:

- What are the success criteria for the project? In business terms? In predictive analytics terms?
- What are the deliverables you want to aim for, such as data models, predictive models, stories, and so on?
- Which resources do you have at hand in terms of workforce (business and technical experts), available data, and available systems? For instance, you'll need a running SAP Analytics Cloud system with enough licenses for both the project team but and your prediction consumers.
- What are the timeline constraints to deliver the project? Can these timelines be met knowing the project resources and constraints?
- What are the data platforms you can rely on? Where is the relevant data currently stored? Will the data be replicated into SAP Analytics Cloud, and, if yes, how? Do you have the proper rights granted to access the data? Will the data be easily available?
- Which kind of predictions are expected to be delivered? How will the predictions be consumed? Is prediction automation required?

- Are there any risks you can identify at the initial stages, and how can you mitigate them?

You must uncover any crucial factors at the beginning of the project that can influence the outcome of the project to avoid losing time and energy during subsequent steps.

Based on the collected information, you can determine the predictive analytics goals. Whereas business goals state the project objectives from a business perspective, you also need to refine these business goals into more technical goals. These predictive goals will also need to come with success criteria. As an example, the success criteria for a forecasting project might consist of dividing the current forecasting error by a factor of two.

Finally, you must produce a project plan that recaps the business goals as well as the predictive analytics goals. This plan should describe all the steps you'll take to achieve the project.

3.2.2   Data Understanding

Let's move on to our next phase. During the data understanding phase, you'll proceed through the following steps, which we'll discuss in the next sections:

1. Collect the data.
2. Describe the data.
3. Explore the data.
4. Check the data quality.

Data Collection

The data collection step consists of acquiring or accessing the data identified as part of the project plan. Depending on the data location, you might want to access and review the data either in SAP Analytics Cloud or directly in the data platform you're relying on. One option consists of acquiring the data into SAP Analytics Cloud (or accessing it live if the data is stored in an on-premise SAP HANA system) and reviewing it there. While SAP Analytics Cloud can't be considered an advanced data exploration and data quality solution, it provides some basic features that can help you during the data understanding phase.

On the other hand, most data platforms, such as SAP HANA, offer data exploration functionalities to help data engineers during the data understanding phase. Based on your project plan and initial assessment, multiple data sources might be required to serve your predictive analytics use case, and that you'll need to group these. During this step, you also need to think of the target data model in SAP Analytics Cloud. Will you use datasets or planning models (only applicable to time series forecasting scenarios)? This modeling choice determines the possibilities you'll have when using this data for predictive analytics and the way you'll report on the predictions. It's good practice to document your findings and choices in a data collection report.

The report should answer the following questions:

- Which data sources do you need to serve your predictive analytics use case?
- Where are these data sources located?
- Which method will you use to connect these data sources into SAP Analytics Cloud? Will you acquire the data into SAP Analytics Cloud and therefore replicate it from the original data sources? Or will you use the live connectivity mechanism to connect to on-premise SAP HANA tables and SQL views?
- Which problems have you identified at this stage? Which solutions have you found to mitigate these problems?

Data Description

In the data description step, you start digging deeper to examine the various properties of the data to answer the following questions:

- What is the data format?
- How many observations do you have in each data source?
- How many columns or variables do you have in each data source?
- What does each column correspond to? Can you name it?
- Should each column be considered a dimension or a measure?
- Did you discover anything specific about the data while describing it?

Based on this analysis, it's recommended to create another short report that contains a description of the data and to document your findings. While this might sound tedious, it's easy to lose track of the project context after a brief period.

Data Exploration

During the data exploration step, you'll explore the data using queries and visualizations. Your analysis should answer the following questions:

- How are your measures distributed?
- What are the values in each of your dimensions?

Datasets in SAP Analytics Cloud offer basic data exploration features. For example, Figure 3.2 shows the data distribution of a measure, and Figure 3.3 shows unique values for a dimension.

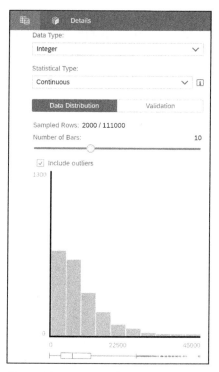

Figure 3.2 Data Distribution of Car Sale Prices (Measure)

Figure 3.3 Unique Values for Car Types (Dimension)

Use your curiosity to dig deeper into the data, and you'll likely make additional findings during this step. Similar to the previous steps, it's recommended that you document your findings in a data exploration report.

Data Quality

In the data quality step, you should answer the following questions to check the data quality:

- Is the data complete? For example, in the context of a time series, you want to make sure the time series is as complete as possible and doesn't contain too many value breaks in the course of the time series.

- Is the data correct, or does it contain errors? Can you spot any outliers in the data?

- Are there missing values in the data? Is it possible to fill these missing values with correct values or not?

The data quality step will result in you creating a data quality report, detailing your findings, and, if any data quality problems exist, listing practical solutions.

You should have a much deeper understanding of your data after this phase. This will help you prepare the data models best to serve your predictive analytics needs.

3.2.3   Data Preparation

There is a famous joke that says predictive analytics is 80% about preparing data and 20% complaining about preparing the data. While the reality might sometimes be less harsh, the condition of the prepared data does impact the accuracy of the predictive results. This is sometimes summarized by predictive analytics practitioners as "garbage in, garbage out."

During the data preparation phase, you'll follow these steps, which we'll discuss in the next sections:

1. Select the data.
2. Clean the data.
3. Enrich the data.
4. Integrate the data.

Data Selection

The data selection step focuses on selecting the data used during the predictive modeling phase. The selection criteria should include the relevance to the predictive analytics goals, as well as quality and technical constraints such as limits on data volume or data types. As an example, if you want to forecast the next 12 months ahead for a given indicator, it's ideal to select five or six years of the past evolution of this indicator, at the monthly level. Note that the data selection should consider dataset columns as well as observations. At the end of this step, you should be able to list the data you would keep or exclude and the rationale for these decisions.

Data Cleaning

During the data cleaning step, you'll raise the level of data quality. There are many different actions you can take there. As we previously mentioned, if time series are incomplete, you should avoid as many breaks as possible in the time series by filling the intermediate, missing data points, assuming they correspond to null values. In addition, dimension members frequently have close names due to typos or incorrect master data management. You need to align these close values to the standard one. Note that smart predict can deal with missing values as part of the classification and regression modeling so you don't need to fill in missing values artificially. The output of this step is a data cleaning report that lists the decisions and actions that were taken to address the data quality problems detected during the data quality check step of the data understanding phase.

Data Enrichment

The data enrichment step includes data preparation operations such as the production of derived variables or transformed values for existing variables. Derived variables are new variables that are built off one or more existing variables of the dataset. The calculation of derived variables and the transformation of existing variable values will need to be documented for traceability and further reference. Note that SAP Analytics Cloud does offer features to clean and enrich data in datasets and planning models. To learn more on dataset transformation features, you can refer to the help page here: *http://s-prs.co/v577110*.

Data Integration

In the data integration step, information from multiple data sources is combined to create new records or values. In most cases, the various data sources will be merged into one through joining. Merged data can also include ad hoc aggregations. SAP Analytics Cloud doesn't offer specific features to handle data integration, so the data integration step must be handled outside of the solution, for instance, by using other SAP solutions such as SAP HANA, SAP Business Warehouse (SAP BW), or SAP Datasphere. Standard data types and data formats are natively handled by SAP Analytics Cloud.

At the end of the data preparation phase, you finalize your data models, alongside a description of the data preparation steps you took to create them.

3.2.4   Predictive Modeling

You've finalized your data models and are ready to use them to create your predictive scenarios and predictive models. The predictive modeling phase will consist of four major steps, which we'll discuss in the following sections:

1. Select the right predictive scenario type.
2. Define a plan to evaluate and compare the predictive models.
3. Create the predictive models.
4. Assess the predictive models.

Select the Right Type of Predictive Scenario

The first step is to select the right predictive scenario type. As discussed in Chapter 2, Section 2.2, in smart predict, you can create three types of predictive scenarios: classification, regression, and time series forecasting. While these three types cover a broad range of business questions addressable by predictive analytics, they don't allow you to, for instance, answer clustering or product recommendation questions.

As a reminder, here are the definitions of the three types of predictive scenarios:

- **Classification**
  This type helps address "who" questions and associate a predicted probability to the corresponding event. Who could win the next game? Who might buy the next product this week? Who might leave the company this year?

- **Regression**
  This type helps predict a numeric value, in the sense of "what" could be a value for a particular object of interest. What could be the sales price for a secondhand car? What could be the payment delay for an invoice?

- **Time series forecasting**
  This type helps predict the evolution of a numeric value over time. What will revenue evolution be over the course of next year on a monthly basis?

Based on your earlier examination of the business question, you should already know at this stage which type of predictive scenario you'll select.

Define a Plan to Evaluate and Compare the Predictive Models

Before you start creating the predictive models, you must define how you'll assess the model accuracy and the relevance of the predictions to fit the business needs. In most cases, you can rely on the performance indicators that smart predict provides you with to evaluate the predictive models. These indicators are computed by internally reserving a set of the actual data and using the predictive model to predict this actual dataset. You might want to evaluate the performance of the predictive model in real-world conditions to estimate the potential performance you could get. For instance, it's common for customers to evaluate the performance of the predictive model by predicting data for periods where they already know the actual values. Another common option is to let some time pass to gather more data points to compare the predictions to what happened later.

Create the Predictive Models

During this step, you first create a predictive scenario that will contain your different predictive models. You can create different predictive models on top of the prepared datasets or planning models. You'll experiment with different predictive model settings. You'll have to iterate between creating predictive models and sophisticating further the base data until you converge to acceptable predictive models. Once this is done, you need to carefully preserve the selected predictive models and their settings, and then describe the logic of your successful experiments. While smart predict stores every predictive model for you in a single predictive scenario, you need to create the right documentation because you might lose track of the predictive model creation history over time.

Assess the Predictive Models

Assessing the predictive models corresponds to confronting your domain knowledge, the predictive analytics success criteria you defined earlier, and your plan to compare and evaluate predictive model experiments. You must summarize the different results obtained, compare the respective qualities of the generated predictive models, and rank them in relation to each other. For this, you can use smart predict standard performance indicators; you can also use ad hoc performance indicators you create in stories.

3.2.5   Predictive Model Evaluation

In the predictive model evaluation, you'll focus on three major steps, which we'll discuss in the following sections:

1. Evaluate your results.
2. Review your process.
3. Determine the next steps.

Evaluate Your Results

Evaluating your results and the performance of predictive models is typically done by the prediction creators using the following standard performance indicators provided by smart predict:

- **Classification**
  Predictive power and prediction confidence.

- **Regression**
  Root mean square error (RMSE) and prediction confidence.

- **Time series forecasting**

  Expected mean absolute percentage error (MAPE), expected mean absolute error (MAE), expected mean absolute scaled error (MASE), expected root mean square error (RMSE), and expected coefficient of determination (R^2).

The performance indicator you choose to evaluate the predictive models should be the one that most closely matches the business objectives defined at the beginning of the project. Customers often create their own performance indicators in the context of stories to evaluate the prediction performance. The rationale for doing this is to create a performance indicator that is close to the way the business expresses its needs and will also evaluate predictions. You can use your predictive model to deliver predictions and compare them to what will happen later if your time and budget constraints allow.

Despite all the excellent work that you've been doing through the previous phases, the performance of your predictive models may not be satisfactory enough. If this is the case, consider the following possibilities:

- **Add more data**

  For classification and regression, if your predictive confidence indicator is too low, this is usually a sign that adding more observations is likely to improve the model. Similarly for time series forecasting, you need to have enough observations for proper evolution patterns to be detected.

- **Create more variables**

  For classification, if your predictive power indicator is too low, this is usually a sign that adding more variables is likely to improve the accuracy of the classification model. For regression, if your RMSE indicator is too low, this is usually a sign that adding more variables is likely to improve the accuracy of the regression model. For time series forecasting, you might notice peaks and valleys in the residuals that could be better explained by additional influencers.

- **Improve the data quality**

  Missing and outlier values in the source data can reduce the predictive model accuracy.

The output from this evaluation step is an assessment of the results with respect to the business goal and success criteria. You summarize the assessment results regarding the business success criteria and provide a final statement as to whether the predictive analytics project meets the initial business objectives.

Review Your Process

You need to conduct a thorough review of the predictive analytics project to determine if there is any crucial factor or task that has somehow been overlooked. Summarize the process and highlight activities that have been missed and/or should be repeated. This review also covers quality assurance issues, so, for example, consider these questions: Did you correctly build the predictive model? Did you only use variables that are allowed for use and that are available for future analysis? This step is needed to build additional confidence and trust in the steps you took.

Determine Your Next Steps

Finally, you'll need to determine the next steps according to the results assessment and the process review. You'll need to decide whether to finish the predictive part of the project and move onto deployment, if that is appropriate, or whether you need to initiate further iterations and set up additional tasks. This step includes the analysis of the remaining resources and budget that influence the decisions. You'll need to describe the decisions about how to proceed, along with the rationale.

3.2.6 Delivering Predictions

Predictions can be used in different ways in SAP Analytics Cloud. The main goal is to provide predictions to prediction consumers so that they can use them in their business context and make decisions based on these predictions. Predictions can be both integrated into stories and exported to external systems, which we'll discuss next.

Integrating Predictions into Stories

The most straightforward place to consume predictions is the stories. Predictions can be exported into datasets (using any predictive scenario type) or planning model versions (specifically using time series forecasting). Stories can be built by story designers off datasets or planning model versions. At the end of the day, prediction consumers can see actuals and predictions side by side in stories, if not budget and forecast in the context of financial planning. They can make decisions based on present and future information. As we previously mentioned, prediction consumers aren't experts in predictive analytics, but they know their business intimately. It's key that prediction creators and story designers can deliver the predictions with enough business context and in a straightforward way so that prediction consumers can understand and use them easily. Smart predict provides several functionalities for prediction consumers to gain trust in the predictions. These capabilities will be explained throughout this book.

Exporting Predictions outside of SAP Analytics Cloud

In some cases, it's not enough to consume the predictions only in the context of SAP Analytics Cloud, so you'll need to export predictions out of SAP Analytics Cloud.

Several features make prediction export possible, with different degrees of automation:

- You can export models' transaction data to SAP Business Planning and Consolidation (SAP BPC), SAP S/4HANA, SAP Integrated Business Planning for Supply Chain (SAP IBP), or OData services. For SAP S/4HANA, you can set up a schedule so that exports recur automatically on a daily, weekly, or monthly basis. This type of export is applicable to time series forecasting only. You can see more information here: *http://s-prs.co/v577111*.

- You can export model data using the Data Export Service application programming interface (API). This type of export is applicable to time series forecasting only. You can find more information here: *http://s-prs.co/v577112*.

- You can export table data as a comma-separated values (CSV) or Microsoft Excel (XLSX) file. Story tables can contain predictions originating from any predictive scenario. You can read more here: *http://s-prs.co/v577113*.

- You can export chart data as a CSV file. Charts can contain predictions originating from any predictive scenario. You can read more here: *http://s-prs.co/v577114*.

3.3   Summary

In this chapter, we walked through the steps required to implement a predictive analytics project in SAP Analytics Cloud, starting with the project stakeholders. We detailed an end-to-end implementation method inspired by CRISP-DM.

We're now ready to proceed with our predictive data modeling in SAP Analytics Cloud. In Part II, we'll focus on time series forecasting, starting with an introduction in the next chapter.

PART II
Time Series Forecasting Models

Chapter 4

Introducing Time Series Forecasting Models

Time series forecasting allows predicting the future values of a quantity that evolves over time. Time series forecasting has become a major asset for planners by accelerating and improving the production of planning forecasts.

In this chapter, we'll start by introducing important notions relating to time series forecasting in Section 4.1. Then, we'll discuss which data sources can be used by the time series forecasting models in SAP Analytics Cloud in Section 4.2. Finally, in Section 4.3, we'll wrap up this chapter by summarizing the different time series forecast workflows.

4.1   What Is Time Series Forecasting?

Time series forecasting is a group of techniques allowing you to predict the evolution of a numeric quantity over time. One focus of time series forecasting is the analysis of the time series to extract patterns such as trends or cycles (see Chapter 5, Section 5.4.2). These patterns are used by the time series forecasting model to calculate the predictions and also help you better understand the behavior of the observed time series.

To begin our discussion, we'll introduce the definitions and concepts that you need to know to have a good understanding of time series forecasting. We'll also provide an overview of two core methods: top-down and bottom-up predictive forecasting.

4.1.1   Key Terms and Concepts

Time series forecasting models can be used in a large variety of business domains to anticipate future needs and act accordingly. Here are a few popular time series forecasting use cases:

- **Financial planning**
  Forecasting sales, expenses, or cash flows enables you to improve the ability of your company plan for future investments.

- **Demand forecasting**
  Forecasting the future demand of a product allows you to minimize your inventory cost, plan for staffing, and budget.

- **Sensor data analysis**
  Forecasting the temperature, humidity, or occupancy rate in your office space saves on costs by adapting heating and cooling power.

Time series forecasting's main assumption is that the patterns that have existed in the past for the quantity to be predicted will continue to exist identically in the future. If, in the past, the predicted quantity has always increased, a time series forecasting model won't be able to predict that the quantity would start decreasing next year.

Let's establish some vocabulary relative to the time series forecasting:

- **Target**
  This is the quantity to be predicted.

- **Actuals**
  A time series forecasting model is trained using historical data. In SAP Analytics Cloud, this historical data is called actuals because it represents what happened in the past.

- **Predictive forecast**
  Forecasting can be a manual activity that doesn't involve predictive algorithms. So, in the rest of this book, we'll specifically use the term *predictive forecast* to name the predictions that are generated by a time series forecasting model.

- **Forecast horizon**
  This is the set of dates associated with the predictive forecast.

- **Forecasting error**
  The forecasting error at a specific date is the difference between the actual value and the predicted value at that date: $e(t) = y(t) - \hat{y}(t)$, where $e(t)$ is the error at the date t, $y(t)$ is the actual value at the date t, and $\hat{y}$ is the predicted value at the date t.

Let's put some of this terminology to work. Figure 4.1 shows an example of a time series forecasting model that predicts the number of air passengers between January 2019 and December 2019. The number of passengers is called the target. Actuals are available from January 2016 to December 2019. We say that the length of the forecast horizon is 12 months (from January 2019 to December 2019).

Figure 4.2 shows how the forecasting error is calculated for July 2017. The predicted value $\hat{y}(2017\text{-}07)$ is subtracted from the actual value $y(2017\text{-}07)$, leading to a forecasting error of $e(2017\text{-}07)$ equal to 157. Note that it's possible to calculate the forecasting error because an actual value is available for July 2017 and because the time series forecasting model can provide "predictions," not only for the forecast horizon (representing the future) but also for the time period where actuals are available (representing the past).

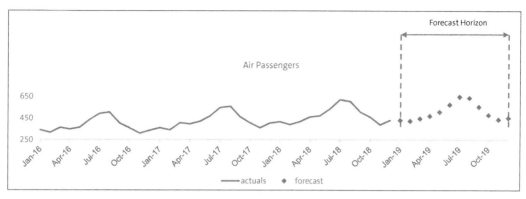

Figure 4.1 Forecasting the Number of Air Passengers

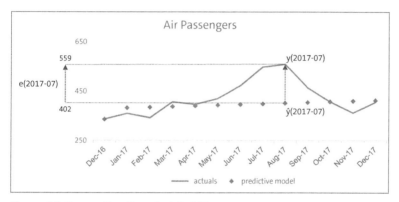

Figure 4.2 Forecasting Error in July 2017

Companies relied on business acumen for years to generate their financial and demand forecast, so why would you want to rely on time series forecasting models instead of human knowledge and wisdom? In short, using time series forecasting models provides a couple of major advantages over manual forecasting:

- **Forecast speed**
  Forecasting is a time-consuming task. With time series forecasting, you can get results in hours instead of weeks.

- **Increased forecast accuracy**
  Experience proves that you'll often get more accurate predictions with time series forecasting algorithms compared to the ones delivered by business experts. Another reason time series forecasting models help get more accurate predictions is the amount of work manual forecast requires. Using predictive models, you can forecast the sales for 1,000 distinct products, while you may not have the workforce to do it manually.

Still, it's a good idea to have the predictive forecasts reviewed by business experts.

Time Series Forecasting versus Regression

Both regression and time series forecasting relate to predicting numeric values, so people often wonder when they should use one or the other. *Regression* (see Chapter 10) is about predicting the value of a numeric variable using related variables. The answered question has no explicit relation to time. However, time series forecasting is about predicting future values of a sequence of values. The answered question is intrinsically related to time. For instance, if you want to predict the possible sales price of a list of cars currently for sale, then you need to use a regression model to determine the relationship between the price and the other car attributes. But if you want to predict the evolution in the future of the price of a car, then you need to use a time series forecasting model.

4.1.2   Top-Down versus Bottom-Up Predictive Forecasting

Most of the time, it's possible to consider your data at different levels of detail. Let's assume you want to forecast the travel expenses for your company. You can consider the time series that relate to travel expenses at the company level, but it's likely that this time series is the result of aggregated data based on country and lines of business (LoBs), for instance. Each detailed time series, corresponding to a data slice—in this example, the time series for each LoB in each country—is called an *entity*.

Having access to the detailed data at the entity level allows for different predictive forecasting approaches:

- **Top-down**
  With this approach, you forecast your travel expenses globally, at the company-wide level. You must then rely on disaggregation rules to determine the detailed forecast at the entity level (per countries and LoB).

- **Bottom-up**
  This is the opposite approach to the top-down approach. With this approach, you create a forecast specifically for each entity you want to consider. The global forecast (company-wide in our example) is calculated by aggregating the forecast for all the entities.

In this book, we'll use the term *entity* indifferently for a time series corresponding to the detailed data slice and for the predictive model that is created to forecast this time series.

Figure 4.3 illustrates the two approaches using a planning model with only two dimensions, country and LoB, and only two members per dimension to simplify the example.

Intermediate approaches are also possible. In the example shown in Figure 4.3, we could create the predictive forecast at the country level. This intermediate approach makes it possible to both aggregate the forecast at the company level and disaggregate at the LoB level.

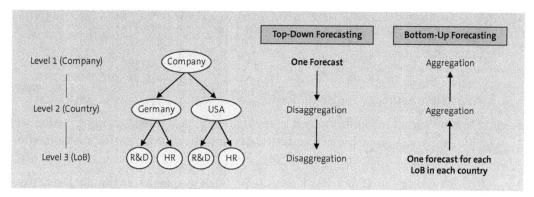

Figure 4.3 Top-Down versus Bottom-Up Forecasting Comparison

A bottom-up approach (i.e., an intermediate approach) often leads to more accurate results compared to a top-down approach. First, the major problem with the top-down approach is that the predicted values must be disaggregated. This can be done manually or automatically, but in both cases, it's based on assumptions that may not be realistic; you don't necessarily know in advance how the forecast values must be disaggregated between the different countries and between the different LoBs.

Secondly, when working with aggregated data, you may be missing some local patterns in the data that are local to some entities and may help increase the prediction accuracy. We'll illustrate this issue in our example in Figure 4.4. Looking at the local time series for human resources (HR), we can see a downward trend as well as some regular high and low peaks. Looking at the local time series for research and development (R&D), we can see an upward trend as well as some regular low peaks. As we'll see in Chapter 9, these patterns can be detected by predictive planning and leveraged to get accurate predictions. All of these specific trends and peaks are lost in the aggregated time series.

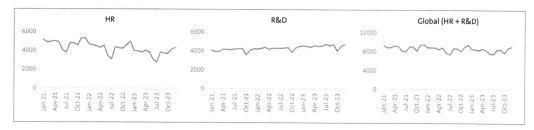

Figure 4.4 Local Time Series versus Aggregated Time Series

Chapter 8, Section 8.6, explains how to choose the best approach based on your specific data.

4.2   Data Sources for Time Series Forecasting Models

Smart predict enables you to use different types of data sources to create time series forecasting models. In this section, we first introduce the specificities of these different data sources with regard to time series forecasting, then we explain how data must be prepared when using datasets.

4.2.1   Data Sources

The time series forecasting models in smart predict can leverage planning models and datasets as data sources. The specificities of each data source are discussed in the following sections.

When working with time series forecasting models, two data sources must be considered:

- **Training data source**
  This is the data source the time series algorithm will use to train a time series forecasting model.
- **Predictions data source**
  This is the data source generated by the predictive model that contains the predictions.

Planning Models

The time series forecasting predictive scenarios can be used with planning models. This integration is called *predictive planning*. Predictive planning provides a tight integration with the planning models and allows you to leverage most of the capabilities of the planning models. More details are available in Chapter 5.

When working with planning models, the training data source and the predictions data source correspond to different *versions* of the planning model, as illustrated by Figure 4.5. Planning model versions allow you to maintain different variations of the planning data. Versions are explained in Chapter 5, Section 5.2.3. It's best practice to have distinct versions to store data—one to store the historical data used to train the predictive model and one to store predictions generated by the predictive model.

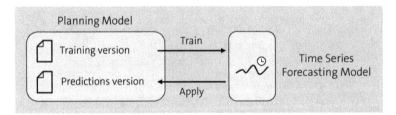

Figure 4.5 Planning Model as Data Source for Time Series Forecasting Model

Datasets

The training data source and the predictions data source are two distinct datasets, as illustrated by Figure 4.6.

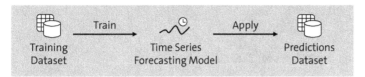

Figure 4.6 Dataset as Data Source for the Time Series Forecasting Model

For a given predictive model, smart predict enforces the technical compatibility between the training and the predictions datasets:

- **Acquired**
  When a time series forecasting model is created using an acquired training dataset, both the application and the predictions dataset must be acquired datasets.

- **Live**
  When a time series forecasting model is created using a live training dataset, both the application and the predictions datasets must be live datasets. In addition, these two datasets must be available in the same SAP HANA instance.

This compatibility is enforced only in the context of a single predictive model. A predictive scenario can contain predictive models trained and applied both with live and acquired datasets, or predictive models trained and applied using different data repositories.

4.2.2   Basic Data Preparation for Datasets

When working with planning models, the data required by the time series forecasting model is transparently read from the planning model structure using the predictive modeling setting defined by the end user. You don't have to care about defining a specific data structure for your planning model to use it for time series forecasting needs.

Conversely, when working with datasets, smart predict requires data to be formatted in a certain way as explained in the following sections.

Basic Time Series Forecasting

When working with datasets, in the simplest cases, your training dataset must follow the minimum structure described in Table 4.1 (where n is the number of observations).

Date	Quantity
Date1	Value1
...	...
$Date_n$	$Value_n$

Table 4.1 Structure of a Training Dataset for Time Series Forecasting

Table 4.2 shows how this data structure can be used for cash flow forecasting.

Date	Global Cash Flow
Jan 2020	653,214
...	...
Dec 2023	685,555

Table 4.2 Dataset Example for Cash Flow Forecasting

Each dataset row corresponds to an observation. Each observation is described by the date of the observation used to order the rows and the measured quantity (a numeric value). The date column must use a format recognized as a date by the datasets; integers are not supported as date columns. As no aggregation capability is available for the datasets, each date in the training dataset must appear only once.

In this simple case, the dates for the predictions are automatically inferred based on the average spacing between the dates that are part of the training dataset.

Forced Forecasting Horizon

If you want to force specific dates for the predictions, you can provide them in the training dataset, as shown in Table 4.3. Doing so can be useful if you want to enforce a forecast granularity that is different from the actual average granularity of the observations. For instance, if your training dataset contains monthly data, but some observations are missing, the inferred forecast granularity may be greater than one month. If you want to get a monthly predictive forecast, you must specify the horizon dates explicitly.

Date	Quantity
$Date_1$	$Value_1$
...	...
$Date_n$	$Value_n$

Table 4.3 Structure of a Training Dataset for Time Series Forecasting (Forced Horizon)

Date	Quantity
$Date_{n+1}$	*<empty>*
...	*<empty>*
$Date_{n+h}$	*<empty>*

Table 4.3 Structure of a Training Dataset for Time Series Forecasting (Forced Horizon) (Cont.)

In Table 4.3, h is the size of the horizon, that is, the number of predicted forecast periods. The rows from $Date_{n+1}$ to $Date_{n+h}$ are only meant to specify the dates of the predictions, so the value to be predicted must be empty.

Table 4.4 shows an example of cash flow forecasting with forced forecasting horizon dates. In this example, because some monthly observations are missing (e.g., the observation for February 2020), a nonmonthly predictive forecast is inferred. However, a predictive forecast will be provided for January, February, and March 2024 because the dates have been explicitly provided without a target value in the training dataset. It's assumed that three forecast periods have been requested.

Date	Global Cash Flow
Jan 2020	456,789
Mar 2020	466,729
...	...
Dec 2023	446,329
Jan 2024	*<empty>*
Feb 2024	*<empty>*
Mar 2024	*<empty>*

Table 4.4 Cash Flow Forecasting Example with an Explicit Horizon

Forecasting Using Influencers

Optionally, you can add influencer columns as additional columns to the dataset. The *influencers* (also known as external regressors) are values that you think are potentially correlated to the target evolution and can be used to improve the accuracy of the predictions. In datasets, the influencers can either be numeric or nominal values (standing for labels). Table 4.5 shows the structure of a training dataset that can be used in the context of time series forecasting.

Date	Quantity	Influencer$_1$	...	Influencer$_m$
Date$_1$	Value$_1$	Influencer value$_{1.1}$	...	Influencer value$_{m.1}$
Date$_2$	Value$_2$	Influencer value$_{1.2}$	...	Influencer value$_{m.2}$
...	...	...	...	...
Date$_n$	Value$_n$	Influencer value$_{1.n}$	...	Influencer value$_{m.n}$
Date$_{n+1}$	*<empty>*	Influencer value$_{1.n+1}$	...	Influencer value$_{m.n+1}$
...	*<empty>*	...	...	...
Date$_{n+h}$	*<empty>*	Influencer value$_{1.n+h}$	...	Influencer value$_{m.n+h}$

Table 4.5 Structure of a Training Dataset for Time Series Forecasting with Influencers

Dates *n+1* to *n+h* are the forecasting horizon, and *h* is the size of the horizon. It's important to note that the values of the influencers must be provided for all the dates of the forecasting horizon. Otherwise, smart predict will assume default values for the influencers, leading to possibly unrealistic predictions.

Table 4.6 shows an example of sales forecasting using the discount percentage as an influencer. On the forecast horizon (January 2024 to February 2024), the expected discount values are provided so the time series forecasting model can consider the discount when calculating the predictions.

Date	Units Sold <target>	Discount <influencer>
Jan 2023	56478	10
Feb 2023	66432	20
...	...	...
Dec 2023	49428	0
Jan 2024	*<empty>*	5
Feb 2024	*<empty>*	5
Mar 2024	*<empty>*	10

Table 4.6 Sales Forecasting Example with Influencers

Forecasting Using Entities

Entities are time series corresponding to different slices of data for which you want to get specific predictions as opposed to a global prediction. For instance, when predicting the sales volume for a product, you may want to get specific predictions for each country. In this case, each country is an entity.

Table 4.7 illustrates the structure of a dataset with one entity column.

Entity	Date	Quantity
Entity value$_{1.1}$	Date$_1$	Value$_1$
...	...	...
Entity value$_{1.1}$	Date$_n$	Value$_n$
...	...	...
Entity value$_{1.k}$	Date$_1$	Value$_1$
...		
Entity value$_{1.k}$	Date$_n$	Value$_n$

Table 4.7 Structure of a Training Dataset for Time Series Forecasting with Different Entities

Table 4.8 shows an example of sales forecasting where the values in the country column define the entities.

Country	Date	Units Sold
Germany	Jan 2020	56,478
...	...	...
Germany	Dec 2023	76,438
...	...	...
USA	Jan 2020	83,721
...	...	
USA	Dec 2023	75,432

Table 4.8 Sales Forecasting Example with Entities

For simplicity, Table 4.7 and Table 4.8 show a case where only one entity column is used and the training dates are the same for all the entities, but smart predict can manage more complex cases:

- **Multiple entities**
  You can have more than one entity column in your dataset. For instance, if you want to get predictions for each product in each country, then you need one column for the countries and one for the products. Smart predict can use up to five entity columns.

- **Different training dates**
  Each entity can have a different set of training dates. While you'll usually use the

same period of historical data for all the entities, the exact set of training dates can also be slightly different for each entity. This may be caused by missing data, by the appearance of new entities (e.g., products that went for sale recently), or by the disappearance of previously existing entities (e.g., products that are discontinued and for which data isn't gathered anymore).

- **Entities and influencers**
  It's possible to combine the use of both entities and influencers.

Finally, note that because aggregation isn't available with the datasets, it's mandatory to use in predictive model setting to specify the columns that define the entity when entities exist in the dataset. Otherwise, the training of the predictive model will end with an error complaining about the dates being duplicated or not properly sorted.

4.3   End-to-End Time Series Forecasting Workflows

The following sections illustrate end-to-end workflows to consume predictive forecasts in stories. We'll cover scenarios when using planning models and when using datasets.

4.3.1   Time Series Forecasting Based on Planning Models

Figure 4.7 illustrates the end-to-end workflow for creating SAP Analytics Cloud stories using predictions generated by a time series forecasting model.

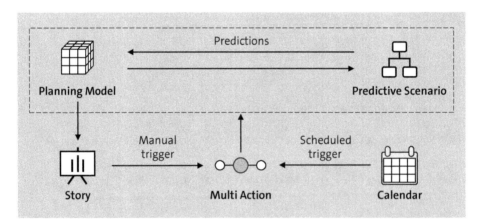

Figure 4.7 End-to-End Time Series Forecasting Workflow for Planning Models

Let's further detail this high-level workflow:

1. You must create two versions in your planning model: one containing the data to train the time series forecasting model and one version (usually empty) that will receive the predictive forecast.

2. You can train a time series forecasting model in a predictive scenario using the training version of your planning model.

3. Using the trained time series forecasting model, you save the predictive forecast into the empty planning version you created previously.

4. You can use a story to display the data you just saved.

5. Delivering a predictive forecast to a story once is great, but you would probably want the predictive forecast to be updated as soon as new actuals are available. Three distinct update workflows are possible depending on your needs:

   – *Controlled predictive forecast*: You can use this workflow if you need to validate the quality of the predictive model before new predictions are available in the story. In this workflow, you can use the smart predict user interface to manually retrain the time series forecasting model, assess the resulting predictive model, and finally save the predictions to the forecast planning version.

   – *Self-service predictive forecast*: You'll use this workflow if you want the story end user to handle the predictive forecast update. In this workflow, you must use a multi action to allow the user of the story to retrain the predictive model and to save the predictive forecast to a given version.

   – *Scheduled predictive forecast*: You'll use this workflow if you want the predictive forecast displayed in the story to be refreshed regularly without requiring end-user involvement. In this workflow, you must use a scheduled multi action.

These three update workflows are explained in further detail in Chapter 5 and Chapter 6.

4.3.2   Time Series Forecasting Based on Datasets

Figure 4.8 illustrates the end-to-end workflow to include predictions generated by a time series forecasting model in stories.

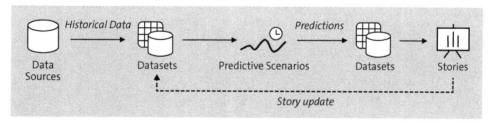

Figure 4.8 End-to-End Time Series Forecasting Workflow for Datasets

The details of this high-level workflow are given here:

1. Identify the data sources used to create the story and those used to train the predictive model. At this step, you must also prepare the data so it can be used for predictive purposes (Section 4.2.2).

2. Enable SAP Analytics Cloud to consume this data by creating acquired or live datasets.

3. Train time series forecasting models in a predictive scenario.

4. Use the trained time series forecasting models to save predictions in a dataset.

5. Consume the dataset in a story.

To update the story with new predictions, some of the steps mentioned must be repeated:

1. If you're working with acquired datasets, then the training dataset must be updated by reimporting data. If you're working with live datasets, you must recreate the training dataset in SAP Analytics Cloud only if its structure has changed. If the structure of your live dataset hasn't changed, then you can move to step 2 directly.

2. More recent data points may be available. You must train a new time series forecasting model to take these new data points into account.

3. Using the refreshed predictive model, you can now generate new predictions to the predictions dataset.

4. If you've overwritten the data of an existing predictions dataset, you don't need to update the story.

4.4   Summary

This chapter introduced time series forecasting models. You've learned what time series forecasting is and the type of business cases it can help with. You've also learned how time series forecasting models can be used with the different data sources available in SAP Analytics Cloud and the high-level workflows that allow you to include predictive forecasts in stories.

With this foundation in place, we'll explain how to use predictive time series forecasting models step-by-step in the next chapter.

Chapter 5

Using Predictive Forecasts in the Planning Process

Forecasting is a key part of the planning activity. The forecasts are traditionally created by experts using their business acumen. But this requires a lot of effort, and the accuracy isn't always as high as expected. What if predictive analytics could help improve the forecasting process?

SAP Analytics Cloud includes powerful planning features. It allows you to set goals for your company's strategic plan, analyze budgets, perform allocations, and compare planning versions while leveraging all the analytics capabilities available in SAP Analytics Cloud.

Smart predict provides time series forecasting capabilities that can be used to improve and accelerate your planning cycles. Thanks to its tight integration with the planning models through the *predictive planning* capability, you can get accurate forecasts faster while remaining autonomous from the IT department.

In this chapter, we'll introduce a travel expense forecast scenario to show the use of predictive forecasting in Section 5.1. Then you'll learn about the fundamentals of planning models in Section 5.2 and how to train time series forecasting models using planning models as data sources in Section 5.3. Section 5.4 and Section 5.5 will describe how to understand your time series forecasting models through reports and how to improve them, respectively. Finally, this chapter will teach you how to save your forecasts (Section 5.6) and use them in a story (Section 5.7).

5.1 Business Scenario

Let's say you work as a financial planning analyst, and you're using SAP Analytics Cloud for your planning activities. As this is the beginning of the year, you're asked to forecast the travel expenses for the coming year. You need to get a forecast for each line of business (LoB) in each country where the company has employees.

To fulfill this task, you used to contact each country responsible and ask them to provide their own forecast. But over time, you've noticed that this approach has many flaws. It's disrupting many company employees who interrupt their daily work to provide a forecast. The forecasts weren't always as accurate as you might expect. This year, you'll do things differently. Using predictive planning, you'll generate predictive forecasts for all the LoBs in all countries based on the history of travel expense data. Doing so, you expect to limit your colleagues' involvement while getting more accurate forecasts in less time.

However, you still want to involve the country responsible during the predictive forecast validation phase. This allows the persons in charge who have specific information to possibly adapt the predictive forecast. The other people in charge who think the predictive forecast is fine will only have to approve the predicted values.

We're assuming a very simple planning model with the following characteristics:

- There is one measure named travel expenses.
- There are two dimensions: country and LoB.
- The time granularity is month.

While the time series forecasting models can be used with datasets, we'll assume planning models as the data source in this chapter. For more information on time series forecasting with datasets, see Chapter 7.

The *travelexpenses.csv* file that allows you to create the SAP Analytics Cloud planning model to support this scenario is available at *https://sap-press.com/5771*. Chapter 2, Section 2.3.2, explains how to create a planning model from a comma-separated values (CSV) file. The examples in this book assume that the planning model is named "Travel and Expenses." We recommend that you use the same name so you can easily follow along with the examples.

5.2   Planning Models

SAP Analytics Cloud offers two types of data models: analytic models and planning models. *Analytic models* are SAP Analytics Cloud objects that act as data sources and contain metadata (data that provides information about other data) that allows you to display the data into a story. A *planning model* is basically an analytic model with the following additional capabilities:

- You can modify the data of a planning model, whereas analytic models are read only.
- The planning models have dimension semantics (organization) that aren't available in analytic models. See Section 5.2.2 to learn about dimensions.
- The planning models have data versioning capabilities. See Section 5.2.3 to learn about versions.

New Model versus Classic Account Model

In SAP Analytics Cloud, two different types of planning models exist: the *classic account model* and the *new model*. The main difference between these two types of models is that the classic account model represents the numeric values as accounts, while the new models represent the number values as measures. You can learn more about the differences between the classic account model and new model at *http://s-prs.co/v577115*. As the new model will eventually replace the classic account model, to keep things simple, we'll always assume that the new model is used in this section. If you're using classic account models, you can still follow along the examples presented in this chapter. Yet, you'll notice some slight differences, such as the term "account" being used instead of "measure" in stories.

Now, let's walk through the different aspects of a planning model.

5.2.1 Measures

A measure is a numeric value or quantity representing something you want to measure, hence the name. As it stores numeric values, a measure can be aggregated, and it can be used in calculations. For instance, cost, price, revenue, and quantity sold are quantities represented as measures in planning models.

We can distinguish two main types of measures:

- **Standard measures**
  The values for these measures are stored in the model. Planning models allow you to modify the values of standard measures by entering data in a planning table (a spreadsheet-like user interface [UI] available in the stories) or by using a script.

- **Calculated measures**
  The values for these measures are the result of a calculation involving other measures or dimensions. Such values can't be changed directly.

5.2.2 Dimensions

A dimension is an element of the model that allows you to categorize or label the transactions stored in the model. A dimension is defined by a set of categorical values called *members*. Dimensions allow you to build perspectives or points of view on the data by grouping and filtering on the members. Country, product, and organization are typical examples of dimensions.

Optionally, the dimension members can be organized into a *hierarchy*. A hierarchy defines relationships between the members. These relationships can be leveraged in stories to choose between detailed views of the data. In SAP Analytics Cloud, there are two types of hierarchies:

- **Parent-child hierarchy**
  A parent-child hierarchy is defined by the members of a single dimension. Therefore, all members of the hierarchy represent the same type of object at all levels.
  Each member of the hierarchy has an attribute pointing to a parent member, thus
  defining a tree structure between the members. This allows some branches of the
  hierarchy to be deeper than others if needed. The exact level of each member within
  the hierarchy is defined implicitly. For instance, the employees of a company can be
  organized using a parent-child hierarchy where the "parent" of an employee is their
  manager. The exact hierarchical level of each employee is defined implicitly by their
  position in their branch.

- **Level-based hierarchy**
  A level-based hierarchy can be used to represent a regular hierarchy with a predefined number of levels. Each level of the hierarchy is defined explicitly by a distinct dimension. Therefore, it's possible to have objects of a different nature at each
  level. For instance, a location could be represented using a level-based hierarchy
  made of three dimensions, Region, Country, and City, each having possibly different
  properties.

Figure 5.1 illustrates the differences between the parent-child and the level-based hierarchies.

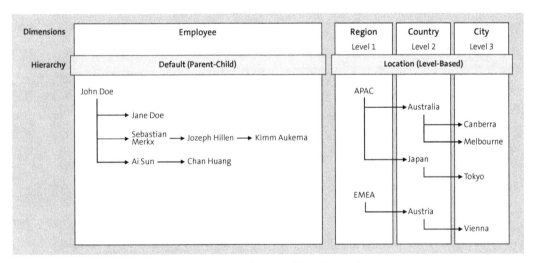

Figure 5.1 Parent-Child and Level-Based Hierarchies Comparison

A given dimension can have multiple hierarchies. In SAP Analytics Cloud, when several
hierarchies exist for a dimension, one of them must be defined as the default hierarchy. The default hierarchy is then used by default in the different workflows using the
planning model, such as the stories. Dimensions can also have member properties.
Member properties allow you to specify attributes specific to each member. For

instance, products may have a weight property, and customers may have a phone number property.

Some dimensions have a specific semantic understood by SAP Analytics Cloud. Each of these semantics corresponds to a predefined type of dimension. Date, account, category, or organization are examples of such dimension types. Other user-defined dimensions that don't correspond to a specific semantic are called *generic dimensions*.

We'll take a closer look at two important types of dimensions in the following sections: the date dimension and the account dimension.

Date Dimension

A date dimension allows ordering transactions over time. The members of the dimension are dates. It's mandatory to have a date dimension representing the date of the transactions in a planning model. This date is referenced in the **Date Dimension Used for Planning** setting. For the sake of simplicity, this is the dimension we'll refer to in the rest of this book when referring to the date dimension. The planning model can contain other date dimensions, but only one is associated with this setting.

The date dimensions have a lot of settings that provide a very high level of customization. In this section, we'll provide an overview of the settings relevant to predictive planning:

- **Date granularity**
  The first parameter you must choose is the date granularity. The granularity defines the most detailed temporal level of the data. Will your date be stored at the day, month, or year level?

  The quality of the time series forecasting models you'll build may be strongly impacted by this choice. Figure 5.2 and Figure 5.3 show the same travel expenses stored using a day granularity and using a month granularity. We can see that when the data is stored at the day level, the time series is very irregular with a lot of days without values for the travel expenses. It's very unlikely that a time series forecasting model could accurately determine travel expenses using this granularity.

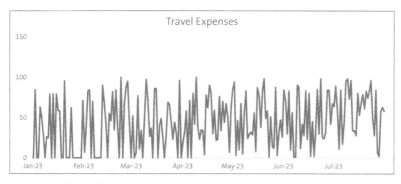

Figure 5.2 Travel Expenses at Day Granularity

On the other hand, using a month granularity, the time series is more regular and even exhibits an obvious increasing trend. Travel expenses will be easier to forecast at a monthly level.

Figure 5.3 Travel Expenses at Month Granularity

The opposite is also possible. By storing the data at the month level, some patterns, which exist at the day level and could be leveraged by a time series forecasting model, may be lost.

As we mentioned in Chapter 4, predictive planning doesn't provide a temporal aggregation capability. The data is always consumed using the lowest temporal granularity available. If you create a planning model specifically for the purpose of predictive forecasting, you need to think about the granularity that will provide the most usable data.

- **Planning time range**
  The planning time range defines the date range available in the planning model. If the planning time range is from 2020 to 2023, dates exist in the model from January 1, 2020, to December 31, 2023. You can enter values between these two dates, but not before and not after. This must be considered when using predictive planning. Let's assume that your planning model contains travel expense data from 2018 to 2022, and you would like to predict expenses for 2023. The time range of the planning model is probably between 2018 and 2022 because it corresponds to the required time range for the data you have. The time range for the planning model must be extended to 2023 or predictive planning won't be able to write predictions for 2023.

  Once it has been defined, the time range can be extended to earlier or future years, but it can't be reduced because of possible data loss.

Account Dimension

The *account dimension's* members define numeric values, representing a quantity: The members of the account dimension, called *accounts*, are basically measures. As such, they have all the settings you can expect from a measure (aggregation type, decimal places, etc.) represented as properties of the dimension. The value of an account can also be the result of a calculation involving other accounts.

In predictive planning, measures and accounts are represented in the same way. Both are just quantities that you can forecast.

As any dimension, the account dimension allows for defining parent-child hierarchies to organize the accounts. The hierarchy of accounts implicitly defines aggregation rules controlled by the account types: the value of the children is added or deducted from the parent account depending on the account type.

New Model versus Classic Account Model

When working with the new model, the numeric values can be represented using either measures only or both accounts and measures. In the latter case, a quantity is represented by the intersection of a specific account with a specific measure. Working directly with accounts is only possible when using the classic account model.

5.2.3   Versions

The *versions* of a planning model allow you to maintain different variations of the planning data. When the data of a version is modified, the data of the other versions remain unmodified.

Why would you need different variations of the same planning model? Well, if you're only interested in analyzing the past travel expenses, then you probably only need one version, representing what happened in the past. But planning is mainly about the future. You would probably want an additional version representing your travel expense budget. Keeping the data for these two versions distinct will enable you to compare them later to answer questions such as "Was the travel budget respected?" You may even want to create more versions for the forecasted travel expenses or for more alternative budgets.

There are two types of versions:

- **Public versions**
  The public versions are available to all the users who can access the planning model. They usually contain data that has been properly validated and is ready to be shared publicly, for instance, in a story.

- **Private versions**
  The private versions, by default, are only available to the user who created them. They usually contain data that isn't ready or not meant to be shared, such as experiments or work in progress. The private versions can be explicitly shared with a set of users, or they can be published, that is, transformed into public versions.

Here is an example of a typical workflow, involving both private and public versions, you may want to implement when using predictive planning:

1. Create an empty private planning version that will receive the predictive forecast.
2. Train a time series forecasting model.
3. Write the predictions of the time series forecasting model to the empty private planning version.
4. Share the planning version that contains the prediction with some reviewers.
5. Once reviewed, publish the version.

5.2.4   Currencies

The planning models allow associating the values of a measure to a specific currency. For instance, the travel expenses for each country can be stored and displayed in the currency of the country. Currency conversion is also supported, allowing to convert values expressed in different currencies to a common currency. For instance, it's possible to convert all the travel expenses to a common currency, for instance the US dollar, and thus get the global sum of the travel expenses across all the countries in that common currency.

How exactly the currency conversion works depends on the exact type of planning models you're using:

- **New model**
  Currency conversion measures must be created to handle the conversion. How the conversion is performed depends on the configuration of the conversion measure.
- **Classic account model**
  How currency relevant values are displayed mainly depends on the configuration of the visualization in the story.

Predictive planning supports currency conversion and enables you, when multiple entities are involved, to forecast each entity either in its local currency or in a common currency. The support of the currency-relevant values with the entities is explained in Section 5.3.6.

5.3   Creating Time Series Forecasting Models with Predictive Planning

In this section, we'll explain how to create a time series forecasting model using a planning model as the training data source. We'll also provide an extensive overview of the settings and how they can be used to get the best out of predictive planning.

5.3.1   Create a Predictive Scenario

Figure 5.4 shows the SAP Analytics Cloud homepage. This is where you'll usually start navigating into SAP Analytics Cloud.

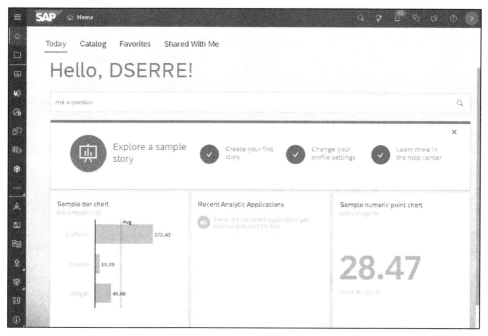

Figure 5.4 SAP Analytics Cloud's Homepage

Starting from the SAP Analytics Cloud's homepage, follow these steps:

1. Click the **Predictive Scenarios** entry ![icon] in the left navigation bar of the UI. The **Predictive Scenarios** entry may be hidden in the **More** menu ![icon] in the navigation bar depending on the space available on screen. The **Predictive Scenarios** button is also available under the **Create** menu of the SAP Analytics Cloud file system ![icon]. If you can't find the **Predictive Scenarios** entry, make sure that you've been granted the proper privileges.

2. Under **Create New**, click the **Time Series Forecast** button, as shown in Figure 5.5.

Figure 5.5 Create a New Time Series Forecasting Predictive Scenario

3. A dialog box called **New Predictive Scenario** will be displayed to let you save the newly created predictive scenario. In the **Name** field, enter "travel expenses prediction", and click **OK**. You can choose to save the predictive scenario to a specific folder. By default, the predictive scenario will be saved in your private user folder.

4. The predictive scenario interface is displayed, as shown in Figure 5.6, and a first time series forecasting model is automatically created for you. You can see the settings for this time series forecasting model in the right-hand side **Settings** panel. For now, the settings are empty.

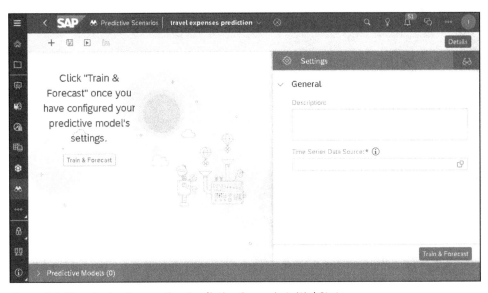

Figure 5.6 Time Series Forecasting Predictive Scenario Initial State

5.3.2   General Settings

Now, let's get started with the different model settings. The **General** section of the time series forecasting model settings is shown in Figure 5.7.

Figure 5.7 General Settings for a Time Series Forecasting Model Based on a Planning Model

Description

Description is a free-form text field for describing the intent of a specific predictive model. While it's optional, it's a best practice to provide a meaningful description for each of your predictive models. You may be sharing your predictive scenario with other colleagues who need to know what each predictive model in the predictive scenario corresponds to. Entering a description will help you properly document your predictive model so your colleagues can easily understand the various predictive models you created. Even if you aren't sharing your predictive scenarios with other colleagues, we encourage you to enter the description of the predictive model. It may be clear to you now what each predictive model corresponds to, but if you come back next month, you may not remember as clearly as today. Will it be clear which predictive model you used to generate your predictions? Entering proper descriptions shouldn't be neglected.

For our example, we'll enter "by country and LoB" as we'll create a time series forecasting model producing forecasts per country and LoB.

Time Series Data Source and Version

The **Time Series Data Source** field allows you to select the data source you want to use to train a time series forecasting model. The training data source setting is mandatory. When working with time series forecasting predictive scenarios, you can use planning models and datasets (acquired and live) as training data sources. Analytic models aren't supported in time series forecasting predictive scenarios because they are read only and therefore don't allow you to save the predictions.

It's mandatory to select the planning **Version** to be used to train the time series forecasting model. To be useful, the time series forecasting model must learn from what happened in the past. You usually want to select a version that contains the actual data. The planning version can be either public or private.

For our example, we'll select the "Travel and Expenses" planning model and the "Actuals" version that contain the travel expenses history.

5.3.3   Predictive Goal

The **Predictive Goal** section of the settings allows you to specify what you want to forecast (see Figure 5.8).

The following sections explain the **Predictive Goal** settings in detail.

Figure 5.8 Predictive Goal Settings

Target

The first setting to be selected in this section is the **Target**. The target is the variable you want to predict. Depending on your planning model setup, you may have to select a measure, an account, or both. Note that neither calculated accounts nor calculated measures (including currency conversion measures) can be used as a target. If you want to forecast the measure C, which depends on A and B, then you must forecast A and B separately (if A and B aren't, in turn, calculated measures).

When working with accounts, predictive planning always uses the default hierarchy. The different accounts of the hierarchy are represented in a flat list in the account selector. The account is displayed in the list using its description, but the identifier is available as a tooltip. You can use the tooltip if you need to differentiate between two accounts that have the same description.

For our example, we'll select the "travel expenses" measure.

Date

The **Date** setting makes it possible to select the date dimension used to order the observations. Usually, you'll select the **Date Dimension used for Planning** (Section 5.2.2). For our example, we'll select the **Date** dimension. Once the **Date** dimension is selected, the **Time Granularity** field is updated. This field is read only. It's meant to remind you of the date granularity. As predictive planning provides no temporal aggregation capability, this corresponds to the granularity of the training data. For instance, if the granularity displayed in **Time Granularity** is **by month**, each data point will correspond to a specific month. The time granularity also applies to the forecast horizon. If the time granularity is **by month**, then each forecast point will correspond to a month.

Number of Forecast Periods

The **Number of Forecast Periods** field allows you to specify the number of data points to be predicted in the future (usually known as the *forecast horizon*). This setting goes hand in hand with the **Time Granularity** setting. For instance, if the **Number of Forecast Periods** is set to **3** and the **Time Granularity** is **by month**, then it means that you'll get a predictive forecast for three consecutive months. The first forecast period always corresponds to the date, as determined by the planning model based on the date granularity, which immediately follows the date of the last training observation (Section 5.3.4). For our example, we'll enter "12" in the **Number of Forecast Periods** field as we want to forecast 12 months ahead.

You may wonder why the forecast horizon must be specified as a model training setting. Why don't we just train a model and specify the number of predictions to be generated at the time they are generated? There are two reasons for that:

- Specifying the length of the forecast horizon allows smart predict to automatically select the model that provides the best performance for this specific forecast horizon.

- Using the smart predict modeling reports, you can check before writing the predictions to a planning version if the chosen forecast horizon is realistic.

There are several things to consider when choosing a number of forecast periods:

- **Does the number of requested forecast periods correspond to your business requirements?**
  As we have seen, the number of requested forecast periods plays a role in the optimization of the time series forecasting model. The best model to predict 12 months ahead isn't necessarily the best model to predict 6 months ahead. If you need only a 6-month forecast, then use this value as a number of forecast periods so you get the best possible time series forecasting model.

- **Is your forecasting objective realistic considering the time granularity of the planning model?**
  The further in the future you want to forecast, the less the forecast has a chance of being accurate. If you need to provide a forecast for the next two years, then it's probably not realistic to work with a day granularity as this would correspond to forecasting 730 points ahead. Working with a month granularity, you would have to forecast only 24 points ahead, which is certainly more realistic.

- **Do you have enough historical data to get a prediction interval for each forecast period?**
  The prediction interval tells you how confident you can be about the prediction for each forecast period (the prediction interval is explained in Section 5.4.1). For each forecast period, you need 5 training points to calculate a prediction interval. For instance, if you want to forecast 12 points ahead, you will need 60 points of historical data in your training dataset. If you have only 55 points in the training dataset, then

you'll get the request for 12 predictions, but only 11 with a prediction interval. The predictive forecast is usable, but the information you need to assess its accuracy isn't complete.

The number of forecast periods is limited to 500 by predictive planning to limit the volume of resources (CPU, memory, etc.) needed to train a time series forecasting model.

Entity

The **Entity** setting allows you to choose between a top-down and bottom-up approach of predictive forecasting (see Chapter 4, Section 4.1). You can select up to five dimensions (or dimension attributes) to define the data slices corresponding to the entities. Figure 5.9 shows what happens if you choose the **country** dimension in the **Entity** field to define the entities. A data slice is first created for each country. Then for each slice, the data is aggregated across all the dimensions not selected in the entity field, except for the date. After the aggregation, each slice is reduced to a time series that we call an entity. A specific time series forecasting model is created for each entity.

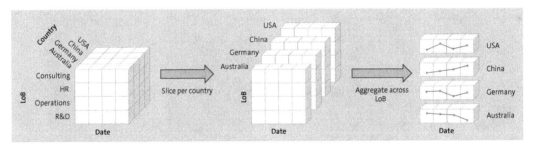

Figure 5.9 Forecasting per Country

By default, an entity is automatically created for each nonempty slice. Figure 5.10 shows an example where both the country and the LoB dimensions are used to define the entities. An entity is created for each combination of country and LoB, except for the human resources (HR) LoB in Australia and the consulting LoB in Germany that have no available data.

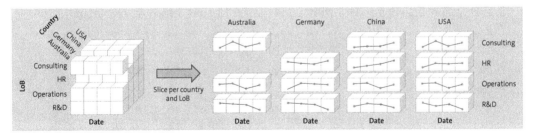

Figure 5.10 Forecasting per Country and LoB

For our example, we'll select the "country" and "LoB" dimensions as we want to get predictions for each LoB in each country.

Predictive planning is limited to a maximum of 1,000 entities per time series forecasting model. If the members of the dimension are organized in a hierarchy, then, by default, the leaf members (members that aren't parent of other members) are used to create entities. This default behavior can be changed by using the **Entity Filters** settings.

Section 5.3.6 details how to use the entities.

Entity Filters

The **Entity Filters** setting allows you to specify a subset of entities to be included in the predictive forecasting scope. This can be useful if you want to ignore some entities because you know that they can't be accurately predicted. For instance, let's assume you're forecasting the expenses per country and a new branch was opened in Germany only 3 months ago. You would probably want to exclude this entity upfront because you know there isn't enough historical data available to train a good enough time series forecasting model. For our example, we'll select countries "USA" and "Germany" to create entities only for those countries. We'll select no LoB explicitly to create entities for all the LoBs.

The entity filters also let you control the predictive forecast granularity. When the members of a dimension used to create the entities are organized in a hierarchy, the entity filter lets you select explicitly the level of the hierarchy to be used for each branch. For instance, let's assume the dimension location has a hierarchy defining multiple levels of geographic groupings. Using **Entity Filters,** you may choose to forecast each US state individually, except for the Midwest, which would be managed as one entity.

5.3.4   Predictive Model Training

The **Predictive Model Training** section contains settings with default values corresponding to the most common use cases that can optionally be refined. We'll discuss the settings in the next sections.

Training Dataset Timeframe

Predictive planning provides two settings, **Train Using** and **Until**, that allow you to specify the range of values to be considered in the training dataset.

The **Train Using** dropdown lets you define the size of the training period. There are two options:

- **All Observations**
  All the observations that exist before the date defined by the **Until** setting are included in the training dataset.

- **Window of Observations**
  Only the observations within the period defined by the user are included in the training dataset.

You can use the **Window of Observations** option to ignore data that is too old as it may reflect behavior that is no longer relevant. This will be discussed in more detail in Section 5.5.1.

Figure 5.11 shows how to use the **Train Using** option to include the past three years of data in the training dataset. Figure 5.12 illustrates the resulting training dataset. As you can see, while observations are available starting from January 2019, the training dataset includes only the observations corresponding to the most recent three years, from September 2020 to September 2023.

Figure 5.11 Settings to Train a Time Series Forecasting Model Using the Past Three Years of Data

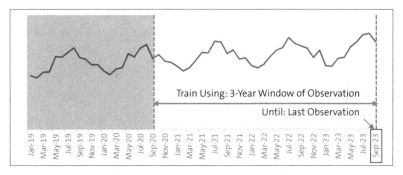

Figure 5.12 Training Dataset Corresponding to the Settings of Figure 5.11

The **Until** option defines the date of the most recent observation to be used in the training dataset. Two options are available:

- **Last Observation**
  Predictive planning will automatically use the most recent observation available in the data as the last observation to be included in the training dataset. This most recent data point is determined across all the entities.

- **User-Defined Date**

  Predictive planning will use the user-defined date to determine the last observation to be included in the training dataset. If no value exists for the provided date, the date corresponding to the most recent observation before the **User-Defined Date** is used instead.

Usually, you want the model to learn from the most recent data, so, in most cases, you'll use the **Last Observation** option. The **Last Observation** option has also the advantage of being dynamic: Every time you retrain the time series forecasting model, the most recent data points will be automatically used, while the **User-Defined Date** option requires you to manually change the date every time. The **Last Observation** option corresponds to most standard use cases and must be used if you plan to automate your predictive forecast using a multi action. The **User-Defined Date** option can be convenient if you want to perform back testing.

Figure 5.13 shows how to use the **Until** option to include all the available data periods until May 2023 in the training dataset. Figure 5.14 illustrates the resulting training dataset. As you can see, while observations are available until September 2023, the training dataset ends with the observation of May 2023 as per the **Until** option.

Figure 5.13 Settings to Train a Model Using All the Available Data Periods until May 2023

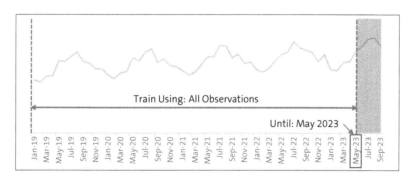

Figure 5.14 Training Dataset Resulting from the Settings of Figure 5.13

For our example, we'll keep the default values for the **Train Using** and **Until** options. **Train Using** must be set to **All Observations** and **Until** must be set to **Last Observation** as we want to train the time series forecasting model using all the available historical data.

Convert Negative Forecast Values to Zero

When forecasting a quantity that would normally always be greater than or equal to zero, a time series forecasting model might predict a negative value. How is this possible? In Figure 5.15, we can see that the travel expenses have decreased steadily for several consecutive months. A time series forecasting model would usually approximate such a time series using a simple linear decreasing function (or a similar function that would prolongate the linear decreasing trend). This works fine for a few months, but after some time, the time series forecasting model will start forecasting negative values if not configured to do otherwise. By enabling the **Convert Negative Forecast Values to Zero** option (see Figure 5.16), you can instruct the time series forecasting model that the values should be converted to zero if it forecasts negative values.

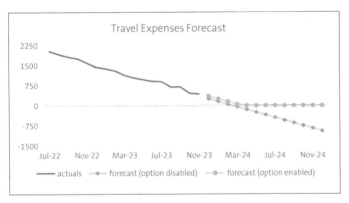

Figure 5.15 Impact of the Convert Negative Forecast Values to Zero Option

Figure 5.16 Enabling the Convert Negative Forecast Values to Zero Option

Note that the **Convert Negative Forecast Values to Zero** option has no impact on the time series forecasting model itself. For example, in Figure 5.15, the time series will be approximated by the same linear function whether the option is enabled or not. Every negative value forecasted by the time series forecasting model is changed to zero. The corrected prediction is used when calculating the error made by the time series forecasting model.

For our example, we'll enable the **Convert Negative Forecast Values to Zero** option as the expenses are always expressed as positive values.

5.3.5   Influencers

The **Influencers** section allows you to specify a set of candidate influencers for your time series forecasting model. Influencers are variables correlated to the target to be predicted. They allow you to better explain the target and therefore can improve the time series forecasting model accuracy. For instance, the number of planned in-person trainings may be correlated to the travel costs in some teams.

The time series forecasting algorithm will consider the influencers and determine if they are helping improve the accuracy of the model. By selecting candidate influencers, you're telling smart predict where potential additional information is available, but you can't force it to use specific candidate influencers that would not be increasing the time series forecasting model accuracy.

For our example, we'll select **events planned**, **training planned**, and **sales pipeline** as candidate influencers, as shown in Figure 5.17.

Figure 5.17 Influencers Configuration

When using a planning model as an input data source, only numeric values (measures or accounts) can be used as candidate influencers. If you want to leverage categorical candidate influencers (e.g., influencers corresponding to the occurrence of corporate events), consider using datasets as the input data source.

Section 5.5.3 further explains the use of influencers to improve the accuracy of your time series forecasting model.

5.3.6   Entities

In Section 5.3.3, we briefly mentioned that the **Entity** setting allows you to choose from a top-down, a bottom-up, or an intermediate predictive forecasting approach. To implement a top-down predictive forecasting approach, the **Entity** setting must remain empty. All the values for the target will be aggregated, and a single time series forecasting model will be built for company-wide travel expenses. To implement a bottom-up predictive forecasting approach, you must select at least one dimension as part of the **Entity** setting.

Figure 5.18 shows a time series forecasting model configured to provide forecasts for each LoB in each country.

Figure 5.18 Entity Configuration

There are additional considerations and impacts of the **Entity** setting, which we'll discuss in the following sections.

Disaggregation Behavior

Bottom-up predictive forecasting is at the lowest level of detail available in the planning model. In practice, this means getting a specific forecast for all the combinations of the members of all the dimensions of the planning model. In our travel expenses example, this means forecasting for every existing combination of country and LoB where data is available. As we'll see in the coming sections, working at this very detailed level is often not desirable or practical. Most of the time, you'll consider only a few dimensions to define the entities. As a result, some disaggregation will happen, and it's important to understand how it works.

Let's assume you use only the country dimension to define the entities. Two cases can be considered:

- **No value is booked at the disaggregation level**
  Figure 5.19 shows what happens in our example when no value is initially available at the LoB level ❶. As there is no weight to guide the disaggregation, the values forecasted at the country level ❷ aren't distributed to the different LoB. Instead, they are distributed to the default member (**Unassigned**) of the LoB level ❸.

Figure 5.19 Forecast Disaggregation: No Initial Values

- **Values are already booked at the disaggregation level**
  Figure 5.20 shows what happens in our example when values are initially available at the LoB level ❶. Values act as weights to guide disaggregation of the values forecasted at the country level ❷. For Germany ❸, one third of the forecasted value is

distributed to the **HR** LoB, two thirds are distributed to the **R&D** LoB, and nothing is distributed to the default member (**Unassigned**).

①	Measures	Travel Expenses
	Date >	2024
Country	**LoB**	
Germany	Unassigned	–
	HR	1
	R&D	2
USA	Unassigned	–
	HR	2
	R&D	1

② Measures	Travel Expenses
Date >	2024
Country	
Germany	100
USA	100

③	Measures	Travel Expenses
	Date >	2024
Country	**LoB**	
Germany	Unassigned	–
	HR	33
	R&D	67
USA	Unassigned	–
	HR	67
	R&D	33

Figure 5.20 Forecast Disaggregation: With Booked or Predefined Values

Currency and Entities

Some measures or accounts may represent values expressed in currencies that depend on a specific dimension. Typically, travel expense currencies depend on the country.

You usually don't want to aggregate values that are expressed in different currencies. For instance, you don't want to sum the travel expenses for Germany expressed in euros and the travel expenses for the United States expressed in US dollars. The only way to get relevant results is to either break down travel expenses by country or convert all the financial values to a common currency. Figure 5.21 shows that the travel expenses are displayed properly only when the country is used as part of the table because each country is associated with a different currency.

Travel and Expenses			Travel and Expenses	
Version	Actual		In USD	
Measures	travel expenses		Version	Actual
country	Germany	USA	Measures	travel expenses
LoB			**LoB**	
Consulting	€17,213.26	$99,161.86	Consulting	
HR	€137,923.94	$344,067.32	HR	
Operations	–	$134,230.13	Operations	134,230.13
R&D	€178,557.70	$274,377.71	R&D	

Figure 5.21 Measure with Multiple Currencies

Two situations must be considered when using a quantity as the target or an influencer whose specific currency depends on a dimension:

- **Classic account model**

  Predictive planning lets you choose between two modes via the **Default Currency** and **Local Currency** radio buttons. With the **Default Currency** mode, all the financial values are implicitly converted into the currency configured as the **Default Currency** in the model, making it possible to sum values originally stored in using distinct currencies. With the **Local Currency** mode, any value is read and written using the associated local currency. In this case, predictive planning forces you to select the dimension with the currency attribute as the entity dimension. This prevents values in different currencies from being aggregated.

- **New model**

  As implicit conversion to a common currency is no longer possible, predictive planning forces you to select the dimension with the currency attribute as the entity dimension. This way, values associated with different currencies aren't aggregated. You can create a currency conversion measure in the planning model explicitly if you want to be able to aggregate values of different entities.

Figure 5.22 shows how predictive planning ensures that values in different currencies aren't summed together.

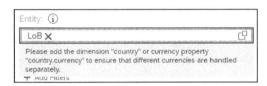

Figure 5.22 Handling Multiple Currencies in Predictive Planning

Note that while the currency isn't explicitly displayed in the modeling reports of predictive planning, both the report values and the predicted values are expressed and must be interpreted using the currency associated with the entity.

Impact of Entities on Influencers

The influencer values are read in the context of each entity, leading to possibly different influencer values for each entity. In most situations, this corresponds to the expected behavior. Sometimes, however, this behavior isn't desirable or possible to implement. For instance, you may want to use the sales pipeline as an influencer for the travel expenses. The sales pipeline is global to all the LoBs. In the planning model, that means the values for sales pipeline are always written to the unassigned member for the LoB dimension. This is a problem if you want to use the LoB dimension to define the entities. The values of the influencer are read in the context of the entity, so predictive planning will read the values of the sales pipeline as LoB = R&D when forecasting the R&D entity. Because values exist only for LoB = Unassigned, no value is returned for the influencer.

In such cases, you must create a calculated measure in the planning model using the RESTRICT or LOOKUP function so the value for LoB is ignored and the value for LoB = Unassigned is always returned. RESTRICT and LOOKUP functions are further explained on this page: *http://s-prs.co/v577116*.

Impact of Entities on the Forecast Horizon

All the entities are generated based on the same settings that you've defined globally in the time series forecasting model. For instance, if you've requested three forecast periods, then all the entities will forecast three periods. We said previously that these three forecast periods would immediately follow the last period available in the training dataset when the **Until Last Observation** option is used. This certainly makes sense when considering a unique time series, but what does it mean for a time series forecasting model with multiple entities, each possibly having a distinct data history?

When the entity setting is populated, predictive planning looks for the most recent training period across all entities, selects the most recent one, and makes it the "overall" most recent training period. The forecast periods for all the entities are generated immediately after this overall most recent training period. This behavior allows you to have a consistent forecast horizon across all entities of the time series forecasting model.

Table 5.1 illustrates how the forecast horizon is determined when multiple entities are created. Let's assume the three entities represented in the table are the only entities in the planning model. Considering all the entities, the most recent date with a booked data point is 2023-03. The following date, 2023-04, is used as the first period for the forecast horizon for all entities.

Date	Travel Expenses		
	Germany	USA	Japan
. . .	. . .	. . .	. . .
2023-01	5,000	8,000	7,500
2023-02	6,000		5,300
2023-03	5,500		
2023-04	$Forecast_{Germany\_1}$	$Forecast_{USA\_1}$	$Forecast_{Japan\_1}$
2023-05	$Forecast_{Germany\_2}$	$Forecast_{USA\_2}$	$Forecast_{Japan\_2}$
2023-06	$Forecast_{Germany\_3}$	$Forecast_{USA\_3}$	$Forecast_{Japan\_3}$

Table 5.1 Forecast Horizon with Multiple Entities

5.4   Understanding Time Series Forecasting Models

Predictive planning provides reports to help you assess the performance of the time series forecasting model and understand how it works. Three reports are available:

- **Overview**
  This is the report displayed by default when the time series forecasting is created with entities. It's available only in this case. The overview report provides aggregated information summarizing the performance of the time series forecasting model.

- **Forecast**
  This report provides detailed performance information for a specific entity (while the overview provides a summary across all the entities).

- **Explanation**
  This report provides insights allowing you to understand the logic used by a specific entity to calculate the predictions.

The reports are displayed as tabs in the main area of the predictive scenario UI. You can navigate to a specific report by clicking the tab header.

When the time series forecasting model is created with entities, the forecast and the explanation reports provide dropdown lists allowing you to display the report for a specific entity. Note that you can think about a time series forecasting model without an entity as a model with a unique entity. Therefore, in this case, the forecast and explanation report are provided for this unique entity.

In Figure 5.23, you can see that the explanation report is displayed for the entity representing the HR LoB in Germany.

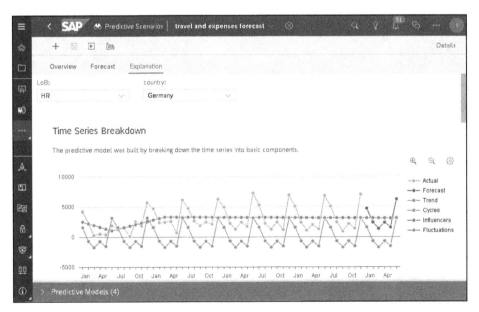

Figure 5.23 Time Series Forecasting Model Reports

The following sections provide a detailed explanation of the model reports for time series forecasting models.

5.4.1   Assessing Model Performance

Using predictive planning, you'll produce predictive forecasts, use them for your financial planning, and possibly share them with other users. It's particularly important to understand how accurate your time series forecasting model is. The following sections explain how to assess the performance of a time series forecasting model in predictive planning using the **Forecast** report, as shown in Figure 5.24.

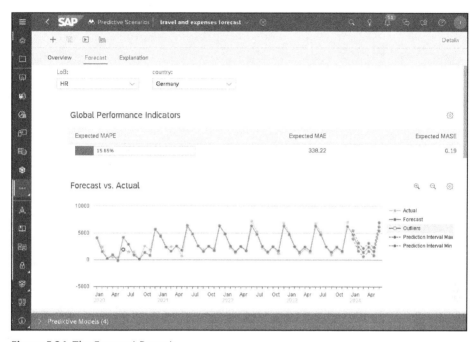

Figure 5.24 The Forecast Report

Global Performance Indicators

The **Global Performance Indicators** visualization of the **Forecast** report (see Figure 5.25) provides standard performance indicators that allow you to assess the model's performance. By default, only the expected mean average percentage error (MAPE) is displayed. You can display other performance indicators using the **Settings** icon of the **Global Performance Indicators** visualization, if you think that another performance indicator is better suited to evaluate the performance of your time series forecasting model.

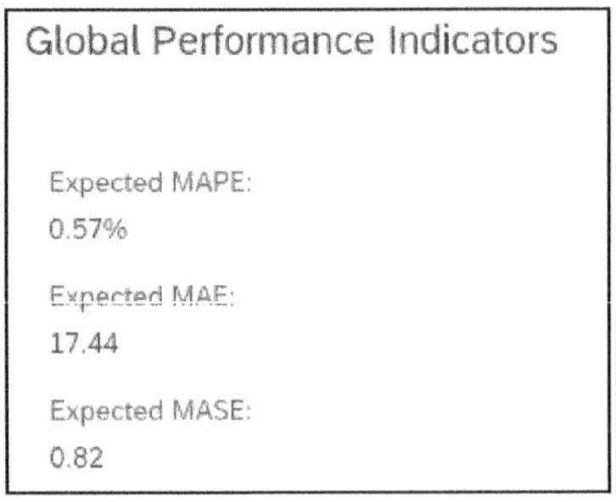

Global Performance Indicators

Expected MAPE:
0.57%

Expected MAE:
17.44

Expected MASE:
0.82

Figure 5.25 Global Performance Indicators

The different performance indicators are calculated so they reflect the performance you can expect when using the time series forecasting models. Therefore, all the names are prefixed by "expected". The exact technique to evaluate the expected performance is explained in Chapter 9, Section 9.4.

Table 5.2 describes available performance indicators and discusses their advantages and drawbacks. We provide the base formula to calculate the standard version of the indicator; note an additional calculation is performed by predictive planning to calculate the expected version. The following is true for all the performance indicators:

- n = number of considered points
- $actual_i$ = actual value
- $predicted_i$ = predicted value

Abbreviation	Description
MAPE	The mean absolute percentage error (MAPE) is the mean of the absolute difference between the actuals and the predicted values, expressed as a percentage. The formula is as follows: $$MAPE = \frac{1}{n}\sum_{i=1}^{n}\left|\frac{actual_i - predicted_i}{actual_i}\right|$$ The lower the MAPE the better. A MAPE of zero denotes a perfect model. The MAPE is expressed as a percentage, which makes it convenient to compare time series forecasting model performances. When the values of a time series are close to zero, the MAPE value can be extremely high, suggesting a bad performance of the time series forecasting model, even though the model is good. When the time series to be forecasted has many values close to zero, we recommend using another performance indicator to evaluate your model.

Table 5.2 Predictive Planning Performance Indicators

Abbreviation	Description
MAE	The mean absolute error (MAE) is the mean of the absolute differences between the actuals and the predicted values. The formula is as follows: $$MAE = \frac{1}{n}\sum_{i=1}^{n}|predicted_i - actual_i|$$ The lower the MAE the better. A MAE of zero denotes a perfect model. The main advantage of the MAE is that it allows you to evaluate the error made by the time series forecasting model in the same unit as the forecasted value. If you're forecasting travel expenses in dollars, then the MAE is also evaluated in dollars. This is also a drawback as the MAEs for different entities aren't comparable: The same MAE, say 100, may be huge for one entity and neglectable for another.
MASE	The mean absolute scaled error (MASE) allows you to evaluate how the time series forecasting model performs compared to a naïve model. This comparison is done by dividing the MAE of the time series forecasting model by the MAE of the naïve model. The formula is as follows: $$MASE = \frac{MAE}{MAE_{naive}}$$ The naïve model is a lag 1 model. A lag 1 is a time series forecasting model that always uses the last known value as the predicted values. The lower the MASE, the better the time series forecasting model performance is. A MASE lower than 1 indicates that the model performance is better than that of a naïve model. A MASE higher than 1 indicates that the model performance is worse than that of a naïve model. The MASE is independent of the scale of the time series and can be used to compare the performance of several time series forecasting models while, unlike the MAPE, not being sensitive to actual values that are close to zero.
RMSE	The root mean squared error (RMSE) is the square root of the mean of squared differences between the predicted and the actual values. The RMSE is expressed in the same unit as the forecasted value. The formula is as follows: $$RMSE = \sqrt{\frac{1}{n}\sum_{i=1}^{n}(predicted_i - actual_i)^2}$$ The lower the RMSE, the better the performance of the time series forecasting model is. A RMSE of zero denotes a perfect model. The RMSE is like the MAE except that it's more degraded by larger errors due to the square. Like the MAE, the RMSE is expressed in the same unit as the forecasted quantity.

Table 5.2 Predictive Planning Performance Indicators (Cont.)

Abbreviation	Description
R^2	The R square (R^2) is the proportion of the variation of the target that is explained by the time series forecasting model.
	Intuitively, the R^2 can be interpreted as a comparison between the considered time series forecasting model and a naïve model that would always predict the mean value of the target. The R^2 represents the percentage of the error made by the naïve model that is explained by the actual model. The formula is as follows:
	$$R^2 = 1 - \frac{\sum_{i=1}^{n}(actual_i - predicted)^2}{\sum_{i=1}^{n}(actual_i - mean(actuals))}$$

Table 5.2 Predictive Planning Performance Indicators (Cont.)

When the time series forecasting model is created with entities, these performance indicators are available in the **Forecast** report for each entity. They are also aggregated across all entities in the **Global Performance Indicators** visualization of the **Overview** report, allowing you to evaluate the global performance of the time series forecasting model. You can evaluate the model performance using the median, the average, the sum, and the third quartile of the performance indicator across all the entities. By default, the **Global Performance Indicators** visualization displays the median expected MAPE and the third quartile of the expected MAPE, but you can choose another aggregation or another performance indicator using the **Settings** icon ⚙ of the visualization.

Figure 5.26 shows an example where the **Global Performance Indicators** visualization was configured to display all possible aggregations of the various performance indicators.

Global Performance Indicators				⚙
Performance Indicators	Median	Average	3rd Quartile	Sum
Expected MAE	8.84	12.81	20.09	89.68
Expected MAPE (%)	0.37	0.33	0.45	2.31
Expected RMSE	30.63	44.38	69.59	310.64
Expected R^2	-67,568,726	-178,590,769.98	-25,878,138.45	-1,250,135,389.84
Expected MASE	0.46	0.39	0.49	2.76

Figure 5.26 Global Performance Indicators Aggregated Over All Entities

Finally, using the **Select Columns** icon ⚙ of the time series forecasting model list (refer to Chapter 2, Section 2.1.2), you can compare several time series forecasting models using performance indicators of your choice.

Forecast vs. Actual

The **Forecast vs. Actual** visualization (see Figure 5.27) provides a more qualitative and visual way of evaluating the time series forecasting model performance by comparing several data series:

- **Actual**
  This time series represents the time series that has been used to train the model.

- **Forecast**
  This time series represents the predictive forecasts provided by the time series forecasting model. The predictive forecasts are available both for the future and for the past, that is, the period of the training data.

- **Prediction Interval Min/Prediction Interval Max**
  Prediction Interval Min and **Prediction Interval Max** (formerly **Error Min** and **Error Max**) represent the lower and higher bounds of the *95% prediction interval*. Each individual predictive forecast has a 95% likelihood to be part of the prediction interval. If you request too many predictions compared to the number of training data points, predictive planning may not be able to provide a prediction interval for all the points. You need five points of historical data for each point to be predicted in the future.

- **Outliers**
  A point of the training dataset is considered an outlier when the forecasting error for this point is abnormally high. Outliers often indicate the occurrence of an event in the past that led to an unpredictable variation of the time series. Whether the forecasting error for a point is normal or abnormal is decided based on the average number of errors made by the time series forecasting model. The error is measured by the residual, that is, the absolute difference between the actual and the prediction. The error is considered abnormally high if the residual for the considered point is strictly higher than three times the standard deviation of the residuals on the training dataset. The outliers are also listed in the **Outliers** tables of the **Forecast** report.

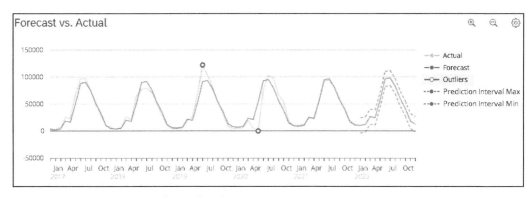

Figure 5.27 Forecast vs. Actual Visualization

Comparing the **Actual** and the **Forecast** time series for the training period helps you visualize how well the time series forecasting model can explain the past data. The **Forecast** time series should be as close as possible to the **Actual** series.

The prediction interval helps you visualize the accuracy that can be expected for the predictive forecast. The smaller the prediction interval the better.

The presence of multiple outliers shows that the time series forecasting model failed to approximate the time series by a distance. This isn't necessarily the indication of a bad time series forecasting model, as outliers are points where the time series doesn't behave as it normally should according to the time series forecasting model. Nevertheless, it can be interesting to investigate the dates and values of the outliers to check if they correspond to one-off incidents, or if they correspond to a regular behavior that was missed by the time series forecasting model. Adding influencers may be interesting to try capture such a regular behavior.

When the **Entity** field is filled, the **Forecast vs. Actual** visualization is provided for each entity.

5.4.2   Time Series Forecasting Model Reports

The **Explanation** report provides visualizations with additional business insights to help you understand how your time series forecasting model works. When the **Entity** field is filled, the **Explanation** report is available for each entity. The visualizations of the **Explanation** report are explained in the following sections.

Time Series Breakdown

The time series forecasting algorithm of predictive planning breaks down the time series to be forecasted into simpler, easier to understand time series, called *components*. These components are used by time series forecasting to calculate the prediction. They also constitute business insights about the time series. The **Explanation** modeling report provides the **Time Series Breakdown** visualization, depicted in Figure 5.28, which shows how each component impacts the predicted values.

Some components may not exist in some time series and therefore different models may show different components (some may have no cycles or no fluctuations for instance).

The predictive models generated by predictive planning can either be based on an additive modeling technique or an exponential smoothing technique. These two modeling techniques are explained in detail in Chapter 9, Section 9.2 and Section 9.3. The exact modeling technique is never mentioned explicitly in the predictive planning reports to avoid introducing terms that may not be understood by all users. Nevertheless, it's possible to differentiate the time series models that use the additive technique and those that use the exponential smoothing technique. In Figure 5.28, the sentence "The predictive model was built by breaking down the time series into basic components" between the chart and its title alludes to the fact that the predictive model is based on an additive technique.

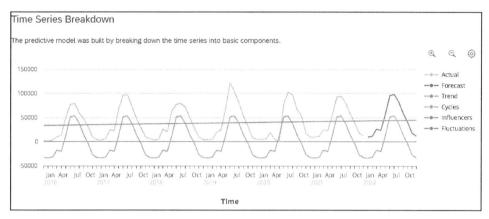

Figure 5.28 Time Series Breakdown Visualization

The **Time Series Breakdown** visualization shows the following components with their impact on the predicted values:

- Trend

  The **Trend** represents the long-term direction of the time series. The nature of the trend depends on the modeling technique. Additive models can either have a single linear trend or several successive linear trends (called *piecewise trend*) if the slope of the trend changes over time. When the models are based on a smoothing technique, the smoothed version of the time series is used as the trend. The trend in Figure 5.28 shows that the travel expenses are slowly increasing on a monthly basis globally.

- Cycles

  The **Cycles** represent patterns that repeat regularly. Figure 5.28 shows that the travel expenses follow the same cycle every year, with high peaks in the summer months and low peaks in winter months. While predictive planning can detect multiple cycles in a time series, the **Cycles** visualization shows their impact summed into a single time series.

- Influencers

  The **Influencers** component shows the impact of the influencers on the predicted values. While predictive planning can detect multiple influencers, this visualization shows their impact summed into a single series.

- Fluctuations

  The **Fluctuations** series represents the impact of the part of time series that depends on past values of the time series, that is, the part of the time series that can be expressed as $y_t = a_1.y_{t-1} + a_2.y_{t-2} + \ldots + a_p.y_{t-p}$.

115

- **Final Residuals**

  Final Residuals represents the part of the actual time series not described by the predictive model. It corresponds to the prediction error. It's not a component of the time series forecasting model, but it allows better visualizing of the error made by the predictive model. You want to make the values of final residuals as small as possible. It's not displayed by default, but you can add it by changing the visualizing settings.

The visualization also shows the **Actual** and the **Forecast** (both in the future and for the training period) for reference.

Independently of the exact nature of the time series forecasting model, the **Time Series Breakdown** visualization always shows the components in an additive form: for any period, the forecast value equals the sum of the values of all components of the time series. For any period t belonging to the training dataset, $forecast_t = trend_t + cycles_t + influencers_t + fluctuations_t$, and $actual_t = forecast_t + residual_t$.

Time Series Component Impact

The **Time Series Component Impact** visualization shows the impact of the various components found by the time series forecasting model in the time series. The impact of a component is the fraction of the forecasted time series represented by this component. The values of the **Impact** column of this visualization always sum to 100%.

If several cycles exist in the predictive model, the table contains one row for each cycle. Likewise, the table contains one row for each influencer that is used in the predictive models. The **Details** column allows you to identify the cycle type or the influencer name.

In the example shown in Figure 5.29, the trend component alone explains 53.34% of the actual values of the travel expenses while the yearly cycle explains 38.64% of the actual values of the travel expenses. The **Final Residuals** row tells us that 8.02% of the actual time series isn't explained by the time series forecasting model.

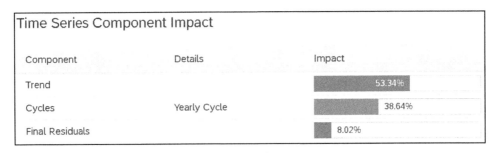

Figure 5.29 Time Series Component Impact Visualization

For each component, the impact is calculated as:

$$Impact(component) = \sum_t |component_t|/SumOfAbsoluteActuals$$

where

$$SumOfAbsoluteActuals$$
$$= \sum_t |actual_t|$$
$$= \sum_t (|trend_t| + |cycle_t| + |fluctuations_t| + |influencers_t| + |finalresiduals_t|)$$

For instance, this is how it gets calculated for the trend component:

$$Impact(trend) = \sum_t |trend_t|/SumOfAbsoluteActuals$$

Impact Of Cycles

The **Impact of Cycles** visualization lets you dig into the details of the cycle impact, period after period. Each orange bar represents a period in the cycle, and the value of the bar corresponds to the impact for this specific period on the predictive forecasts. This visualization can be used for two major purposes:

- Understanding the logic used by the predictive model to calculate the predictive forecast.

- Getting business insights about the time series to be forecasted. Which months of the year have the highest travel expenses, and which have the lowest travel expenses?

Figure 5.30 tells us that, for instance, in January, travel expenses decrease by about 35,000 while they increase by about 50,000 in June.

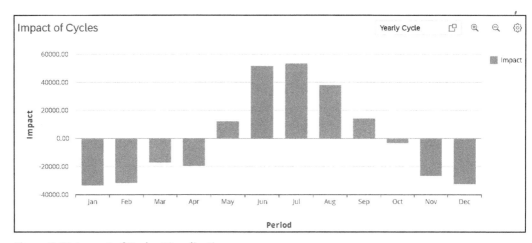

Figure 5.30 Impact of Cycles Visualization

Impact of Numerical Influencers

The **Impact of Numerical Influencers** visualization lets you explore how influencer values impact the predicted time series. The x-axis of the chart represents the influencer values, while the y-axis represents the impact of the influencer value to the predictive forecast.

Figure 5.31 shows the influence of the number of in-person training days planned to the forecasted travel expenses for the HR LoB in the United States. We can notice a negative linear correlation between the number of planned training days and the travel expenses: The more training days are planned in a given month, the lower the travel expenses will be. Looking at the exact values, you can tell that when there is no training day planned in a given month, the predicted travel expenses increase by 591.91, while they decrease by 757.80 when there are five training days planned during the month.

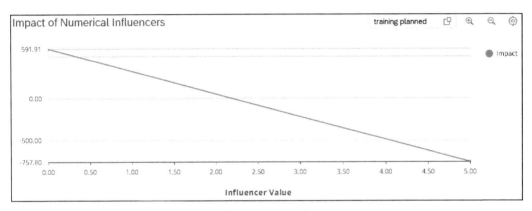

Figure 5.31 Impact of Numerical Influencers Visualization

Predictive planning can capture more complex relationships between the influencers and the target, resulting in multiple segments in the **Impact of Numerical Influencers** visualization.

Fluctuations

The **Past Target Value Contributions** visualization shows how the time series is impacted by the recent past, that is, how the forecasted value for a data point is impacted by the previous data points. This visualization corresponds to the detailed explanation of the component named fluctuations in the **Time Series Breakdown** visualization. It's displayed only if a fluctuations component is detected in the time series.

The negative values on the x-axis represent the number of data points in the past, called a lag. A value of –1 means one point before the forecasted value and a value of –2 corresponds to two data points in the past. The bar height represents the relative impact of each lag as part of the fluctuations component: A value of 80% means the lag represents 80% of the impact of the fluctuations component, not 80% of the forecasted value.

In the example of Figure 5.32, the target is influenced by the previous two values. Considering a prediction at date t, the point at $t-1$ accounts for about 75% of the fluctuations component and the point at $t-2$ accounts for the remaining 25% of the fluctuations component.

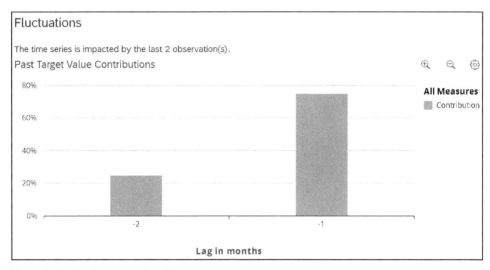

Figure 5.32 Fluctuations Visualization

Forecast Breakdown

The **Forecast Breakdown** visualization represents the impact of each component of the predictive model to a given forecasted period. The **Forecast Breakdown** is available as part of the **Forecast** report.

While most of the visualizations in the modeling reports explain the global behavior of the model, the **Forecast Breakdown** focuses on explaining individual predictive forecasts, that is, a predictive forecast for a specific period. For instance, you may use it to understand what component of the predictive model had the most positive or negative impact on the prediction.

The **Forecast Breakdown** is presented as a waterfall chart where each bar is a component of the time series forecasting model associated with the component value for the predictive forecast period. The height of each bar represents the impact of the component on the forecasted value. A positive bar height means that the contribution of the component increases the forecasted value, while a negative bar height means that the contribution of the component decreases the forecasted value. The last bar, named **Total**, represents the forecasted value. The value of the **Total** bar equals the sum of the value of the model components. The components are ordered based on their decreasing impact on the prediction (from the biggest impact to the lowest impact).

Figure 5.33 shows the **Forecast Breakdown** of the predicted travel expenses for the German HR LoB for May 2024. This chart tells us that the predicted value at this date is mostly impacted by the trend. The trend sets a base forecasted value of 2962.76. The fact that May corresponds to the fifth month of the half-yearly cycle decreases the forecasted value by 1491.52. That one corporate event is planned in May 2024, and the sales pipeline's value slightly increases the forecasted value.

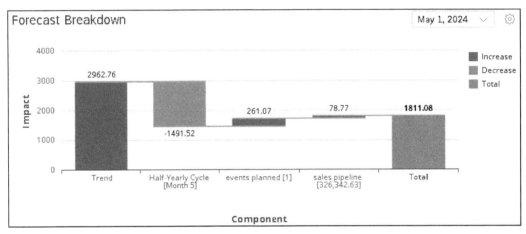

Figure 5.33 Forecast Breakdown Visualization

5.5   Improving Time Series Forecasting Models with Predictive Planning

Despite predictive planning being as automated as possible, there are still situations where human judgement is needed to improve the quality of the predictive model or review how well it fits your business requirements. The following sections provide hints to help you improve your time series forecasting models.

Keep track of your different experiments using the capabilities provided in the **Predictive Scenarios** screen:

1. Open the **Predictive Models** table at the bottom of the screen.

2. Open the context menu of a predictive model you would like to start from, and click **Duplicate**.

3. Select the copy of the predictive model created in the previous step.

4. Change some settings, for instance, add influencers.

5. In the predictive model description, replace the default description to document your experiment: "added 2 influencers".

6. Train the predictive model.

Repeat all of these steps for each experiment you do with different predictive model settings.

5.5.1   Finding the Optimal Training Dataset Size

One crucial point when training a time series forecasting model is finding the right trade-off for the training dataset size. On one hand, having enough past data points is needed so the predictive model can identify long-term patterns. For instance, predictive planning needs to see a cycle being repeated at least three times in the data to identify it as a cycle. If you think you have yearly cycles in your data, you'll need to provide at least three years of training data at the monthly level to predictive planning so it can identify these cycles. Predictive planning also requires enough training data so it can produce a prediction interval for the forecast points. For each forecasted point, 5 more training data points are required to calculate a prediction interval. For instance, if you plan to forecast 12 points in the future, you need at least 60 past data points to calculate a prediction interval for all the predictions. Note that this requirement is expressed using the number of data points as it's independent of the time granularity.

On the other hand, learning from data that is too old can be counterproductive. Time series forecasting assumes that patterns which existed in the past will repeat similarly in the future. But behaviors evolve, and it's unlikely that patterns that existed 10 years ago are still relevant today.

Here are some recommendations to handle this trade-off best:

- Always be sure you have enough historical to get a prediction interval for all the forecast points. Still, you should keep the size of the forecast horizon reasonable: The longer the forecast horizon, the more training data points you need to get a prediction interval.

- Be sure that the size of the training data is enough for cycles to be fully repeated. When working with a month granularity, this requires having at least three years of training data to properly detect yearly cycles. But it's probably not worth going beyond five years of training data as it's more than what is needed to detect patterns.

- If you have more training data than needed to detect cycles and get a prediction interval for all the predictions, try reducing the size of the training data incrementally. Train a first time series forecasting model using the **Train Using: All Observations** option. Then train a second time series forecast model using, for instance, five years of historical data. Compare the two predictive models. If the predictive model with the smallest training size provides the same accuracy and has detected the same component as the first one, then use the model with the smallest training size. You can repeat this process, reducing the size of the training data each time, until the predictive model no longer improves.

5.5.2   Filtering Entities

When forecasting for several entities, some entities can't be forecasted properly, which usually happens for the following reasons:

- **The entity is new**
  If an entity didn't exist until recently, there may not be enough historical data to extract a trend or cycles. Consequently, the entity can't be forecasted properly. For instance, it may be challenging to forecast the travel expenses for the new site your company has opened in France just three months ago.

- **The entity doesn't exist anymore**
  Such entities won't get data updates in the future and should not be forecasted anymore. For instance, your company may have closed the LoB for large accounts last year. In this case, the problem isn't that the entity can't be forecasted properly, but that it should not be forecasted at all as it will no longer be relevant in the future.

- **The entity has a lot of missing data points**
  Missing data can happen for several reasons. Possibly the travel expenses weren't recorded for some months, or the travel expenses for two consecutive months were aggregated. Whatever the reason, if there are too many missing data points, it may not be possible to create a time series forecasting model that can predict the entity correctly.

These entities that can't be forecasted accurately should be excluded from the predictive model using the **Entity Filters** option (Section 5.3.3).

Usually, you won't know upfront which entities should be excluded, including those that are too recent, terminated, or have data quality issues. We recommend training a baseline predictive model to identify the entities that should be excluded. In this baseline predictive model, you'll try to identify the different types of entities and check if they should be excluded:

- **Low accuracy entities**
  Have a look in the reports for the entities with the lowest accuracy (based on the performance indicator you've chosen). Look at the **Forecast vs. Actual** visualization. This may help identifying intermittent entities that should be excluded from the predictive model. You may also decide to exclude an entity if the predictive forecast doesn't seem to fit the actual as expected.

- **Perfectly fitted entities**
  You should also look at entities where the error number is zero or close to zero. Such high accuracy is sometimes the sign of an entity that you may want to exclude from the predictive model, especially very recent entities with very few data points.

A low accuracy or an accuracy that is "too good to be true" doesn't necessarily mean that an entity must be excluded. These are only clues that should draw your attention to that entity. You must use the reports provided by predictive planning and your judgment to decide if it makes sense to keep or exclude the entity.

When hierarchies are involved, the **Entity Filters** option also allows you to choose the specific node(s) of the hierarchy to be used to create an entity. Let's assume you've trained a time series forecasting model that produces a travel expenses forecast for each LoB in each country. It turns out that the travel expenses volume for Belgium, Netherlands, and Luxembourg (i.e., the Benelux region) is rather low, and the entity doesn't show any specific pattern, resulting in a poor model accuracy for these countries. Using the **Entity Filters** option, you can choose to forecast the Benelux region as a whole (assuming it exists in the hierarchy) while still forecasting all countries other than the Benelux ones individually.

5.5.3   Adding Influencers

One way to improve the accuracy of the predictive model is to use influencers. With the influencers, you can consider factors that are external to the time series to be predicted but that may influence its values. For instance, knowing that employees often travel for corporate events or conversely aren't able to travel due to trainings, you may want to use the number of corporate events and the number of internal trainings as influencers.

It's important that you remain selective with the candidate influencers. The time series forecasting algorithm will try finding correlations between the candidate influencers and the target. If you provide too many candidate influencers, it's highly likely that the algorithm will find correlations, including accidental ones. As a rule of thumb, you should prioritize only influencers that make sense to you. Can you explain why the target would be impacted by the influencer? If not, you shouldn't use that influencer.

Another rule of thumb is to keep only influencers that have enough impact on the target. It's not worth keeping an influencer that decreases the MAPE by 0.1% or whose impact is 1%.

We recommend you include the predictors one by one into the predictive model:

1. Train a predictive model without any influencers.
2. Introduce one influencer, and train another predictive model.
3. Evaluate the predictive model.
4. If the model accuracy is significantly improved and the influencer impact on the model is significant, then you can keep this influencer. Otherwise, you should discard it.
5. Repeat the same process using another influencer.

5.6   Saving Predictive Forecasts

Predictive planning doesn't let you write the predictive forecasts to a public version. You need to create at least one private version and save the predictions to it. This workflow lets you review the quality of the predictive forecast before it's made publicly available. This section will teach you step-by-step how to save the predictions of a time series forecasting model to a private planning version.

5.6.1   Creating a Private Version

Let's detail how to create this private planning version:

1. Create a new story by clicking the **Stories** icon ▦ in the main navigation bar to the left of the screen.
2. Choose the type of layout you want for your story. You can choose either **Responsive** or **Canvas**.
3. You'll be prompted to choose a **Design Mode Type**. Select **Optimized Design Experience** (this is the default choice).
4. Click the **Insert • Table** button ▦ in the top toolbar.
5. You'll be prompted for the selection of a data source. Select the planning model you want to work with.
6. Be sure the table is focused and click the overflow button ⊡ in the **Tools** section of the top toolbar.
7. In the dropdown menu that opens click **Version Management**. The **Version Management** panel shown in Figure 5.34 opens to the right of the screen.

Figure 5.34 Version Management UI

8. Click the **Create Blank Private Version** button ⊞ next to the **Private Versions** header.
9. Provide a name for the new private version, and click **Create** to finalize the creation.

Note that creating a story and creating a table are mandatory steps to manage the versions of a planning model: These capabilities aren't available in the planning model editor.

Some version management shortcuts are also available in the context menu when right-clicking the version column in the table (called **Category**).

5.6.2   Saving Forecasts into a Private Version

Once you've created a private version, you're ready to save the predictions:

1. In the predictive planning toolbar, click the **Save Forecast** icon [icon]. The **Save Forecast** dialog opens (see Figure 5.35).

2. In the **Private Version** dropdown list, select the private version you want to save the predictions to.

3. Click **Save**.

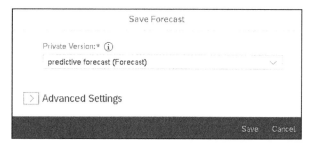

Figure 5.35 Save Forecast Dialog

The predictions are saved directly into the measure used as the target in the selected version. The predictions are written for all the entities in the predictive model. By default, the predictions are saved only for the forecast horizon. If you want to compute custom performance indicators, you can request the predictions for the training period to be saved as well using **Save Forecast Values for Past Periods** in the **Advanced Settings**. Chapter 8, Section 8.4, explains how to use this option to create ad hoc performance metrics.

You can monitor the progress of the **Save** operation in the **Predictive Models** list at the bottom of the screen. The value for the predictive model in the **Status** column is **Applying** when the operation is in progress. When the operation is finished, the value of the **Status** column changes to **Applied**.

> **Keep Actuals and Predictive Forecasts Separated**
>
> Saving the predictive forecasts to the version that was used to train the time series forecasting model is discouraged. While it may seem a solution to avoid multiplying the number of versions and isn't actively prevented by predictive planning, it should not be considered a best practice. Methodologically speaking, it's a best practice to always keep the actual version of data (what has happened) and the predictive forecast version of data (what might happen) separated. Technically speaking, nothing differentiates the data points corresponding to the predictions from the data points corresponding to the actuals. The next time the time series forecasting model will be applied or trained, the new data points will be considered by the predictive model, inducing a "shift" of the forecasting horizon.

5.7 Including Predictive Forecasts in a Story

The predictive forecast is now stored in a version of your planning model. Let's explore different ways of displaying the predictive forecast to story end users.

5.7.1 Including Predictive Forecasts in a Table

Planning tables are frequently used to show the delta between two versions. For instance, you may have a budget for travel expenses (stored in its own version), and you may want to compare this budget to the predictive forecast to check for each entity if it will be over budget or within budget over the course of the year. This section will guide you through the steps for creating a planning table showing the percentage difference between the predictive forecast and the budget. Figure 5.36 illustrates the result we'll work toward.

Version	predictive forecast										
Measures	travel expenses										
LoB	Consulting							HR			
country	Germany				USA			Germany			
Cross Calculations	Budget	Forecast		Delta	Budget	Forecast		Delta	Budget	Forecast	
Date											
⌄ 2024	€7,200	€7,797	-8.3%		$28,000	$26,960	3.7%		€38,000	€42,298	-11.3%
⌄ Q1 (2024)	€1,800	€1,705	5.3%		$7,000	$7,142	-2.0%		€9,500	€10,151	-6.9%
Jan (2024)	€600	€553	7.8%		$2,333	$2,406	-3.1%		€3,167	€3,373	-6.5%
Feb (2024)	€600	€572	4.7%		$2,333	$2,401	-2.9%		€3,167	€3,393	-7.1%
Mar (2024)	€600	€580	3.3%		$2,333	$2,335	-0.1%		€3,167	€3,385	-6.9%
> Q2 (2024)	€1,800	€1,855	-3.1%		$7,000	$6,810	2.7%		€9,500	€10,111	-6.4%
> Q3 (2024)	€1,800	€2,070	-15.0%		$7,000	$6,503	7.1%		€9,500	€10,764	-13.3%
> Q4 (2024)	€1,800	€2,167	-20.4%		$7,000	$6,505	7.1%		€9,500	€11,271	-18.6%

Figure 5.36 Difference between Budget and Forecast Versions

First, you must add a planning table to a story by following these steps:

1. Create a new story by clicking the **Stories** icon ⊞ in the navigation bar.
2. Choose the type of layout you want for your story. You can choose either **Responsive** or **Canvas**.
3. You'll be prompted to choose a **Design Mode Type**. Select **Optimized Design Experience** (default choice).
4. Click the **Insert • Table** icon ⊞ in the top toolbar.
5. You'll be prompted for the selection of a data source. Select the planning model you want to work with.

> **Builder Panel**
>
> From now on, these step-by-step instructions will mention settings that are displayed in a separate panel called **Builder**. If this panel isn't displayed, be sure to choose **View • Right Side Panel** in the toolbar.

Then, you can set up the layout of the table. Here's how to set up the layout corresponding to Figure 5.36, but any other layout will do:

1. In the **Rows** section, as shown in Figure 5.37, click **Add Dimensions**, and select the **Date** dimension.

2. Set everything else as columns. In the **Columns** section, click **Add Dimensions** to successively add the version (the corresponding dimension is called **Category** if you're working with the classic account model), the **Measures** or **Accounts**, the **LoB** dimension, and the **country** dimension.

3. Choose the quantity to be displayed. In the **Filters** section, click **Accounts** or **Measures** (depending on the setup of your planning model), and select the **travel expenses** measure/account.

4. Choose the version to be displayed. In the **Filters** section, click **Version**, and select the version where you've saved the predictive forecast.

Figure 5.37 Predictive Forecast Table Layout

Now, you must set up a few cross calculations. *Cross calculations* are simply standard calculated measures that implicitly take a measure as parameter. For instance, we want to calculate the difference between the budget and the forecast version for the travel expenses measure. The calculated measure we'll create for that purpose will never reference the travel expenses measure explicitly. Instead, it will reference a kind of placeholder measure called **Measure Values** (or **Account Values** for a classic account model) that serves as the parameter and will be replaced later by a real measure or account.

In the **Columns** section, click **Add Dimensions**, and select **Dimensions · Cross Calculations**. The **Measure Values** column header has appeared, but the content of the table remains unchanged because **Measure Values** is a pseudo measure that takes the value of the measure (or account) selected in the table (in this case, travel expenses).

Now let's create a cross calculation that represents the budget value:

1. In the **Cross Calculations** token, click the ⊡ icon to open the context menu, and click **Add Calculation**. The **Calculation Editor** appears, as shown in Figure 5.38.

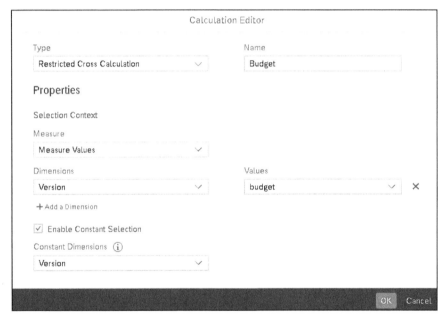

Figure 5.38 Restricted Cross Calculation for Budget

2. In the **Type** dropdown, select **Restricted Cross Calculation**. A restricted cross calculation allows you to enforce the value of some dimensions to remain constant in the calculation independently of the value selected in the visualization for these dimensions.

3. In the **Name** field, enter "Budget".

4. In the **Measure** dropdown, select **Measure Values**. This allows the version restriction to apply to any measure or account.

5. In the **Dimensions** dropdown, select **Version** because we want to force a specific version to be used in the calculation independently of the table configuration.

6. Open the **Values** dropdown, and click **Select by Member**.

7. Select the version that contains the budget, and click **OK**.

8. Select **Enable Constant Selection**, and select **Version** in the dropdown. This is the option that allows the version used in the calculation to remain independent of the version displayed in the table.

9. Click **OK** to validate the creation of the cross calculation.

Create another restricted cross calculation named "Forecast" for the version with the predictive forecast. Repeat the same list of steps, but in the **Values** dropdown, select the version that contains the predictive forecast.

Finally, you must create a last cross calculation to calculate the difference between budget and forecast:

1. In the **Cross Calculations** token, click the [•••] icon to open the context menu, and click **Add Calculation**.

2. In the **Type** dropdown, select **Calculated Cross Calculation**. This is what allows you to enter a formula using standard operators and functions.

3. In the **Name** field, enter "Delta".

4. In **Edit Formula**, enter "([#Budget]-[#Forecast])/[#Budget]".

5. Click **OK** to create the cross calculation.

The table is almost ready to use. We just need to clean and format it before we're done.

You'll probably want to remove the **Measure Values** column, which is redundant with the **Forecast** column. In the **Filters** section, click the **Cross Calculations** token, and deselect **Account Values**.

Next, let's format the **Delta** column as a percentage by following these steps:

1. In the **Columns** section, click **Story Calculations** to open the menu.

2. Hover over **Delta**, and click the **Edit Formatting Options** icon, as shown in Figure 5.39.

3. In the **Formatting** dialog (see Figure 5.40), deselect **Use number formatting of Measure dimension**. Then, deselect **Use unit of underlying measures**.

4. In the **Scale** dropdown, select **Percentage**.

Figure 5.39 Edit the Cross Calculations' Formatting Options

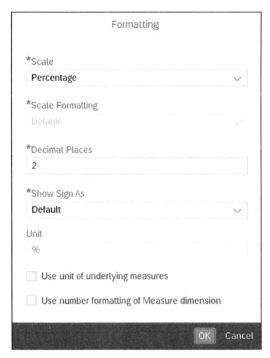

Figure 5.40 Formatting Options for the Delta Cross Calculation

Finally, let's display a green bar in the table when the budget is greater than the forecast and a red bar when the forecast is greater than the budget:

1. In the table header, click one of the **Delta** headers. Right-click the same header to open the context menu.

2. In the table context menu, click **In-Cell Chart**, as shown in Figure 5.41. Bars appear in the **Delta** columns.

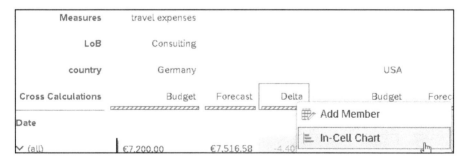

Figure 5.41 In-Cell Chart Menu Item

3. Click one of the cells in the **Delta** column. The **Builder** panel now displays a **Chart Structure** section.

4. Open the **Comparison** dropdown menu, and click **Variance Bar**, as shown in Figure 5.42.

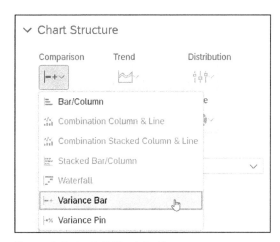

Figure 5.42 In-Cell Chart Options

5.7.2   Including Predictive Forecasts in a Time Series Chart

In this section, you'll learn how to use a time series chart to compare the future evolution of the travel expenses per country. Figure 5.43 shows the expected result.

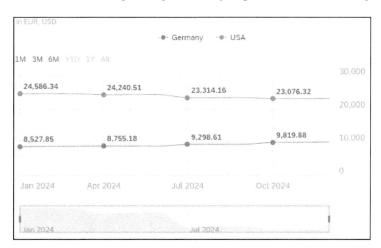

Figure 5.43 Travel Expenses Forecast Per Country

Let's walk through the steps:

1. Open an existing story or create a new one. Refer to Section 5.7.1 for instructions about how to create a story.

2. In the toolbar, click **Insert · Chart**.

3. If you've created a new story, you'll be prompted for the selection of a data source. Select the planning model you want to work with.

4. In the **Builder** panel, open the **Currently Selected Chart** dropdown, and select **Time Series**, as shown in Figure 5.44.

5. In the **Measures** section, select **travel expenses.**

6. In the **Time** section, select the **Date** dimension.

7. In the **Color** section, click **Add Dimension**, and select **LoB.**

8. In the **Filters** section, click the **Version** token, and select the version corresponding to the forecast. Deselect all the other versions, and click **OK** to validate.

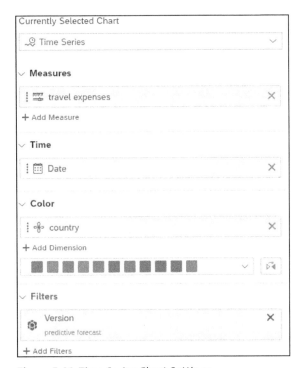

Figure 5.44 Time Series Chart Settings

5.8   Summary

In this chapter, we listed planning concepts useful in time series forecasting. You've learned how to create, evaluate, and improve a time series forecasting model using a planning model as data source. Finally, we've guided you through the creation of a story to display the predictions of the time series forecasting model.

In the next chapter, we'll explain how these instructions can be automated using multi actions.

Chapter 6

Automating the Production of Predictive Forecasts

The automation of repetitive, tedious, or time-intensive tasks is critical for efficient and streamlined business operations. SAP Analytics Cloud enables you to automate actions and, as a result, your predictive forecasts.

In this chapter, we'll introduce the *multi action*, an SAP Analytics Cloud object that lets you automate tasks related to planning models. We'll first explain what multi actions can be used for in Section 6.1. Then, in Section 6.2, we'll describe the steps required to create a multi action to automate the inclusion of a predictive forecast in stories. Finally, we'll present different ways to trigger a multi action in Section 6.3.

6.1 Introducing Multi Actions

Let's assume you need to update your predictive forecast for future travel expenses every month. This involves multiple complex steps such as preparing the data stored in the training version, training a time series forecasting model, saving the predictive forecast to the planning model, and possibly performing detailed data allocation. These steps must be repeated identically, in the same order, every month. Updating the predictive forecast manually is tedious and error prone. It makes sense to automate this workflow, and this is precisely what the multi actions are designed for.

Multi actions let you automate actions performed on one or several planning models. Different types of actions, such as running an existing data action or updating a predictive forecast, are available for automating complex workflows. The individual actions that are part of the multi action are called *steps*. Steps are executed as a sequence in the order they have been created. Usually, a power user is responsible for creating the multi action, while multiple users will leverage it in stories or applications.

Figure 6.1 shows an example of a multi action to forecast travel expenses.

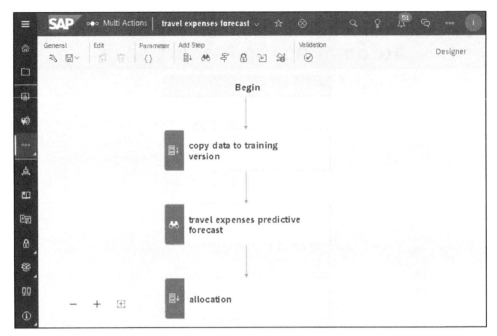

Figure 6.1 Multi Action with Three Steps

Multi actions support *parameters*. Parameters are variables that can be referenced in the multi action. Parameters allow the users of multi actions to customize the execution by providing their own values. The value of a parameter can either be a numeric value or the member of a dimension. One typical use of parameters is to let the user choose a specific input or output version when a specific step is executed.

There are two ways to execute a multi action:

- **Scheduled execution**
  You can schedule the execution of a multi action using the SAP Analytics Cloud calendar (Section 6.3.1). The multi action is then executed automatically at a fixed date and time. You can then set up recurrent schedules, for instance, to run the multi action every Monday morning.

- **Manual execution**
  You can allow story users to execute a multi action by clicking on a button, called a multi action trigger, in the story (Section 6.3.2).

6.2   Creating Predictive Steps in Multi Actions

Before creating a multi action, you first need to create a time series forecasting scenario containing at least one predictive model. What is the reason for this? Multi actions are meant to orchestrate the execution of existing assets; they aren't meant to create new assets. More specifically, multi actions aren't meant to create predictive scenarios and predictive models. It's key to validate a predictive model in predictive planning using the modeling reports before you use it productively. Once you've validated the benefits that a predictive model is bringing, you can automate the delivery of predictive forecasts using a multi action.

Recurrent Forecast

You probably want to automate your predictive forecast because you want it to be updated on a regular basis, for example, monthly. The ability to consider new data points and shift the forecast horizon accordingly is provided by the **Until: Last Observation** option of the time series forecasting model (see Chapter 5, Section 5.3.4). If you use the **Until: User-Defined Date** option, then for every run of the multi action, the same training data will be considered and therefore the same time series forecasting model will be trained.

Let's create a multi action that delivers predictive forecasts into stories:

1. In the main navigation bar, click the **Multi Actions** icon .
2. Click the **Create New · Multi Action** button. The multi action designer opens and shows an empty canvas.
3. In the toolbar, click the **General · Save · Save** button to save the multi action. Save the multi action in your personal folder, and name it "travel and expenses forecast".

Figure 6.2 shows the state of the multi action designer immediately after the multi action is created.

Figure 6.2 Empty Multi Action Designer Screen

One of the settings of the predictive step is the output version. The *output version* is the version of the planning model that will receive the predictive forecast. You can select a version explicitly, but you may want to allow users to write the predictive forecast in their own private version (private versions can't be selected in the multi action designer). In addition, there may be no version that you can select yet. It's usually a better idea to use a parameter to allow version choice. So let's create a version parameter:

1. In the multi actions top toolbar, click the **Parameter · Show Parameter List** icon . A **Parameter List** panel opens.

2. In the **Parameter List** panel click the **Create Parameter** link. The **Parameter List** panel is replaced by the **Parameter Detail** panel, as shown in Figure 6.3.

3. In the **ID** field, provide a name for your parameter. As it will be used to select the output version, let's call it "outputversion".

4. Be sure that **Parameter Type** is set to **Member** and that **Single-Model Parameter** is selected (defaults).

5. Click the **Model** dropdown, and click **Select other model**. In the dialog box, select the "Travel and Expenses" planning model that contains the quantity you want to forecast.

6. Open the **Dimensions** dropdown, and select the **Version** dimension.

7. Be sure that **Cardinality** is set to single (only one member of the **Version** dimension can be selected), and keep the default for all the other settings.

8. Click **Done** to validate the creation of the parameter.

9. In the toolbar, click the **General · Save · Save** button to save the multi action.

Figure 6.3 Version Parameter Settings

We're now ready to create a predictive step in our multi action:

1. In the toolbar, click the **Add Step · Add Predictive Step** icon. A node is added to the multi action canvas, and a **Step Details** panel is opened with the details of the predictive step, as shown in Figure 6.4.

2. Enter a name for the predictive step in the **Step Name** field, which, in our example, is "travel expenses predictive forecast".

3. Click the **Predictive Scenario** dropdown, and click **Select other predictive scenario**. In the dialog box, select the predictive scenario that contains the predictive model you want to automate. For this example, we're using **travel and expenses forecast**, which is the predictive scenario we created in Chapter 5, Section 5.3.

4. Click the **Predictive Model** dropdown, and select the time series forecasting model you want to automate. For this example, we're using **by country and LoB**, which is the time series forecasting model we have created in Chapter 5, Section 5.3. The **Corresponding Planning Model** field is updated, which lets you know the planning model used to train the predictive model.

5. Click the **Available Parameters** icon next to the **Save Forecast To Version** field. In the dropdown, select the **outputversion** field.

6. In the toolbar, click the **General** · **Save** and then the **Save** button to save the multi action.

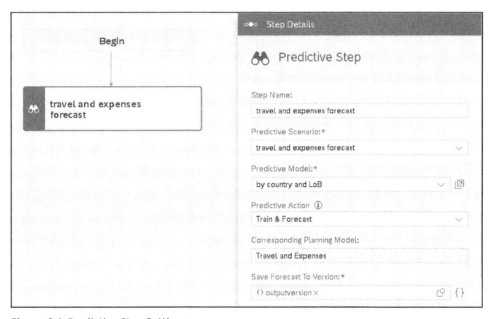

Figure 6.4 Predictive Step Settings

What does the **Train & Forecast** value for the **Predictive Action** field mean? When a predictive step runs, it will automatically perform a time series forecasting model training operation and a forecast saving operation. The predictive model referenced by the **Predictive Model** field will be trained using the settings you defined in predictive planning, and then the resulting predictive forecast will be saved to the version referenced in **Save Forecast To Version**.

This is a simple multi action. For a real use case, you might want to add a data preparation step before the predictive step and a forecast postprocessing step after the predictive step. For instance, you might run a data action before the predictive step to fill future influencers values and another data action after the predictive step to perform allocation of the predictive forecast to dimensions that weren't selected to define the entities.

Other Uses of the Predictive Step

While this chapter focuses on using multi actions to automate a forecast update, predictive steps can be used for other use cases. Here are two examples of what can be achieved using a predictive step in a multi action:

- **Predictive what-if simulation**
  Time series forecasting models with influencers can be used to produce forecasts corresponding to different hypotheses for the influencers in the future. For instance, you can use a predictive model to simulate the travel expenses based on the increase, decrease, or stability of the oil price. Using multi actions, you can run the simulations directly from the same story where you edit the simulation hypotheses and visualize the simulation results. The predictive step of the multi action must be configured with an **Apply Only** action, allowing you to produce forecasts without having to retrain the predictive model systematically.

- **Overcome the 1,000 entities limitation**
  A single predictive planning time series forecasting model can handle a maximum of 1,000 distinct entities. Let's assume you want to forecast the demand for 1,000 products in five regions. This corresponds to forecasting 5,000 distinct entities, which isn't feasible with a single time series forecasting model. What you can do is create one time series forecasting model for each region and use a multi action to produce the forecasts, so you don't have to manage each predictive model separately. In the multi action, you must create one predictive step (using the **Train & Forecast** action) for each of the five predictive models. Now you can forecast the 5,000 entities by just running the multi action.

6.3   Using Multi Actions

Depending on your needs, you may want the execution of the multi action to be scheduled or triggered manually by story users. This section explains how to implement the different possible approaches.

6.3.1   Scheduling Multi Actions

You want the story that displays your predictive forecast to remain up to date, which usually means you want the predictive forecast to be updated regularly. If the time granularity of your planning model is month, it probably means that new actuals will be available each month and, consequently, the predictive forecast can be updated every month. Of course, you can trigger the update manually every month. But if you forget to trigger the update (or if you're on vacation), then the story consumers are left with an outdated forecast. The problem is even worse if the time granularity of your planning model is set to week or day. Having the update triggered automatically is much more convenient.

This automatic scheduled update is made possible by the SAP Analytics Cloud calendar. Let's see how to schedule the execution of a multi action:

1. In the main navigation bar, click the **Calendar** icon 📅. The calendar is displayed.
2. In the toolbar, click **General**, and then click the **Create** icon ⊞∨. In the dropdown menu, click **Multi Action Task**.

First you must give a name to the task and configure the event that will trigger the task (i.e., trigger the multi action), as shown in Figure 6.5:

1. Enter a name for the task in the **Event Name** field.
2. Select **Time** in the **Start By** dropdown list. This will allow us to start the task at a specific date and time. Note that other options are available for more complex needs, such as starting the task based on the status of another calendar task.
3. In the **Start Date** field, select the date you want the task to be executed for the first time.
4. Click the **Add Recurrence** link to configure the recurrence of the task.

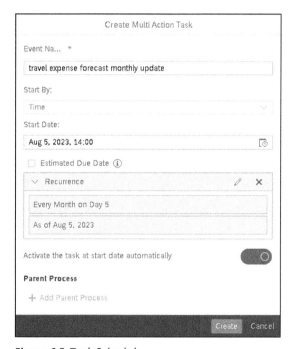

Figure 6.5 Task Schedule

5. In the **Recurrence Settings** dialog box, if you want the forecast to be updated every month, choose **Month** in the **Recurrence Pattern** dropdown, and enter "1" in the **Every** field. In the **Day** field under **Start On**, enter "5". This field is very important because it allows you to consider the data availability delay. Updating the planning model takes time, and the data for the previous month is likely unavailable on the first day of the new month. In this example, we assume that the planning model is updated between the first and fourth day of the month, so a new forecast can be calculated on the fifth day of the month.

6. Click **OK** to close the **Recurrence Settings** dialog box.

7. Click **Create** to create the task.

The multi action task is now created, but it's not ready to run yet. It must be configured and activated first:

1. Scroll down to the **Multi Action** section.

2. Open the **Multi Action** dropdown, as shown in Figure 6.6, and click **Select other multi action**. Using the **Select Multi Action** dialog, select the multi action you want to schedule. In our example, we select **travel and expenses forecast**, which is the multi action we created in Section 6.2.

3. An explicit value must be provided for all the parameters. For instance, assuming you want to schedule the multi action created in Section 6.2, you must point to a specific version for the **outputversion** parameter (this parameter was created in the multi action in Section 6.2).

4. Click the **Update** button to validate the configuration and activate the task. Click **OK** to close the information message.

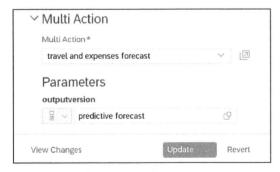

Figure 6.6 Multi Action Task Settings

6.3.2   Triggering Multi Actions

Sometimes, it's not possible to schedule the execution of a multi action. For instance, you may want to allow the user to change the value of some parameters. It could also be that your planning model is updated on an irregular basis, and it's not possible to configure a recurrence. In such cases, the solution is to provide a button in the story, called a *multi action trigger*, which allows a story user to run the multi action.

As with any element of a story, the trigger is visible to all the users who have the view privilege granted on the story. You may be worried that any user can run the multi action and update the predictive forecast. Fortunately, all the usual privilege validations on the planning model, the versions, and the predictive model still apply. The multi action performs a prevalidation step so that the multi action starts running only if all the steps can be completed based on the current user privileges.

Let's set up a multi action trigger:

1. Open an existing story referencing a planning model, or create a new story.
2. Click the **Insert · Add** button. In the dropdown menu, click **Planning Actions · Multi Action Trigger**.

A button is added to the story canvas, and a **Builder** panel is opened, as shown in Figure 6.7. Now, you must configure the trigger:

1. Provide values for the **Label** and **Description** fields. The values of these fields are displayed in the trigger to allow the story user to know what the trigger is meant for. In our example, the trigger is for a multi action that updates the travel expenses forecast.
2. Be sure the **Always run in background** option is deselected, so that the story is updated automatically when the multi action has finished running.

Figure 6.7 Multi Action Trigger Configuration

3. Open the **Multi Action** dropdown, and click **Select other multi action**. Using the **Select Multi Action** dialog box, select the multi action to be triggered. In our example, we select **travel and expenses forecast**, which is the multi action we created in Section 6.2.

4. You can configure the parameters, but it's optional. You would probably want to set **Input** to **Prompt** so the story users can customize the execution of the multi action. At this step, you can also select a value for the prompt that will be proposed as the default value when running the multi action.

Figure 6.8 shows the resulting trigger.

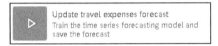

▷ Update travel expenses forecast
    Train the time series forecasting model and
    save the forecast

Figure 6.8 Multi Action Trigger

To run the multi action, the story viewer must click the blue play button. A dialog box will appear allowing the story viewer to select values for the parameters. For our example, you'll select the **predictive forecast** version as the value for the **outputversion** parameter, as shown in Figure 6.9, so the predictive forecast is written to the predictive forecast version.

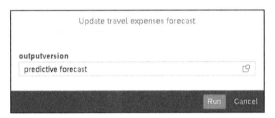

Figure 6.9 Multi Action Run Configuration

Any issue detected during the prevalidation step is displayed in the dialog box.

6.4   Summary

In this chapter we introduced the multi actions that enable you to automate the production of predictive forecasts. Through a step-by-step example, you've learned how to create a multi action to update a predictive forecast and the different ways to run a multi action.

In the next chapter, we'll switch away from our focus on time series forecasting for planning models to discuss time series forecasting for datasets.

Chapter 7
Time Series Forecasting Models Using Datasets

You've learned how to use time series forecasting with planning models. But what about scenarios where you want to perform a quick forecast on a dataset without designing a complex planning model? This is possible with smart predict.

In this chapter, we'll discuss how to use time series forecasting models on top of datasets. We'll start with a business scenario in Section 7.1, and then you'll create datasets and learn how to validate them in Section 7.2. You'll learn how to create time series forecasting models on top of datasets in Section 7.3. You'll assess your time series forecasting model and learn how to perfect it in Section 7.4 and Section 7.5, respectively. Finally, you'll see how to save your predictive forecasts (Section 7.6) and learn the diverse ways you can integrate predictive forecasts in stories (Section 7.7).

7.1 Business Scenario

You're responsible for US national parks. You must make sure that visitors enjoy the best experience when visiting nature jewels such as Yosemite National Park and Yellowstone National Park. Throughout this chapter, you'll create a time series forecasting model to do the following:

- Predict future visits at the national park level.
- Report on your predictive forecasts in a story and relate them to actuals and latest trends.
- Aggregate your predictive forecasts at the national level.

Datasets need to have a specific structure so that they can be used in the context of time series forecasting. Chapter 4, Section 4.2, covers the data structure expected for these datasets and the data preparation steps to obtain them.

We provide you with a prepared dataset, and you'll just need to acquire the data into SAP Analytics Cloud, as detailed in Section 7.2.1. You can find the files supporting this business scenario here: *https://sap-press.com/5771*. Take a first look at the dataset named *US National Park Visit Forecasting.csv* to see that the dataset contains the monthly recreational visits for different national parks in the past years. The dataset will make it possible to do entity-based forecasting as you'll be able to create predictive forecasts for the coming months for each national park.

To keep it simple and illustrate the use of datasets, we've chosen to use a dataset in the rest of the chapter; note that you can also create a planning model on top of the provided data.

7.2   Creating and Editing Datasets

This section will walk you through creating and editing datasets. You'll first learn how to create a dataset, and then you'll see the editing possibilities.

7.2.1   Creating the Training Dataset

You'll first navigate to the **Datasets** area, using the left navigation bar. Then, under **Create New**, click the **From a CSV or Excel File** option, as shown in Figure 7.1. Note that you use this option as the base data part of a comma-separated values (CSV) file. If you want to acquire the data from SAP Business Warehouse (SAP BW), SAP HANA, or any database supported by SAP Analytics Cloud, you will then use the **From a Data Source** option.

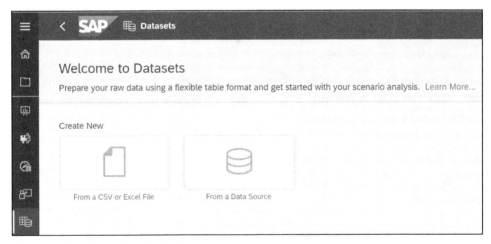

Figure 7.1 Creating a New Dataset

Under **Choose File From**, select **Local System**. Then, click the **Select Source File** button, and select *US National Park Visit Forecasting.csv*. The rest of the options in the dialog will be set automatically, and you should have a similar dialog to the one represented in Figure 7.2.

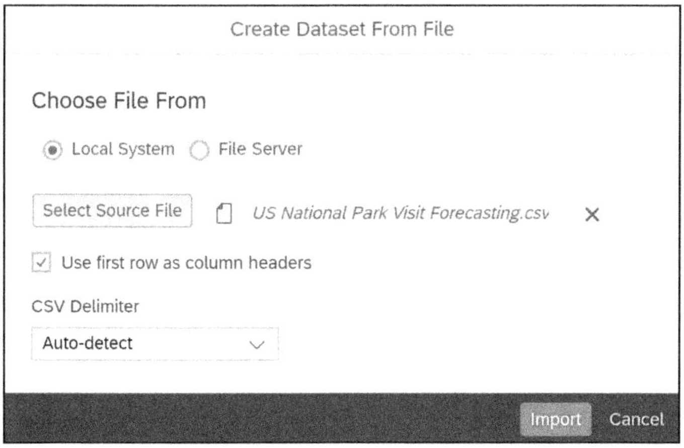

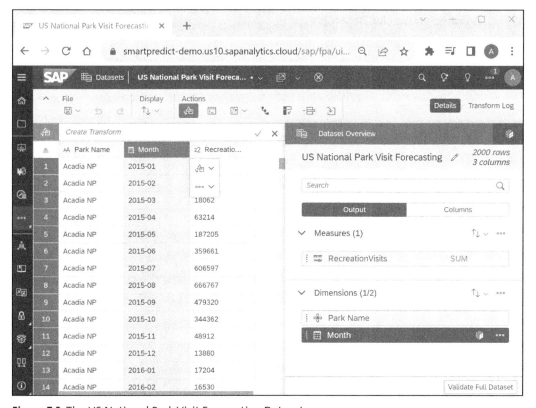

Figure 7.2 Filled Dataset Creation Dialog

Once you click **Import**, you'll need to save your dataset to a specific location in the SAP Analytics Cloud file system. Data will be uploaded, and the dataset windows will be opened for you, so that you can start working with it (see Figure 7.3).

Figure 7.3 The US National Park Visit Forecasting Dataset

Once the dataset window is opened:

- You should check that your dataset columns have been correctly recognized as either measures or dimensions. The number of recreational visits is indeed a measure, while the park name and the month correspond to dimensions.

- You can also use the right-side **Details** panel to check that the proper information (data type, statistical type, conversion format, aggregation type, scale) has been recognized for the different dataset columns.

- Finally, you can click **Validate Full Dataset** to make sure your dataset's data is fully valid.

Once you're done with these basic checks, don't forget to use the **File • Save** option to save your dataset.

7.2.2   Additional Dataset Considerations

Once you've created your dataset, there are some additional factors and possibilities to consider. We'll discuss them in the next sections.

Acquired versus Live Datasets

As detailed in Chapter 2, Section 2.3, datasets can either be acquired (data is replicated from a variety of data sources to SAP Analytics Cloud) or live (dataset's data stands for an equivalent table or SQL view in an on-premise SAP HANA system). Both types of datasets can be used in the context of time series forecasting scenarios.

Validating Datasets

As you did in Section 7.2.1, when you're using a dataset in the context of time series forecasting scenarios, you'll use the dataset editor to perform a few initial checks before you can create a time series forecasting scenario on top of this dataset:

- Make sure that the structure of the dataset corresponds to your forecasting needs.

- Make sure that your dataset's data is valid. You can use the **Validate Full Dataset** feature to do so.

- Make sure that the different dataset variables are handled properly, whether it comes to their nature (dimension of measure), their types (data type, statistical type), or other relevant information.

Sampled Data

When your dataset contains more than 2,000 rows, the following are true:

- Only 2,000 sampled rows from your dataset are visible.

- The data distribution of the different variables will be based on these 2,000 sampled rows.

> While this sampling is necessary to maximize performance on huge datasets, you should be cautious not to be misled by this incomplete information. You might need to use complementary data exploration tools to get a complete picture of the data.

Manipulating Datasets

You can leverage all the dataset capabilities to transform your datasets as you see fit. Some of these capabilities include the following:

- Creating data transformations
- Transposing columns to rows
- Removing duplicated rows
- Reimporting more recent data from a given data source for acquired datasets (live datasets always present the latest information available in SAP HANA)

You can read more about the data wrangling, data mapping, and data transformation capabilities of the datasets here: *http://s-prs.co/v577117*.

7.3   Creating Time Series Forecasting Models on Datasets

This section walks you through the creation of a time series forecasting model using a dataset as the training data source. You'll be provided with an overview of the different settings.

> **Time Series Forecasting on Datasets versus Planning Models**
>
> Most of the time, series forecasting model creation settings are identical when you're creating time series forecasting models on top of datasets or planning models. Therefore, throughout this section, we'll refer you to Chapter 5 where some of the specific settings have been covered in more detail. Major settings differences are detailed at the end of this section.

You first need to create a time series forecasting scenario by following these steps:

1. Click the **Predictive Scenarios** 🔍 entry on the left navigation bar of the user interface. The **Predictive Scenarios** entry could be found in the **More** ⚬⚬⚬ menu in the left navigation bar depending on the real estate available on your screen. Predictive scenarios can also be created by opening the **Files** entry of the left navigation bar, clicking the **+** button of the toolbar, and selecting the **Predictive Scenarios** entry. If you can't find the entries for create predictive scenarios, make sure that you've been granted the proper privileges.

2. Click the **Time Series Forecast** button in the **Create New** section, as shown in Figure 7.4.

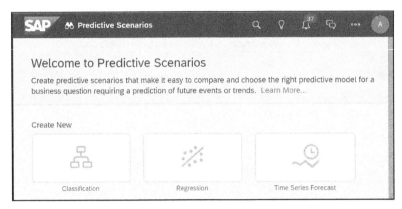

Figure 7.4 Create a New Time Series Forecasting Predictive Scenario

3. The **New Predictive Scenario** dialog box appears to let you save the newly created predictive scenario. In the **Name** field, enter "US National Park Visit Forecasting", and click **OK**. You can choose to save the predictive scenario to a specific folder. By default, the predictive scenario will be saved in your private user folder.

4. The predictive scenario interface is displayed, and a first time series forecasting model is automatically created for you. You can see the settings for this time series forecasting model in the right-hand **Settings** panel. For now, the settings aren't fully set, as shown in Figure 7.5.

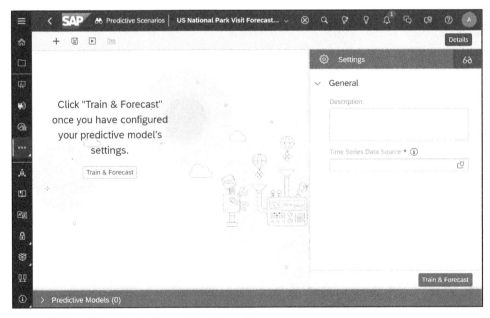

Figure 7.5 Your Time Series Forecasting Scenario

The next sections explain the different time series forecasting model settings. You'll enter them as you progress through the settings explanations.

7.3.1   General Settings

The **General** section of the time series forecasting model settings is represented in Figure 7.6.

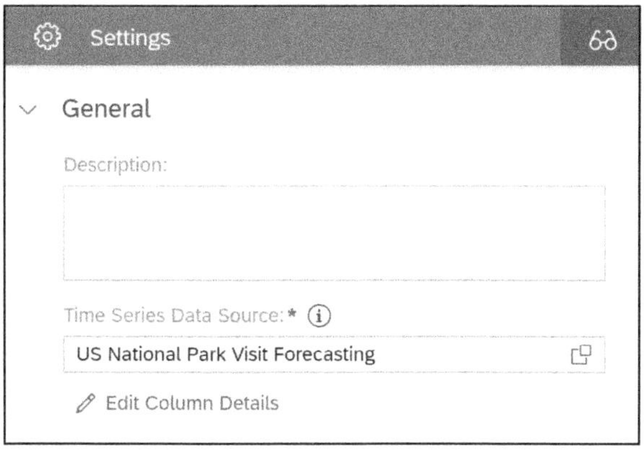

Figure 7.6 General Settings for a Time Series Forecasting Model Based on a Dataset

Let's review these key settings:

- **Description**
  The **Description** field is a free-form text field that allows you to describe the intent of a time series forecasting model. While filling this field is optional, we recommend you provide a meaningful description for each of your time series forecasting models (for more details, see Chapter 5, Section 5.3.2).

  For our example, enter the description as: "This is my first predictive model for US National Park visit forecasting."

- **Time Series Data Source**
  The **Time Series Data Source** field allows you to select the data source you want to use to train a time series forecasting model. This setting is mandatory. Select the training dataset **US National Park Visit Forecasting** you created in Section 7.2.1.

Note that once you've selected your training dataset, you can edit the dataset column details by clicking on the **Edit Column Details** hyperlink.

7.3.2   Predictive Goal

The **Predictive Goal** section of the settings allows you to specify the column in the training dataset that you want to forecast and your forecasting goals (see Figure 7.7).

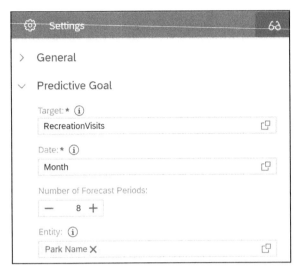

Figure 7.7 Predictive Goal Settings

We'll explain the **Predictive Goal** settings in more detail:

- **Target**
  The target variable is the variable you want to predict. You'll usually select one of your dataset measures.
  Select **RecreationVisits** as your target.

- **Date**
  The **Date** setting makes it possible to select the date dimension used to order the observations. Forecasts will depend on the inner date granularity of your data. For instance, if your dataset contains daily observations, forecasts will be done daily. Chapter 4, Section 4.2, covers the basics while in Chapter 8, Section 8.3, we cover the topic of time granularity in more detail.
  Select **Month** as your date.

- **Number of Forecast Periods**
  The **Number of Forecast Periods** field allows you to specify the number of observations to be predicted in the future (known as the *forecast horizon*). Section 5.3.4 details the corresponding forecast period based on other settings. Chapter 5, Section 5.3.3, details what must be considered when choosing several forecast periods. The

number of forecast periods can't exceed 500 to limit the volume of resources (CPU, memory, etc.) needed to train a time series forecasting model.

Set the number of forecast periods to "8". You'll forecast the May to December 2021 visits.

- **Entity**

  Through the **Entity** setting, you can select up to five dimensions (or dimension attributes) to define the data slices corresponding to the entities. We already detailed in Chapter 5, Section 5.3.3, how entities are handled in the context of smart predict. It's quite different with datasets as they are flat data tables. You need to make sure that the datasets are prepared up front to match your entity-based forecasting scenario. Dataset structures are discussed in Chapter 4, Section 4.2. You can generate up to 1,000 entities per time series forecasting model. Note that the **Entity Filters** setting isn't offered in the context of datasets.

  Set **Park Name** as the entity variable. This is the only possible choice, as we have a dataset composed of multiple parks (entities) and we want to generate one time series forecasting model per park.

7.3.3   Predictive Model Training

The **Predictive Model Training** section is set to default settings. You can refine these settings to have more control over the time series forecasting model (see Figure 7.8).

Figure 7.8 Predictive Model Training Settings

Let's take a closer look at these settings:

- **Train Using** and **Until:**
  Smart predict provides two settings, **Train Using** and **Until**, that allow you to specify the dates to be included in the training dataset. We discussed these settings in detail with examples in Chapter 5, Section 5.3.4.

  For our business scenario, you'll set the following settings:
  - **Train Using** should be set to **All Observations**.
  - **Until** should be set to **Last Observation**.

- **Exclude As Influencer**
  This setting makes it possible to exclude candidate influencers. As we've discussed in Chapter 5, influencers are variables correlated to the target to be predicted. They allow you to better explain the target and therefore can improve the time series forecasting model accuracy. By default, all dataset columns not set as either **Target**, **Date**, or **Entity** will be considered potential influencers. Numerical and categorical columns can be used as candidate influencers when training time series forecasting models on top of datasets.

  You can refer to Chapter 5, Section 5.3.5, if you want to better understand how to consider influencers to improve the accuracy of your time series forecasting model.

  In the context of our business scenario, we don't use influencers, so you don't need to change this setting.

- **Convert Negative Forecast Values to Zero**
  By enabling this option, you can instruct the time series forecasting model that if it forecasts negative values, they should be converted to zero values. The use of this option is further detailed in Chapter 5, Section 5.3.4.

  For our business scenario, you'll turn on **Convert Negative Forecast Values to Zero** as having negative visit forecasts doesn't make sense.

7.3.4   Datasets versus Planning Models

Figure 7.9 shows the compared settings that need to be entered when using a planning model (left side) or a dataset (right side) as a data source to train the time series forecasting model. The detailed breakdown can be found in Table 7.1.

The major differences are the following:

- When selecting a planning model, the data **Version** needs to be selected as well.
- The **Time Granularity** and **Entity** filters settings are available only in the context of planning models.
- Influencers must be included when using planning models and excluded when using datasets.

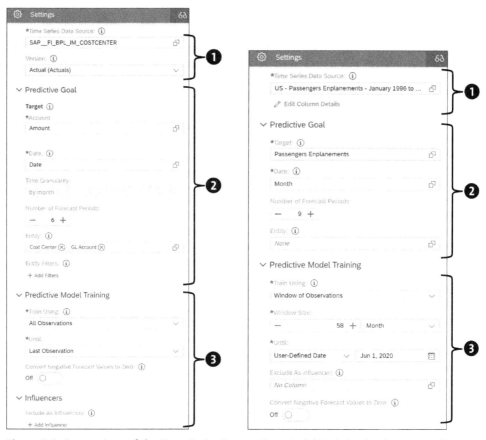

Figure 7.9 Comparison of the Time Series Forecasting Model Training Settings According to the Data Source Used

	Forecasting Using Planning Models	Forecasting Using Datasets
❶ Time Series Data Source	<ul><li>Planning model</li><li>Planning model version</li></ul>	<ul><li>Dataset</li></ul>
❷ Predictive Goal Forecasting Using Datasets	<ul><li>Target</li><li>Date variable</li><li>Time granularity</li><li>Number of forecast periods</li><li>Entities help create predictive models based on dimension combinations</li><li>Entities can be filtered to focus the forecasting scope</li></ul>	<ul><li>Target</li><li>Date variable</li><li>Number of forecast periods</li><li>Entities help create predictive models based on dimension combinations</li></ul>

Table 7.1 Comparison Breakdown

	Forecasting Using Planning Models	Forecasting Using Datasets
❸ Predictive Model Training	■ Data history window that's used for training ■ Convert negative forecast values to zero ■ Influencers are included	■ Data history window that's used for training ■ Convert negative forecast values to zero ■ Influencers are excluded

Table 7.1 Comparison Breakdown (Cont.)

You're now ready to create your time series forecasting model. Click the **Train & Forecast** button so that your time series forecasting model gets trained.

7.4   Understanding Time Series Forecasting Models Based on Datasets

Smart predict provides multiple reports to help you assess the performance of the time series forecasting model and understand how it works. The following sections provide a quick overview of these reports. A more detailed explanation of these reports is provided in Chapter 5, Section 5.4.

7.4.1   Assessing Model Performance

Using smart predict, you can deliver predictive forecasts in datasets that will be used in stories and consumed by end users. It's particularly important that you understand how accurate your time series forecasting model is. We've covered these reports in detail in Chapter 5, Section 5.4.1, so we'll provide a quick recap here:

■ **Global Performance Indicators**
  The **Global Performance Indicators** visualization of the **Forecast** report provides standard performance indicators that allow you to assess the model's performance. Figure 7.10 shows an example of the **Global Performance Indicators** visualization you obtain in your time series forecasting model. You can see the value of the median **Expected MAPE** is 108.84%. This means that half of the parks have an **Expected MAPE** inferior to 108.84%, while the other half have an **Expected MAPE** superior to 108.84%.

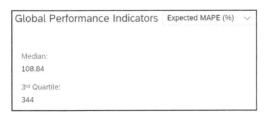

Figure 7.10 Global Performance Indicators

You can refer to Chapter 5, Section 5.4.1, where performance indicators are described in detail, including their advantages and drawbacks.

- **Forecast vs. Actual**
  The **Forecast vs. Actual** visualization (see Figure 7.11) provides a more qualitative and visual way of evaluating the time series forecasting model performance by comparing several data series: the actual, forecast, prediction interval min (formerly error min), prediction interval max (formerly error max), and outliers. The **Actual** and **Forecast** series are close, which is the sign of an accurate predictive model. In our example, we can spot at least one outlier in April 2020 as the park was closed during the peak of the COVID-19 pandemic. The time series forecasting model predicts 166,551 visitors, hence the outlier (major difference between reality and prediction). Finally, you can see the predictions for the rest of year 2021 with the **Prediction Interval Min** and **Prediction Interval Max** series.

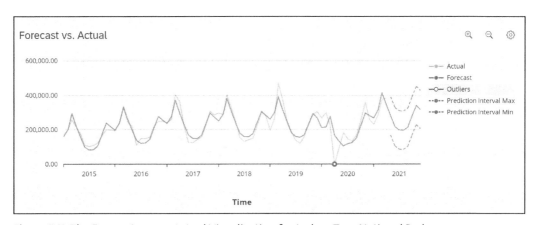

Figure 7.11 The Forecast versus Actual Visualization for Joshua Tree National Park

7.4.2   Time Series Forecasting Model Reports

The smart predict modeling reports provide visualizations with additional business insights to help you understand how your time series forecasting model works. When the **Entity** field is used, these reports are available for each entity. We've covered these reports in detail in Chapter 5, Section 5.4.2, so we'll provide a quick recap here:

- **Time Series Breakdown**
  The time series forecasting algorithm of smart predict breaks down the time series to be forecasted into simpler, easier to understand time series, called *components*. These components are used by the time series forecasting to calculate the forecast. They also constitute business insights related to the time series. The **Time Series Breakdown** visualization (see Figure 7.12) shows how each component impacts the predicted values and is available as part of the **Explanation** modeling report.

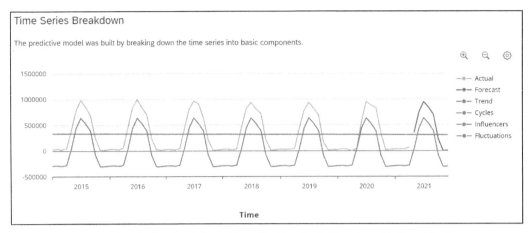

Figure 7.12 Time Series Breakdown Visualization for Yellowstone National Park

- **Time Series Component Impact**

  The **Time Series Component Impact** shows the impact of the various components found by the time series forecasting model when modeling the time series. The impact of a component is the fraction of the forecasted time series represented by this component. The values of the column **Impact** of this visualization always sum to 100%.

  In the example of Figure 7.13, the trend component alone explains 73.14% of the actual values of the travel expenses, while the yearly cycle explains 18.19% of the actual values of the travel expenses. The **Final Residuals** row tells us that 8.67% of the actual time series isn't explained by the time series forecasting model.

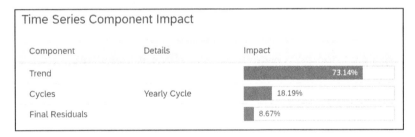

Figure 7.13 Time Series Component Impact Visualization

- **Impact of Cycles**

  The **Impact of Cycles** visualization lets you dig into the details of the cycle impact, period after period. Each orange bar represents a period in the cycle, and the value of the bar corresponds to the impact for this specific period on the predictive forecasts. This visualization can be used for two major purposes:

  - Understand the logic used by the time series forecasting model to calculate the predictive forecast.

- Get business insights about the time series to be forecasted. What are the months of the year with the highest visits or the lowest visits?

- **Impact of Numerical Influencers**
  The **Impact of Numerical Influencers** visualization lets you explore how influencer values impact the predicted time series. The x-axis of the chart represents the influencer values, while the y-axis represents the impact of the influencer value to the predictive forecast.

- **Past Target Value Contributions**
  The **Past Target Value Contributions** visualization shows how the time series is impacted by the recent past, that is, how the forecasted value for a data point is impacted by the previous data points. This visualization is displayed only if a fluctuations component is part of the time series forecasting model.

- **Forecast Breakdown**
  The **Forecast Breakdown** visualization represents the impact of each component of the time series forecasting model to a given forecasted period. The **Forecast Breakdown** is available as part of the **Forecast** report. In the example shown in Figure 7.14, the **Total** forecasted value (349,754.67) is broken down into the **Trend** contribution (311,424.61) and the **Yearly Cycle [May]** contribution (38,330.06).

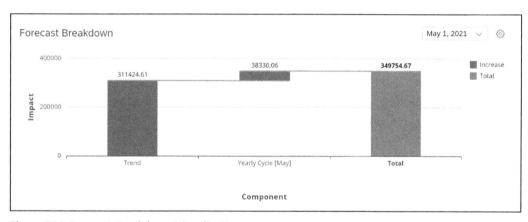

Figure 7.14 Forecast Breakdown Visualization

7.5   Improving Time Series Forecasting Models Based on Datasets

Although the use of smart predict is as automated as possible, there are still situations where your judgement is needed to improve the quality of the time series forecasting model or review how well it fits your business requirements. The following sections provide you with some quick hints to help you improve your time series forecasting models. We provided these tips in detail in Chapter 5, Section 5.5, so we'll only provide a quick review for our discussion here.

Keep track of your different experiments using the capabilities provided in the predictive scenarios:

1. Open the **Predictive Models** table at the bottom of the screen.
2. Open the context menu of a time series forecasting model you would like to start from, and click **Duplicate**.
3. Select the copy of the time series forecasting model created in the previous step.
4. Change some settings; for instance, add influencers.
5. In the time series forecasting model description, replace the default description to document your experiment; for instance, enter "added 2 influencers".
6. Train the time series forecasting model.

Repeat all of these steps for each experiment you do with different time series forecasting model settings.

7.5.1   Finding the Optimal Training Data Size

One crucial point when training a time series forecasting model is finding the right trade-off for the training dataset size. Chapter 5, Section 5.5.1, details additional recommendations to handle this trade-off.

7.5.2   Filtering Entities

When forecasting for several entities, some entities may not be forecasted properly. Chapter 5, Section 5.5.2, elaborates more on the diverse types of entities you can find. **Entity Filters** isn't available as part of the smart predict time series forecasting model settings when the source of the time series forecasting model is a dataset. Therefore, such entities either have to be manually removed, or you can also use the dataset editing features to remove the rows corresponding to such non-forecastable entities.

7.5.3   Adding Influencers

One way to improve the accuracy of the time series forecasting model is to use influencers. With the influencers, you can consider factors that are external to the time series to be predicted, but that may influence its values. Chapter 5, Section 5.5.3, elaborates more on how you can leverage influencers. It's important that you remain selective with the candidate influencers.

7.6   Saving Predictive Forecasts

Once your time series forecasting model has been trained and improved, you're ready to save your predictive forecasts into the predictions dataset. Figure 7.15 represents the process of training a time series forecasting model and delivering predictive forecasts to the predictions dataset. First of all, you need to create a training dataset, train a time series forecasting model based on specified user settings, and then deliver the predictions to the training dataset.

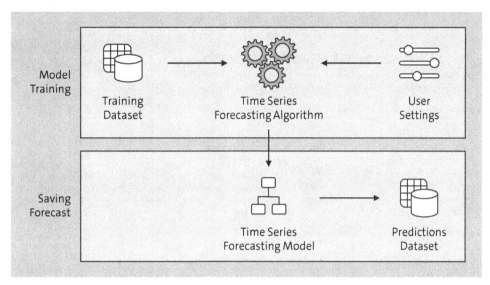

Figure 7.15 Time Series Forecasting Process

Let's walk through the steps to save your predictive forecast based on a dataset:

1. Click the **Save Forecast** icon, as shown in Figure 7.16.

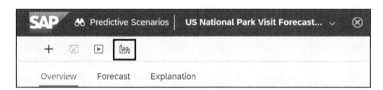

Figure 7.16 Save Forecast Icon

2. In the **Save Forecast** dialog shown in Figure 7.17, choose a location to save your predictions dataset, and name it "US National Park 2021 Forecasted Visits".

Figure 7.17 Save Forecast Dialog

Your predictive forecasts for the rest of the year 2021 will be saved into the predictions dataset.

3. Next, open this dataset so that you can take a quick look (see Figure 7.18).

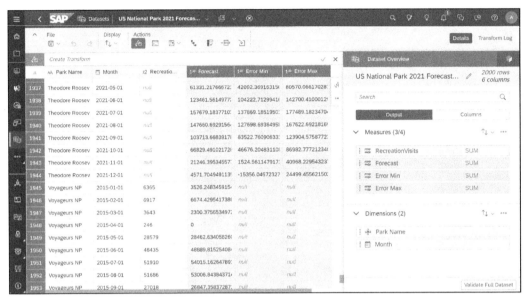

Figure 7.18 Predictions Dataset

The predictions dataset contains six columns, four measures, and two dimensions:

- **Park Name** and **Month** are the training dataset original dimensions. Note the **Month** values have been augmented with months ranging from May 2021 to December 2021.

- **RecreationVisits** is the training dataset original measure. This measure contains the historical values for park recreation visits.

- **Forecast**, as the name hints, contains the recreation visit forecasts.

- **Error Min** and **Error Max** contain the lower and upper bounds, respectively, of the prediction intervals for the forecasted months.

7.7 Including Predictive Forecasts in a Story

To integrate predictive forecasts in a story, you need to create a story that uses the predictions dataset as its main model or blend the predictions datasets to other data models in the context of preexisting stories. Here you'll create a story from scratch, leveraging the **Forecast**, **Error Min,** and **Error Max** information.

Go to the **Stories** area of the left side navigation bar. Choose **Canvas**, as shown in Figure 7.19. Select the default entry **Optimized Design Experience**, and click **Create**. Save your story to your working folder where you saved the datasets and the predictive scenario. Name the story "US National Park 2021 Forecasted Visits".

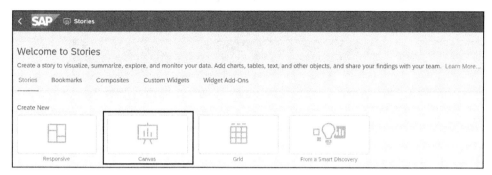

Figure 7.19 Create a New Canvas Story

Next you'll click on the **Add New Data** entry under the **Tools** menu (see Figure 7.20). Select the predictions dataset **US National Park 2021 Forecasted Visits**. Save your story.

Figure 7.20 Add a Dataset to a Story

In the next subsections, you'll see how to report on predictive forecasts in a table and in a time series chart.

7.7.1 Report on Predictive Forecasts in a Table

You'll first rename your initial story page, currently named Page_1, as "Table". Next, you'll insert a new table by clicking the **Table** icon, as shown in Figure 7.21.

Figure 7.21 Insert a Table

You'll configure the **Builder** corresponding to the table, as shown in Figure 7.22:

- Under **Rows**, place the dimension **Month**.
- Under **Columns**, place **Measures**.
- Under **Filters**, filter **Measures** on **Forecast** and **Month** on the range going from May to December 2021.

Figure 7.22 Configuring the Builder for the Table

You can now visualize your forecasted recreational visits at the national level for the rest of the year 2021 in the table you just configured (see Figure 7.23). According to the predictions, more than 66 million visits are expected at the national level for the rest of the year 2021.

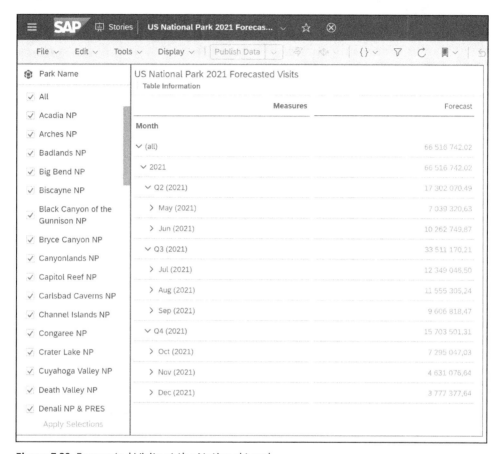

Figure 7.23 Forecasted Visits at the National Level

You can add an input control related to **Park Name** if you want to visualize this information per national park. First create the input control as shown in Figure 7.24, and then select the **Park Name** dimension, followed by **All Members** so that all parks are shown in the input control.

Figure 7.24 Creating an Input Control

Figure 7.25 shows the expected visits for Yosemite, a little more than 3 million for the rest of the year.

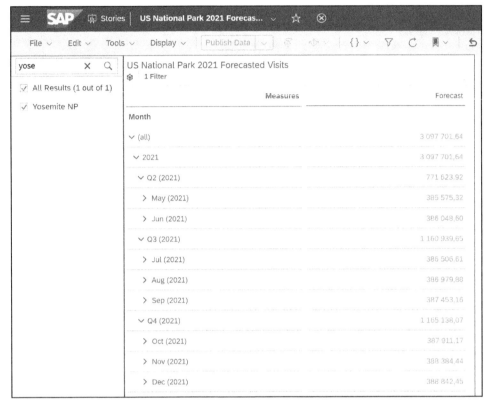

Figure 7.25 Expected Visits for Yosemite

Don't forget to save the story when you're done.

7.7.2   Report on Predictive Forecasts in a Time Series Chart

You'll now add a time series chart to report on the number of forecasted visits visually. Create a new page, and name it "Time Series Chart". Insert a new chart by clicking the **Chart** icon, as shown in Figure 7.26.

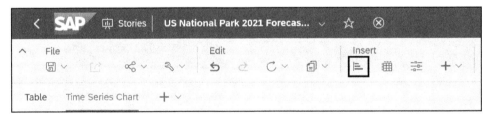

Figure 7.26 Insert a New Chart

Set the **Builder** corresponding to the time series chart as shown in Figure 7.27 to report on **Forecast**, **Error Min**, and **Error Max** for May to December 2021:

- Under **Measures**, place the measures **Forecast**, **Error Min**, and **Error Max**.
- Under **Time**, place the dimension **Month**.
- Under **Filters**, filter **Month** on the period ranging from May to December 2021.

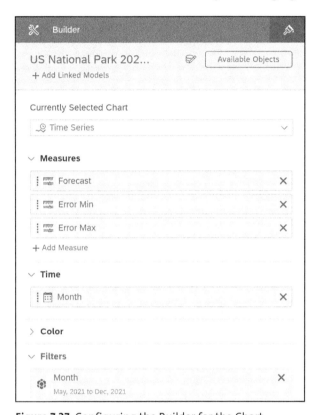

Figure 7.27 Configuring the Builder for the Chart

You can then refine the styling as you want to make the chart display nicer, for instance, by editing the series colors and patterns, as shown in Figure 7.28.

The outcome is shown in Figure 7.29.

Figure 7.28 Color Configuration

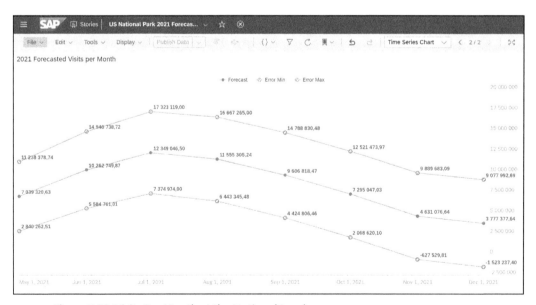

Figure 7.29 Visits Per Month at the National Level

You can improve your story in diverse ways:

- You can report both on the tables and in the time series chart on actuals and predictive forecasts and then compare them.
- You can input controls per page or global to the story to be able to filter on national parks.
- You can also forecast periods where you know what happened (e.g., the most dramatic COVID-19 periods) and see what the predictions were saying about 2020 visits versus what happened.

7

7.8   Summary

To summarize, we've seen the end-to-end workflow of time series forecasting based on datasets, from creating datasets, to setting time series forecasting models and delivering predictive forecasts, and finally to using predictive forecasts in the context of stories.

In the next chapter, we'll provide some tips and tricks for adapting to advanced scenarios when working with time series forecasting models.

Chapter 8

Best Practices and Tips for Time Series Forecasting Models

So far, our examples of time series forecasting have been simple for illustrative purposes. However, your organization's real-world requirements may be more advanced. This chapter will equip you with all you need to face complex situations.

This chapter provides best practices, hints, and tips to help you adapt to advanced situations when doing time series forecasting. We'll cover the following topics:

- Pushing entity limits (Section 8.1)
- Missing data in time series (Section 8.2)
- Time granularities (Section 8.3)
- Custom performance indicators (Section 8.4)
- What-if simulations (Section 8.5)
- Data forecast level (Section 8.6)

8.1 Going Beyond 1,000 Entities

By default, time series forecasting scenarios are limited to 1,000 entities. Depending on your business scenario, crossing multiple dimensions in the **Entity** field can lead to the creation of more than 1,000 entities. Let's imagine a sales forecasting use case where you want to forecast the sales of 100 products across 100 countries. Assuming you sell every product in every country, crossing the **Product** and **Country** dimensions in the **Entity** field will lead to the creation of 10,000 entities, which exceeds the limitation. So, what can you do in such a situation?

There are two major ways you can go ahead, which we'll examine in the next sections. The first way is to forecast by batch of 1,000 entities. The second way is to aggregate to predict and disaggregate to plan.

8.1.1   Forecast by Batch of 1,000 Entities

The first way is to divide the data so you can run several time series forecasting models, each running a maximum of 1,000 entities. We'll explain how in the context of planning models and datasets.

Using Planning Models

Let's go back to our sales forecasting example. When you cross two dimensions of the planning model in the **Entity** field, you must handle the full combined dimensionality. On top of this, you can use the **Entity Filters** feature to divide the data into smaller data chunks to fall back to time series forecasting models that stay within the limit of 1,000 entities. For instance, you can filter the **Product** dimension and keep only 10 products out of the 100, or you can filter the **Country** dimension and keep only 10 countries out of the 100. With this approach, you can create 10 separate time series forecasting models with different **Entity Filters** sets, each staying within the limit of 1,000 entities. You can write back the predictive forecasts to a single output version and combine your predictive forecasts across the 10,000 entities (see Figure 8.1).

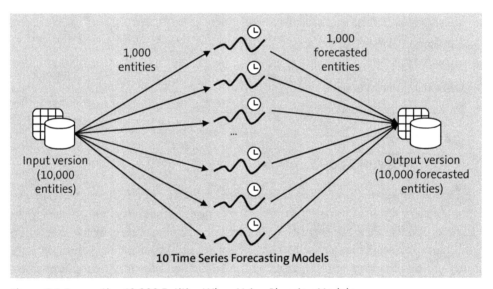

Figure 8.1 Forecasting 10,000 Entities When Using Planning Models

You can automate the processing of your different time series forecasting models using predictive steps in a single multi action. For instance, in a single multi action, you can chain 10 predictive steps where each step handles the forecasting of 1,000 entities. Note that there is a limit to the "forecast by batch of 1,000 entities approach" based on practical experience: It's difficult to go beyond 10,000 entities when you execute these steps in sequence into a single multi action.

Using Datasets

When you're using datasets, you can't make use of the **Entity Filters** feature. The only way you can handle such a scenario is to split your data up front. Back to our earlier example, you'll need to split the overall data table into 10 different datasets, each having data equivalent to 1,000 entities. You'll then need to create 10 separate time series forecasting models, each of them based on one of these different datasets. You'll create 10 separate prediction datasets that you can report on in a single story (see Figure 8.2).

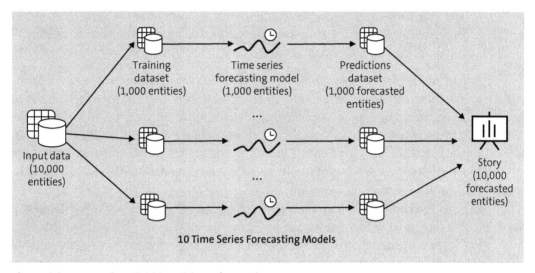

Figure 8.2 Forecasting 10,000 Entities When Using Datasets

Unfortunately, it's not possible to automate such an approach when using datasets. Every time series forecasting model forecasting step must be handled manually.

8.1.2   Aggregate to Predict and Disaggregate to Plan and Report

The second way is to aggregate to predict and disaggregate to plan. By *aggregate to predict*, we mean that the predictions aren't generated based on the most granular data, but rather on pre-aggregated data. By *disaggregate to plan*, we mean that once the predictions have been generated at the aggregated level, they can be disaggregated at the level where planners expect to work.

Once again, we'll explain this method for both planning models and datasets.

Using Planning Models

Let's imagine your 100 products are grouped into 10 distinct product categories, each including 10 products. You can also imagine that the 100 countries are grouped into 10 regions, each of these regions including 10 countries. You can then create predictive forecasts at the level of product category and country or product, and region. In both cases, you would stay within the limit of the 1,000 entities.

Let's decompose this approach step by step:

1. First, you need modeled hierarchies or attributes for product categories or regions.

2. You can set your **Entity** with products and countries and use the **Entity Filters** feature to filter on specific product categories or regions.

3. In the time series forecasting process, data will first be aggregated at the desired level (product category–country, product-region, or product category–region) and forecasted at this level. You'll get entities for *product category A – France, product 1 – Europe*, or *product category A – Europe*.

As part of the predictive forecast saving step, predictive forecasts will be saved to the proper hierarchy nodes, say *product 1 – Europe*. But because the Europe region has 10 children, including France, Germany, and others, the forecasted value for Europe will also be automatically disaggregated to the 10 children. If your predictive forecast equals 100,000 sales for product 1 in a given month, then each *product 1 – European country* cell will receive 1/10 of the overall sales, meaning 10,000 sales each. It could be that this "equal value" disaggregation approach isn't the most appropriate for your scenario as you know you usually realize 20% of your sales in France and 30% in Germany. In this case, you can prepopulate the output version where you'll be saving the predictive forecasts with weighted data to influence the disaggregation process. You can read more about this disaggregation approach in Chapter 5, Section 5.3.6. It's possible to automate such an approach with a multi action (see Chapter 6), including preparing the output version (using a data action step) and creating the predictive forecasts (using a predictive step).

Using Datasets

The approach described in the earlier section isn't applicable to datasets. You can, of course, make sure to aggregate the base data in a different way in your dataset, for instance, building your dataset based on product categories and countries or products and regions. You can predict your forecasts at this level. But then, you'll face a tough time deriving the high-level predictions to the base dimension granularity that people expect to report on. This proves the richness of using planning-enabled models as they allow this type of workaround.

8.1.3   Compared Approaches

Table 8.1 details the pros and cons of different approaches when using planning models.

Approaches	Number of Time Series Forecasting Models	Complexity of Creation and Maintenance	Can Be Automated?
Forecast by batch of 1,000 entities (using planning models)	As many as batches of 1,000 entities	High	Yes
Forecast by batch of 1,000 entities (using datasets)	As many as batches of 1,000 entities—the same for datasets	Very high	No
Aggregate to predict, disaggregate to plan and report (using planning models)	Depends on the specific dimensionality at play, but can be just 1	Medium	Yes

Table 8.1 Going beyond 1,000 Entities: Compared Approaches When Using Planning Models

You can also think of combining both approaches when using planning models, for instance, forecasting multiple batches of product category/country, product/region, and so on. You must adapt this generic guidance to your business scenario.

When you're using datasets, only one approach is possible, as detailed in Table 8.2.

Approaches	Number of Time Series Forecasting Models	Complexity of Creation and Maintenance	Can Be Automated?
Forecast by batch of 1,000 entities (using datasets)	As many as batches of 1,000 entities—same for datasets	Very high	No

Table 8.2 Going beyond 1,000 Entities: When Using Datasets

8.2   Handling Time Series with Missing Data

Let's start with a few definitions:

- **Zero**
  The period exists, and there is a value equal to zero that is present for this period (e.g., March 2023 exists in the data, and the corresponding value is 0).

- **Blank**
  This is a period for which no data point is available (e.g., March 2023 doesn't exist in the data, alongside the corresponding value). This missing data point could also

correspond to a missing zero. There are varied reasons why these data points could be blank, as we'll detail in Table 8.3.

- **Discontinued time series**
  This time series has values entered for a continuous period and then contains only blank periods (e.g., filled periods for January 2015 to December 2020, "blank" periods since January 2021). See Figure 8.3 for an example of a discontinued time series. An example of a discontinued time series is the evolution of product sales when a product is no longer for sale at a given point in time.

- **Emerging time series**
  This time series has values filled for a given period, usually up to the present, while it had blank periods before (e.g., filled periods for January 2020 to February 2022, "blank" periods before January 2020). See Figure 8.4 for an example of an emerging time series. For instance, this could correspond to a new product that started selling recently on the market.

- **Intermittent time series**
  This time series has a substantial number of zeros, meaning a mix of time periods filled with values (> = 0) and time periods corresponding to zero values. See Figure 8.5 for an example of an intermittent time series.

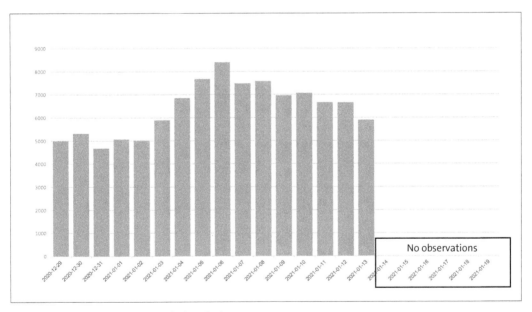

Figure 8.3 Discontinued Time Series

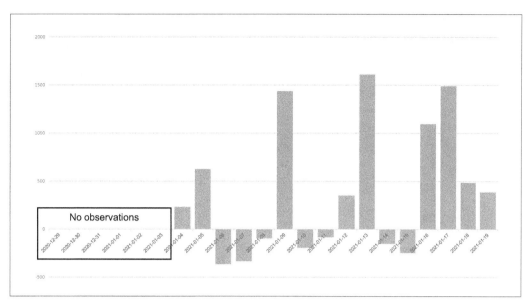

Figure 8.4 Emerging Time Series

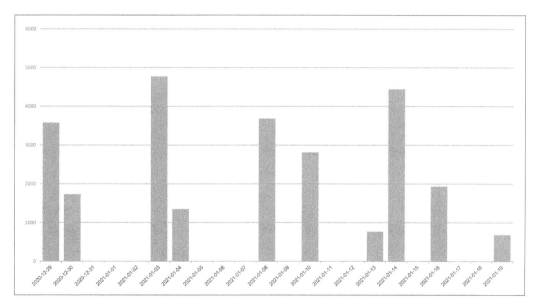

Figure 8.5 Intermittent Time Series

Table 8.3 details the major reasons for missing data.

Case	Reason
Missing "0"	If data was extracted from a transactional system, the absence of a transaction for a given period may denote that the period should be associated to a 0 value. For example, no sales transaction on 2021-01-01 means "0 sales were done on 2021-01-01".
"Normal" missing value	There is no data for some periods, and associating zero values with these periods would not be correct, as these missing values are normal. This might correspond with a given product no longer being for sale, for instance.
Data quality issues	There could be many reasons for this, but here are a few examples: ■ The data point exists but it wasn't entered in the system. ■ Two distinct periods were aggregated. ■ Data was lost during the data building process.

Table 8.3 Major Reasons for Missing Data

We'll now make a few recommendations to handle time series with missing data.

The first thing you need to do is check the nature of the different time series. You should also measure the percentage of missing values you have across the data range you use for training the time series forecasting models. This should give you a good sign of what to expect with the time series and the remediation measures you can take. The lower the percentage of missing values in the time series, the better.

You have different ways to check the percentage of filled data:

■ If you're using an entity-based time series forecasting model, you can check the **Record Count** per entity in the **Overview** tab of your time series forecasting model (see Figure 8.6). If you have a single time series forecasting model, you can see the **Record Count** in the **Predictive Models** list.

■ You can create ad hoc stories based on your training data to report on the number of filled data periods per different time granularities.

Here are a few remediation measures you can take based on your initial data exploration and analysis:

■ You need to gauge the percentage of zeros in an intermittent time series. An intermittent time series with too many zero values is typically not a great fit for predictive forecasting as the time series forecasting model will tend to average zeros, filled values, and flat, averaged predictive forecasts.

- You should discard discontinued time series as they are most probably no longer relevant to your business case once you've confirmed the missing observations do correspond to this time series being effectively discontinued.

- You should not replace blanks with zeros at the beginning of emerging time series, as it's normal that such periods are missing.

All Entities (62)				
Name	Creation Date	Expected MAPE	Influencer Count	Record Count
Acadia NP	Dec 3, 2023 15:38:43	28.76%	0	76
Arches NP	Dec 3, 2023 15:38:43	74.06%	0	76
Badlands NP	Dec 3, 2023 15:38:43	17.68%	0	76
Big Bend NP	Dec 3, 2023 15:38:44	20.48%	0	76
Biscayne NP	Dec 3, 2023 15:38:44	157.82%	0	76
Black Canyon of the Gu...	Dec 3, 2023 15:38:44	41.09%	0	76
Bryce Canyon NP	Dec 3, 2023 15:38:44	348.99%	0	76
Canyonlands NP	Dec 3, 2023 15:38:44	71.23%	0	76
Capitol Reef NP	Dec 3, 2023 15:38:45	55.02%	0	76
Carlsbad Caverns NP	Dec 3, 2023 15:38:45	113.39%	0	76

Figure 8.6 Record Count per Entity

When you're replacing blanks with zeros, it's important that you can evaluate the percentage of zeros in your time series. Having an important percentage of zeros in a time series isn't the best avenue to success as time series forecasting models aren't good at predicting based on a mix of zeroes and filled values.

8.3   Considering Time Granularities

Time series forecasting scenarios support several types of time granularities. Depending on your predictive forecasting needs, you might need to handle the data with different time granularities. In the next sections, we'll detail time granularities that can be used in datasets and planning models. We'll finish with a few recommendations on how you can handle time granularities best.

8.3.1   Using Datasets

When building your datasets for time series forecasting, you can use the following time granularities:

- Yearly
- Quarterly
- Monthly
- Weekly
- Daily
- Hourly
- Per minute
- Per second

Time series forecasting models created on top of datasets expect a date per each period to learn on. If you want to forecast your monthly sales, you need to provide a date per month in front of the sales for the corresponding month.

If you don't need to forecast per hour, per minute, or per second, you can stick to the generic date format YYYY-MM-DD where YYYY stands for years, MM stands for month, and DD stands for day of the month.

If you need to forecast per hour, per minute, or per second you'll need to use the longer date format YYYY-MM-DD hh:mm:ss where hh stands for hours from 0 to 24, mm stands for minutes from 1 to 59, and ss stands for seconds from 0 to 59.

Let's cover this through a few examples. You can create time series forecasting scenarios where the date granularity can be the following:

- Year expressed as YYYY
- Quarter expressed as YYYY-Q or YYYY-QQ, for instance, YYYY-1 or YYYY-01 for the first quarter of a given year YYYY
- Month expressed as YYYY-MM
- Weekly data in the date format YYYY-MM-DD taking, for instance, the first day of the week to fill out the characters DD (moving week)
- Day (calendar dates) expressed as YYYY-MM-DD
- Hour expressed as YYYY-MM-DD hh:01:01 where YYYY-MM-DD hh is variable (moving hour)
- Minute expressed as YYYY-MM-DD hh:mm:01 where YYYY-MM-DD hh:mm is variable (moving minute)
- Second expressed as YYYY-MM-DD hh:mm:ss (moving second)

These are the most common time granularities, yet the date format is flexible, so you can imagine forecasting at the semester level or forecasting every 15 minutes, for instance.

8.3.2   Using Planning Models

When you create a planning model, you must choose from the following base time granularities:

- Year
- Quarter
- Month
- Week
- Day

If the planning model's lowest level of time granularity is monthly, then a time series forecasting model created on top of this planning model will deliver monthly predictive forecasts. You need to take this into consideration when creating your planning model.

Example

Let's consider an example scenario:

- The granularity of the date dimension of your planning model is defined as monthly.
- You have data for the months from January 2019 to December 2023—five years of data.
- You ask for 12 forecasts.

In this case, predictive forecasts will be generated from January 2024 to December 2024.

You can't forecast per hour, minute, or second when using planning models.

8.3.3   Additional Recommendations

You can forecast more time granularities when you're using datasets over planning models, particularly at the hour, minute, or second level, but also for uncommon time granularities. If you look after year, quarter, month, week, or day, you can use either datasets or planning models.

You might not be sure what the best level is to use to forecast; for instance, in the business of retail, you might be unsure whether you should forecast sales at the daily, weekly, or monthly level to be the most precise when it comes to daily sales planning. In general, it's recommended to forecast at the level at which you expect to consume the predictive forecasts. So, if you want to forecast daily sales, it's better to use a daily time granularity. However, nothing prevents you from experimenting and drawing your own conclusions as to the best approach to take.

Note that the more granular the data, the more time this will take to generate your predictive forecasts. The maximum number of forecast periods that can be set in the user interface is restricted to 500 to prevent any performance issues.

8.4   Creating Ad Hoc Performance Indicators

As we presented in Chapter 5, time series forecasting models come with standard performance indicators by default (see Chapter 5, Section 5.4, for more details). However, for a number of reasons, you might need to calculate your very own performance indicators to evaluate the performance of time series forecasting models.

To calculate a performance indicator to evaluate the potential future performance of a time series forecasting model, you need to be able to compare the forecasts to real values (i.e., actuals). The actuals are obviously known only for the past period. That means that we need forecasts "in the past" (the training data partition) where the actuals are known. You can see an illustration of this in Figure 8.7 where the past forecasts are on the left ❶ and the future forecasts ❷ start in January 2021.

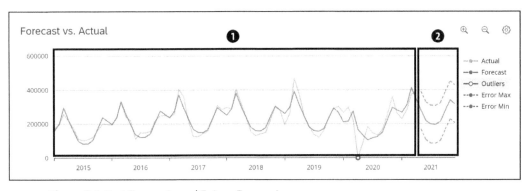

Figure 8.7 Past Forecasts and Future Forecasts

The first step consists of saving predictive forecasts for past periods, and then a custom performance indicator can be built in the context of planning models or stories. We'll walk through these steps in the following sections.

8.4.1   Saving Forecasts for Past Periods

When you're saving your predictive forecast, either in the predictive scenario (see Figure 8.8) or in a predictive step in a multi action (see Figure 8.9), you can turn on the **Save Forecast Values For Past Periods** option. When doing this, you'll save predictive forecasts not only for future periods but also for past periods (training period) (refer to Figure 8.7).

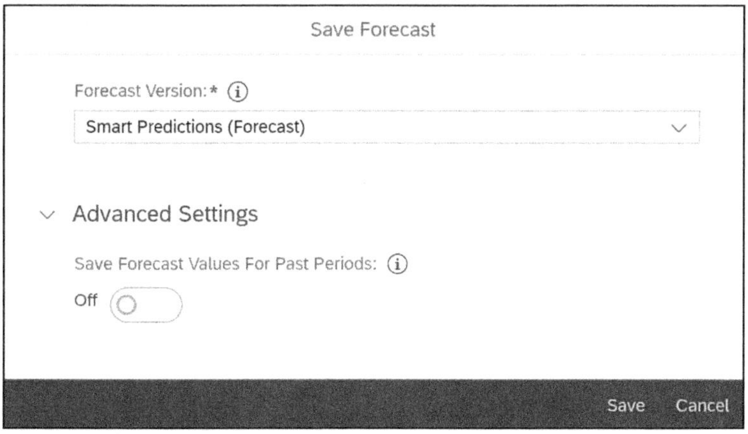

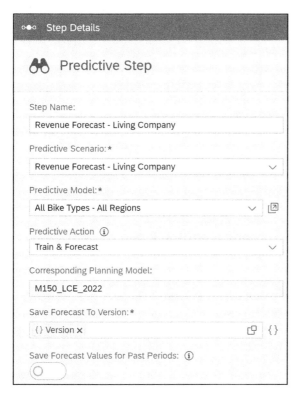

Figure 8.8 Save Forecast Values for Past Periods in Time Series Forecasting Scenarios

Figure 8.9 Save Forecast Values for Past Periods in Multi Action Predictive Steps

8.4.2   Custom Performance Indicators

It's difficult to provide generic recommendations for what you'll need to do as it depends on the type of indicator you want to calculate. In all cases, you'll need to compare actuals and forecasts for the past periods (as actuals aren't available for future periods). Calculated measures, restricted measures, and aggregations will be a great help for you to achieve your goals.

> **Tip**
>
> The blog at *http://s-prs.co/v577118* walks you through creating a custom performance indicator.

8.5   Generating What-If Simulations

Influencers can help increase the accuracy of predictive forecasts. When you're using influencers that aren't in your control because you can't know their future values for sure, you can generate multiples forecasts based on different scenarios to decide what you think is the most plausible version of the future or plan for different outcomes. This type of scenario planning is also known as *what-if simulation*.

What-if simulations are used in a planning context to figure out the future value of business indicators based on different hypothetical business scenarios, for instance:

- What would your revenue be this year if you gave the same commercial discounts as last year? What if you gave no discounts?
- What if your advertising budget gets reduced? How would that affect your product sales?
- What would be the number of bikes hired tomorrow in your city if it rains? What if it doesn't rain?

As an example, let's imagine that you want to forecast the number of bike hires in a city in the next month. Your daily bike hire predictions will be influenced by some weather-related conditions, more specifically, the amount of rain and the temperature during the day.

You want to get predictions for the 30 coming days. You can have some precise weather forecast you can use for tomorrow, even for the entire week to come. But there is no way you can get a weather forecast you can trust for the 30 days to come. In all cases, you would be using unreliable input to generate predictive forecasts.

So, what can you do? You can perform a predictive what-if simulation where you create multiple predictive forecasts based on different hypotheses. For instance, you can perform a what-if simulation using three simple scenarios (or hypotheses), as shown in Figure 8.10:

- **Median scenario**
  A median scenario will allow a predictive forecast to be generated based on some standard assumptions on the weather conditions (weather will be like what happened the past year).

- **Pessimistic scenario**

  A pessimistic scenario will allow a predictive forecast to be generated based on pessimistic assumptions about the weather (worse than expected weather conditions).

- **Optimistic scenario**

  An optimistic scenario will allow a predictive forecast to be generated based on optimistic assumptions about the weather (better than expected weather conditions).

Note that there can be as many scenarios as hypotheses you want to have.

To implement these scenarios, you'll need to vary the part of the data that corresponds to the future values of the influencers. You need to prepare as many separate planning input versions to train the time series forecasting models as hypotheses you're making. What will differ between these versions is the future value of influencers. When you're saving the predictive forecasts to separate output versions, you can report on the different output versions to have your different hypotheses.

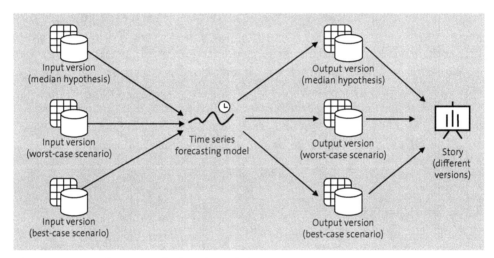

Figure 8.10 Overall Process of What-If Simulation

Further Resources

If you want to explore complementary resources about what-if simulations powered by predictive planning, refer to the following resources. We described the general principle of what-if simulations, but it's still interesting to get complementary perspectives, such as these:

- This blog walks you through more details regarding predictive planning and what-if simulation: *http://s-prs.co/v577119*.

- This blog provides an end user perspective on what-if simulations: *http://s-prs.co/v577120*.

- This blog walks you through the automation of what-if simulations: *http://s-prs.co/v577121*

8.6   Forecasting Data at the Right Level

There are many situations where you might wonder about the best way to approach a time series forecasting problem and obtain the best results. When using datasets, you must define your data up front, and it has a set granularity. You can't aggregate it differently, so it's even more important that you think ahead about the best approach to minimize the number of iterations. When you're using planning models, you have the luxury to play with more flexible entity definitions as well as entity filtering. You also need to find the best way of forecasting given constraints that can come from SAP Analytics Cloud or from the inner nature of your data. In the next subsections, we discuss the different points to consider.

8.6.1   Maximizing Forecasting Accuracy

The theory and literature tend to prove that when you have a specific predictive forecasting goal in mind (meaning you know the level at which you expect the predictive forecasts to be delivered on), say forecasting your expenses per division, it's better to stick to this exact level of granularity as opposed to forecasting at a higher level (then disaggregating your predictive forecasts) or forecasting at a lower level, if you want to maximize your forecasting accuracy. If you forecast at a too high level, you might lose some nuances that exist in the original data. If you forecast at a too granular level, you might be fooled by local patterns and get trapped in the curse of dimensionality (see *https://en.wikipedia.org/wiki/Curse_of_dimensionality*) and data becomes sparse and unforecastable.

8.6.2   Data Quality Is Key

The data will condition what you can do with it or what you should not do with it. Imagine you decide for a certain data granularity, generate many entities, and many of them are in error or show warnings. You need to take a closer look at the data and ask yourself a few questions:

- Do I have enough data periods filled?
- Do I have breaks in certain time series?
- Is the entirety of my data forecastable as is, or do I need to have different treatments for various parts of my data?

Professor Rob Hyndman (see *https://en.wikipedia.org/wiki/Rob_J._Hyndman*) is a worldwide forecasting expert. In a recent podcast (see *http://s-prs.co/v577122*), he shared some interesting practical advice, in particular, this quote:

> *Anything can be forecasted, but not everything can be forecasted well.*

He listed five conditions describing something that can be forecasted well. Here is a summary:

- **You understand the factors that contribute to its variation.**
  For instance, if you want to forecast the future employee expenses for your company, you know that the evolution of these expenses will be heavily conditioned by the number of employees. You need to consider this as part of your data model.

- **A lot of data is available.**
  We touched on this in earlier chapters. You can't forecast 30 months ahead if you only have 12 months of historical data; this doesn't make sense.

- **The forecasts can't affect the thing you're trying to forecast.**
  This is so there is no feedback—your forecasts don't make a difference to the outcome of the thing you're forecasting. This is what makes currency exchange and stock value evolution so hard to forecast.

- **The future is like the past.**
  For instance, let's say the travel expenses for a company drop 90% from one month to the other due to sanitary conditions. Suddenly, the future of travel expenses isn't going to be like the past, and we enter "new normal" conditions.

- **There is little natural or unexplainable variation.**
  You can describe the variables that relate to what you want to forecast. If you're doing a good job, you can totally model the evolution of the output variable and explain this evolution with the time series forecasting model.

This is an interesting piece of advice to consider. You should think of these recommendations and examine the data with great scrutiny through your forecasting experiments.

8.6.3   Predictive Planning versus Planning

While time series forecasting is fully part of the planning cycle, predictive planning and planning aren't the exact same activities. It's not because you want to plan and get predictive forecast numbers at a given level of data that you necessarily need to predict at this same level. For instance, business will tell you that they need to get predictions at the level of each product and each country where they sell certain products. This represents 100,000 combinations to forecast. Then, you need to see if you can predict at a higher level, say product categories per country, and then cascade the predicted numbers to the most granular levels where a business is expecting them. It's one example where predictive planning and planning aren't done on the same level of data.

8.6.4   Scalability

As we previously explained, the number of entities you can create with a single time series forecasting model is 1,000 entities maximum in one go. While you can bypass this limit to a degree by chaining multiple predictive steps into a multi action (Section 8.1.1), there is a limit to this approach, and the maximum order of magnitude you can achieve is in the ballpark of several thousand entities.

8.6.5   Key Takeaways

To sum up this section, here are the major points you need to consider:

- What is the exact thing I want to forecast? This will condition the optimal level where you should maximize your forecasting accuracy according to literature.
- Can I forecast this well? This is where the data and its inner qualities or deficiencies will come into play.
- Do I need to align my predictive planning and planning activities?
- Is this forecasting scenario generating too many entities and thus can't be forecasted in SAP Analytics Cloud? Can I use approaches to cope with the product limitations?

Through these questions, you should stick to your common sense, try out multiple experiments and approaches, and keep a strong focus on the source data and the corresponding accuracy of your time series forecasting models.

8.7   Summary

Through this chapter, we provided you with best practices, hints, and tips to adapt to advanced situations that you can face when performing time series forecasting. We hope you feel equipped to progress with confidence in your time series forecasting implementation projects.

To conclude our discussion of time series forecasting, in the next chapter, we'll look at the underlying data science techniques.

Chapter 9

The Data Science behind Time Series Forecasting Models

So far, we've discussed the general principles of time series forecasting, and we've seen how it can be implemented in SAP Analytics Cloud using a time series forecasting scenario. We hope this introduction has motivated you to dig deeper into the machine learning techniques used behind the scenes.

9

This chapter unveils the automated time series forecasting techniques. In Section 9.1, we'll first briefly describe the process that creates a time series forecasting model. Then, in Section 9.2 and Section 9.3, we'll provide details about the two major methods used by smart predict to create candidate predictive models. Finally, we'll explain how the best time series forecasting model is selected among the different candidate predictive models in Section 9.4.

9.1 End-to-End Process

When you train a time series forecasting model in smart predict, a multitude of candidate predictive models are trained under the hood. These candidate predictive models enter a competition where the winner is the one that will have the best performance with respect to the complexity. This winning predictive model is the one you see in the smart predict modeling reports and that you can use to generate predictive forecasts. The other candidate predictive models are discarded after the training process. This process is illustrated by Figure 9.1.

The candidate predictive models are either based on an additive modeling technique or on an exponential smoothing technique. These predictive modeling techniques are explained in more detail in the following sections.

While different predictive modeling techniques are involved, the modeling reports in smart predict are designed to provide a consistent user experience. Whether the winning predictive model is an additive model or an exponential smoothing model, the same visualizations are displayed and convey the same information.

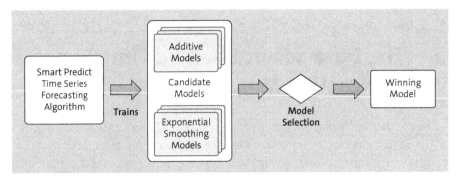

Figure 9.1 Smart Predict Time Series Forecasting Process

9.2   Additive Modeling Technique

With the *additive modeling technique*, the time series is broken down into components. *Components* are time series corresponding to patterns that a human can easily understand. This predictive modeling technique is called "additive" because the time series equals to the sum of its components:

Time series = Trend + Cycles + Influencers + Fluctuations + Residual

Let's quickly define these components (they are explained in more detail in the coming sections):

- **Trend**
  The trend represents the general evolution of the time series. In smart predict, a trend will always be detected.

- **Cycles**
  Cycles correspond to patterns that repeat in the time series over time. A given time series can have multiple cycles or no cycles at all.

- **Influencers**
  An influencer is a variable that is correlated to the time series to be predicted. A given time series forecasting model can contain multiple influencers or no influencers at all.

- **Fluctuations**
  Fluctuations represent the part of time series that depends on past values of the time series. A given time series may or may not have fluctuations.

- **Residual**
  The residual is the part of the time series that can't be explained by the time series forecasting model.

  Because the residual can't be modeled, it's not a component of the predictive model:

Predictive model = Trend + Cycles + Influencers + Fluctuations

Time series = Predictive model + Residual

As illustrated in Figure 9.2, the different components of the additive model are determined iteratively: the trend first, then the cycles, and finally the fluctuations. At each step, the detected component is subtracted from the time series. In the next step, the time series forecasting algorithm works on what is left of the actual time series.

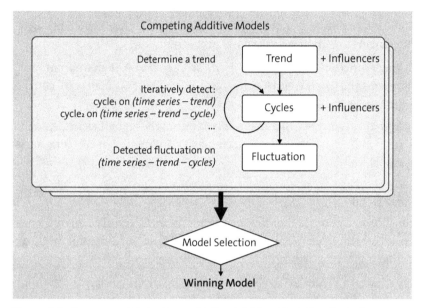

Figure 9.2 Component Detection with the Additive Modeling Technique

The detection of the influencers isn't a step by itself. In fact, some influencers may be determined during the trend detection step, and others may be determined during the cycles detection step. This is explained in more detail in Section 9.2.1 and Section 9.2.2. However, this inner relationship of the influencers to the trend and to the cycle detection steps had been made invisible in the smart predict modeling reports to avoid confusion.

Now, let's take a closer look at each additive modeling component.

9.2.1   Trend

The trend is the general evolution of the time series. It's the first component determined during the predictive modeling process. At this stage, smart predict doesn't complete the choice of the best possible trend; it simply puts in the competition a set of candidate predictive models that each include a different type of trend. There are a few types of trends, which we'll discuss in the following sections.

Linear Trend

A linear trend assumes that the value of the time series depends on time. Under the hood, the linear trend and the influencers are determined in the same step. A smart predict regression model is trained to determine the relationship between the time series values y_t (target of the regression model), the time t, and the influencers $X_1...X_2$ (both used as explanatory variables for the regression). The resulting regression model is a function $trend_t = A_0 + A_1.t + B_1.X_1 +...+ B_n.X_n$ where $A_0, A_1, B_1...,B_n$ are constants determined by the regression model. As the regression algorithm discards the variables that don't have a significant contribution (variable selection), any of the coefficients A_0, A_1, and $B_1...B_n$ can be equal to 0. There are two parts in this function:

- $A_0 + A_1.t$ is a linear function of t. If either A_0 or A_1 isn't equal to 0, then this part of the function represents the linear trend for the time series. If both A_0 and A_1 are equal to 0, then the time series has no linear trend.

- $B_1.X_1 +...+ B_n.X_n$ depends on the influencers only. If one of the B_i coefficients isn't null, then the corresponding X_i variable is detected as an influencer of the time series forecasting model.

Piece-Wise Linear Trend

A piece-wise linear trend assumes that the time series followed several different linear trends over time. This allows us to consider the change of general direction or disruptions that occurred in the time series.

The time series shown in Figure 9.3 used to be increasing from January 2020 to July 2021. Then, it decreased from July 2021 to April 2022. Since April 2022, the time series has been increasing again. This time series has followed different long-term trends that don't correspond to a single linear trend. Using a piece-wise linear trend allows you to consider these changes so that the most recent identified long-term direction is used to forecast future values.

Figure 9.3 Piece-Wise Linear Trend versus Linear Trend

The initial phase of a piece-wise trend detection consists of finding points correspond-ing to a shift of regime in the time series. These points are referred to as *change points*.

Then, for each time interval delimited by two change points (the first and last point of the time series being considered as change points), the linear trend detection process, as explained in the previous section, is applied. All the other subsequent modeling steps remain unchanged, as they don't depend on the nature of the trend.

Lag 1 Trend

The lag 1 trend (aka L1 trend) assumes that at a given point in time, the value of the time series depends on the earlier value of the time series. The predicted trend value at time t is equal to the time series value at time $t–1$: $trend_t = y_{t–1}$.

Figure 9.4 shows a lag 1 trend. We can see how the trend follows the time series while lagging one point behind.

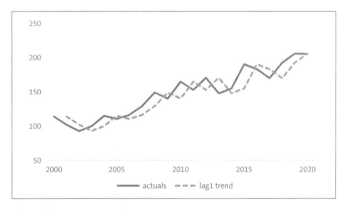

Figure 9.4 Lag 1 Trend

Simple Modeling Hypotheses

As we've seen, only three trend types are tested by smart predict: linear, piece-wise lin-ear, and lag 1. Why not test more complex types of trends such as quadratic trend (trends that have a variable increase or decrease rate) or lag 2? Testing fewer hypothe-ses comes with several advantages:

- **Improved predictive model interpretability**
  Complex trends are more difficult to interpret. It can be difficult to make sense out of a high order lag trend or complex polynomial trends. Testing fewer and simpler hypotheses leads to more interpretable predictive models.

- **Increased predictive model accuracy**
  Extensive benchmarks have shown that limiting the number and complexity of the hypotheses in competition doesn't reduce the accuracy of the predictive models. Using simpler hypotheses even tends to increase the predictive model robustness,

that is, the ability of the predictive model to generalize in the future the pattern it discovered in the training data.

- **Reduced training time**
  Testing fewer and simpler hypotheses also reduces the time needed to train a time series forecasting model.

9.2.2   Cycles

Cycles are recurrent variations of a time series. In smart predict, we consider two main cycle types:

- **Seasonal**
  Such cycles have a recurrence based on calendar time units such as day, month, or year.
- **Fixed length**
  Such cycles recur on a set number of observations. Because the observations aren't necessarily evenly spaced out, the cycle duration (in days, months, etc.) isn't constant.

The cycles are detected on the detrended time series. The detrended time series is the time series where the trend detected in the previous step has been removed. Smart predict tests all possible cycles and keeps cycles that improve the predictive forecast accuracy. The time series is split into two datasets. The training dataset is used to detect cycles, and the validation dataset to check their accuracy. The following process happens for each candidate cycle c_i:

- Temporarily include c_i in the predictive model and fit it on the remaining time series.
- Generate the predictions and compare the predictions to the actuals on the validation set.
- If the predictive forecast is improved, then keep c_i in the predictive model and subtract c_i from the time series. Otherwise, discard c_i from the model.
- Repeat the cycle detection process with the next candidate cycle c_i.

The cycle detection process stops when there is no significant cycle to add to the predictive model.

As all the fixed-length cycles are tested iteratively, by increasing the size of the tested cycle at each iteration, it's important to have a limit in the size of the cycles. This is especially true when the number of observations in the training dataset is large. Having a size limit reduces the number of cycles to be tested, minimizing training time. The maximum length of a cycle is equal to $min(\frac{|train\ set|}{12}, 450)$, where *train set* is the number of observations in the training datasets. As a rule of thumb, a cycle must appear at least three times entirely in the historical data to have a chance to be detected.

9.2.3   Influencers

An influencer in smart predict is a variable that allows you to predict the time series using information that comes on top of the existing time series data. Such variables are also known as external variables or external regressors.

You can use influencers to improve the accuracy of your time series forecasting model. By detecting the trend, the cycles, and the fluctuations, the time series forecasting model extracts patterns that are part of the time series, that is, patterns that depend only on time. But the values of some time series can also be influenced by external factors that can be only detected when using influencers. For instance, the travel costs can be influenced by the oil price, the amount of ice cream sold can be influenced by the outside temperature, and most financial planning key performance indicators (KPIs) are influenced by various ongoing macroeconomic factors.

In smart predict, the variables you select as influencers are only candidate influencers. While some of them may be useful to determine the future values of the time series, others may not. Smart predict checks if all the selected variables improve the accuracy of the time series forecasting model. Only the variables that improve the predictive forecast accuracy actually become influencers, that is, take part in the calculation of the predicted forecasts.

As opposed to what happens for the other predictive model components, there is no specific influencer detection step. Instead, the influencers are detected either as part of the trend detection step or as part of the cycle detection step. We alluded to this in Section 9.2.1 and Section 9.2.2.

Note that you must provide the future values of the influencers (the values over the forecast horizon) to get predictive forecast values that are influenced by the influencer values. It's possible to train a time series forecasting model without providing the future values of the influencers as only the past values are used. You'll even get accurate detailed influencer contributions. If you don't provide future values for the influencers, smart predict will generate predictions using default values for the influencers: the mean for the numerical variables or the most represented value for the categorical variables.

9.2.4   Fluctuations

After the trend, the cycles, and the influencers have been detected, smart predict tries to detect any remaining autoregressive components in the time series, called fluctuations. In an *autoregressive component* of a time series, a value for a given point in time depends on earlier values.

An autoregressive model is computed on what is left from the time series after removing the trend, the cycles, and the influencers. The equation for such an autoregressive model is $y_t = a_1.y_{t-1} + a_2.y_{t-2} + \ldots + a_p.y_{t-p}$, where y_t is the value of the time series at time t, p is the order of the autoregressive model, and $a_1,\ldots,a_p$ are the weights associated with the different time lags. In smart predict, the order of the autoregressive model is limited to 2. This leads to a simplified equation: $y_t = a_1.y_{t-1} + a_2.y_{t-2}$. The rationale to limit the order is to increase the predictive model interpretability for the following reasons:

- Cycles are easier to interpret than fluctuations and usually make more sense. Limiting the detection of fluctuations increases the detection of cycles.

- The higher the order of the autoregressive components, the harder the understanding.

9.3   Exponential Smoothing

Besides the additive models, smart predict also leverages the *exponential smoothing technique*. An exponential smoothing model is basically a complex moving average. While a moving average would give an equal importance to all the observations considered, exponential smoothing gives more weight to the most recent observations. More precisely, the weight of the observations decreases exponentially as older observations are considered.

One major difference between the additive predictive models and the exponential smoothing predictive models in smart predict is that the influencer detection isn't supported by the exponential smoothing models.

Next, we'll explain the different exponential smoothing models that smart predict adds to the predictive model competition.

9.3.1   Simple Exponential Smoothing

The *simple exponential smoothing* method works well for time series with no trend and no cyclic patterns. It's relevant to forecast disrupted time series that don't show any clear pattern.

The main assumption of simple exponential smoothing is that the only component of the time series is its level, that is, the average value of the time series over a period of time. The forecast is assumed to be equal to the level at the most recent known time point: $F_{t+1} = L_t$ where F_t is the forecasted value at time t, and L_t is the level at time t.

Figure 9.5 shows the monthly forecast of a time series from January 2023 to December 2023 using the simple exponential algorithm. The level is a smoothed version of the time series. You can see that all the predicted values are equal to the most recent calculated level, ignoring the trend and seasonality of the time series.

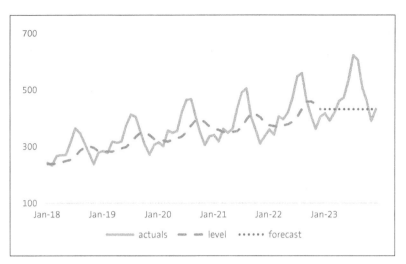

Figure 9.5 Forecast Using Simple Exponential Smoothing

L_t can be calculated using the *level updating equation*: $L_t = \alpha Y_t + (1 - \alpha)L_{t-1}$. The previous level value is updated with the value of the most recent data point Y_t using a weighted average where α and $1 - \alpha$ are weights. The equation is initialized with L_1 equals to Y_1, which is the first value of the time series.

α is known as the *smoothing factor*. It's a parameter controlling the rate at which the past observations' influence decreases. This smoothing factor is set between 0 and 1, so $0 \leq 1 - \alpha \leq 1$. Smoothing factor values closer to 1 reduce the weight of the oldest data and give a greater importance to recent data. Smart predict calculates a value for α that optimizes the accuracy of the predictive model.

The equation to calculate the level can be rewritten as $L_t = \alpha Y_t + \alpha(1 - \alpha)Y_{t-1} + \alpha(1 - \alpha)^2 Y_{t-2} +$. Notice that the weights are decreasing exponentially as older observations are considered, hence the name exponential smoothing.

Note that there is no level component displayed as such in the smart predict reports. In smart predict, the level is represented as the trend of the time series, so the reports remain consistent independently of the predictive modeling technique used under the hood.

9.3.2   Double Exponential Smoothing

Double exponential smoothing (aka Holt's exponential smoothing) is an improvement over simple exponential smoothing as it can detect trends. Double exponential smoothing assumes that the time series is made of both a level and a trend. The forecast equation is a combination of the most recent known level and the most recent known trend. Double exponential smoothing works well when the time series has a trend and no seasonalities.

The level and trend can be combined in an additive fashion to capture linear trends or in a multiplicative fashion to capture exponential trends. In smart predict, both hypotheses are tested by adding one candidate model corresponding to each hypothesis to the internal predictive model competition.

This leads to two the following forecasting equations where h is the number of requested forecast points:

- Additive trend: $F_{t+h} = L_t + hT_t$
- Multiplicative trend: $F_{t+h} = L_t \times (T_t)^h$

Figure 9.6 shows the monthly forecast of a time series from January 2023 to December 2023 using the double exponential algorithm and assuming an additive trend. You can see that the forecast follows the increasing trend of the time series starting from the most recent calculated level.

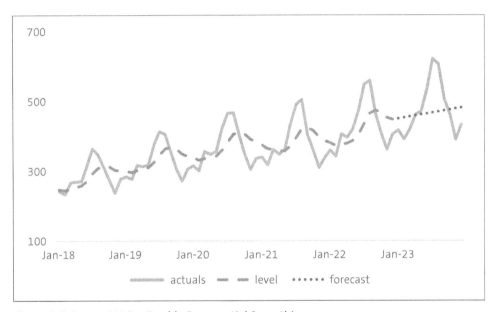

Figure 9.6 Forecast Using Double Exponential Smoothing

Two updating equations are needed, one for the level and one for the trend:

- The level updating equation is very similar to that of the simple exponential smoothing, except that the previous level is adjusted by adding a trend: $L_t = \alpha Y_t + (1 - \alpha)(L_{t-1} + T_{t-1})$. α is the smoothing factor as explained for the simple exponential smoothing.
- The trend updating equation updates the previous trend by adding a weighted difference between the most recent level estimates: $T_t = \beta(L_t - L_{t-1}) + (1 - \beta)T_{t-1}$. $L_t - L_{t-1}$ is the different in level between $t{-}1$ and t, and can be interpreted as the local slope of the time series between $t{-}1$ and t. Therefore, based on the formula, the trend is

updated by combining the previous trend with the current slope of the time series. This means that the trend is an estimation of the slope of the time series adapted over time. The parameter β allows you to control how fast this adaptation is allowed to occur.

Smart predict calculates values for α and β that optimize the accuracy of the predictive model.

9.3.3   Triple Exponential Smoothing

Triple exponential smoothing (aka Winter's exponential smoothing) is an improvement over simple and double exponential smoothing that can detect both trends and seasonalities. The forecast equation is a combination of the most recent level, the most recent trend, and the most recent cycle values. Triple exponential smoothing works well when the time series has a seasonality.

Seasonalities can be combined to the level and trend in an additive fashion to capture seasonalities with a constant amplitude, or in a multiplicative fashion to capture seasonalities with a variable amplitude. In smart predict, both hypotheses are tested by adding one candidate model corresponding to each hypothesis to the internal predictive model competition.

This leads to two forecasting equations, where h is the number of requested forecast points and M is the size of the cycles in number of observations (M is determined by smart predict):

- Additive seasonality: $F_{t+h} = L_t + hT_t + S_{t+h-M}$
- Multiplicative seasonality: $F_{t+h} = (L_t + hT_t)S_{t+h-M}$

For the sake of simplicity, we'll focus only on the cases where the trend is additive and the seasonality is multiplicative.

Figure 9.7 shows the monthly forecast of a time series from January 2023 to December 2023 using the triple exponential algorithm and assuming an additive trend and a multiplicative seasonality. You can see that the forecast follows the increasing trend of the time series and its yearly seasonality starting from the most recent calculated level.

Three updating equations are needed, one for the level, one for the trend, and one for the seasonality:

- **Level updating equation**
  This equation is modified to take the seasonality into account: $L_t = \alpha(Y_t \div S_{t-M}) + (1 - \alpha)(L_{t-1} + T_{t-1})$. α is the smoothing factor as explained for the simple exponential smoothing. Y_t / S_{t-M} allows you to remove the seasonal component of the value of Y_t.
- **Trend updating equation**
  This equation is the same as the one for double exponential smoothing.

- **Seasonality updating equation**
  The equation for multiplicative seasonality is $S_t = \gamma(Y_t \div L_t) + (1 - \gamma)S_{t-M}$. $Y_t \div L_t$ is the detrended value of Y_t. Therefore, the seasonality is updated by combining the most recent seasonality with the detrended value of Y_t. The parameter γ controls how fast the seasonality is updated.

Smart predict calculates values for α, β, and γ that optimize the accuracy of the predictive model.

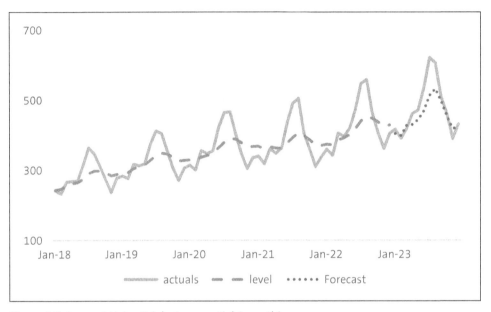

Figure 9.7 Forecast Using Triple Exponential Smoothing

9.3.4   Damped Trend

Exponential smoothing methods usually detect trends that are reliable in the short term. However, these methods can lead to steadily increasing or decreasing trends that may not be realistic in the long term. This can lead to over optimistic or over pessimistic forecasts (depending on the trend direction). To counter this problem, the double exponential smoothing technique has been improved with *damped trends*. A damped trend is a linear trend whose slope gradually decreases until it becomes almost flat. The speed at which the slope decreases is controlled by an additional parameter φ, called the *damping factor*. The damping factor is between 0 and 1. Values of the damping factor closer to 0 make the trend slope decrease faster. When the damping factor is equal to 1, the trend remains linear. The damping factor value is determined automatically by smart predict. Benchmarks show that damped trends are more realistic for long-term forecasting.

Figure 9.8 illustrates the difference between a linear and a damped trend.

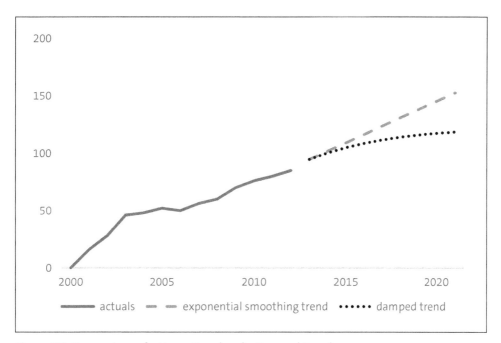

Figure 9.8 Comparison of a Linear Trend and a Damped Trend

9.4   Predictive Model Selection

Once the candidate time series forecasting models corresponding to different predictive modeling hypotheses have been trained, it's possible for smart predict to calculate their respective performance metrics. Based on these performance metrics, a winning predictive model is decided.

The historical data is split into two parts:

- **Training dataset**
  Of the data, 75% corresponds to the oldest observations and is used to train the time series forecasting models that enter the competition.

- **Validation dataset**
  The remaining 25% corresponds to the most recent observations and is used to assess the accuracy of the time series forecasting models.

Predictions are generated for each candidate predictive model, and performance metrics are calculated by comparing the predictions to the actual time series values in the validation set. Because the validation set wasn't used to train the predictive models, the estimated accuracy isn't biased.

One specific performance metric, the *expected mean absolute error* (expected MAE), is used to choose the predictive winning model. It's derived from the MAE, which is the mean of the absolute difference between the predicted values and the actual values. The MAE is calculated as follows:

$$MAE(h) = \frac{1}{n}\sum_{i=1}^{n} |predicted_{i+h} - actual_{i+h}|$$

Here, n is the number of considered points and h is a parameter allowing you to shift the considered slice of data (the standard MAE formula corresponds to $MAE(0)$).

The expected MAE provides a better estimate of the performance that can be expected in the future by averaging the MAE calculated for different horizons:

$$Expected\ MAE(H) = \frac{1}{H}\sum_{h=1}^{H} MAE(h)$$

Here, H is the forecast horizon requested in the setting of the predictive model in smart predict.

To balance accuracy and interpretability, the following rules apply to the selection of the winning predictive model:

- The predictive model with the best expected MAE is selected as the winning model.
- In case of a tie with a 5% tolerance, then the simplest predictive model is selected as the winner.

Expected Performance Metrics

The modeling reports in smart predict show various standard performance metrics prefixed with "expected." The idea is always to provide an estimation of the performance that can be expected when using the time series forecasting model. The principle to calculate the expected version of the performance metric is also always the same: The performance metric is calculated for different horizons and the results are averaged. Given an error metric E, $Expected\ E(H) = \frac{1}{H}\sum_{i=1}^{H} E(h)$.

9.5   Summary

In this chapter, we've unveiled the data science behind the time series forecasting models. First, we touched on the idea of model competition. Then, we explained how the additive models and the exponential smoothing models, the two types of time series forecasting models supported by smart predict, are created. Finally, we explained how the winning model is determined.

In the next chapter, we'll switch away from the time series forecasting model and introduce the classification and regression models.

PART III

Classification Models and Regression Models

Chapter 10

Introducing Classification Models and Regression Models

Classification models and regression models serve fundamentally differ-
ent purposes but share some similarities in their data sources, workflow
in predictive scenarios, and underlying data science. For this reason,
we've bundled these models in this final part of the book.

Classification models are used to predict the category an object of interest or an event belongs to. They can be used in many use cases, including cross-sell, attrition prediction, and fraud prediction. *Regression models* are used to predict the values of a numeric variable for an object of interest. Regression models are useful for a large variety of use cases, including financial predictions, customer sales predictions, and customer value estimation.

In this chapter, we'll introduce the classification models in Section 10.1 and the regression models in Section 10.2. We'll then discuss how these two types of models relate to the data sources in SAP Analytics Cloud in Section 10.3. We'll wrap up this chapter in Section 10.4 by explaining the various steps involved when working with classification models and regression models.

10.1 What Is Classification?

First, let's explain what a classification model can be used for. We'll also introduce a few useful concepts to get a deeper understanding of how classification models work in smart predict.

10.1.1 Key Terms and Concepts

A *classification model* (also called classifier) allows you to categorize objects of the same nature, based on their attributes. A classification algorithm searches for relationships between the categories to be predicted and the attributes. In more formal terms, the classification model is a function $f(x_1, ..., x_n) = y$, where $(x_1, ... , x_n)$ are attributes of an object of interest, and y is the category or class predicted for this object. We call this prediction the *predicted category*.

Figure 10.1 illustrates the principle of a classification model that classifies customers into two categories, the customers who will buy shoes and the customers who won't buy shoes.

Extracting the relationships that exist between the variable to be predicted and the other variables is called *predictive model training*. During training, the classification model learns from past examples where the variable value to be predicted is known. This learning principle is called *supervised learning*.

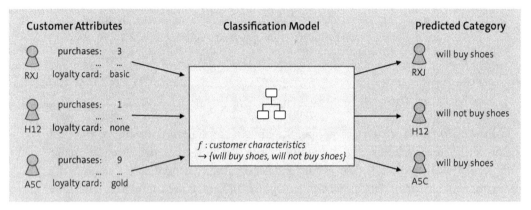

Figure 10.1 Classification Model Example

In a business environment, you often need to predict the occurrence of an event or the category an object of interest belongs to. You've probably been confronted at least once with one of these business questions (or analogous questions):

- Which of my customers will buy shoes?
- Can I identify in advance the customers who are about to end their subscription?
- Which employees are likely to leave the company I work for?

Let's consider the following business question: Which of my customers will buy shoes? Answering this question requires classifying each customer, based on their attributes, into one of these two categories: the customers who will buy shoes and the customers who won't buy shoes.

In this example, the concept of customer is the *object of interest*, and "will buy shoes" is the event to be predicted, which is called the *target*. Each value of the target is called a *category* (or sometimes class) because it represents a classification category.

One specific occurrence of the object of interest, for instance, one specific customer along with the customer's attributes, is called an *observation*. The set of all the observations—in our example all the customers considered—is called the *population*.

Finally, the *classification algorithm* creates a classification model by learning from past data. We'll cover this distinction in more detail in Section 10.4.

Classification versus Clustering

Classification is often mistaken for clustering because both are about taking objects and putting them into groups, but they are completely different algorithms and answer different questions. With *classification*, you have a set of predefined categories, and you want to predict which category a new observation belongs to. *Clustering*, on the other hand, consists of grouping objects by similarity. The groups don't belong to a specific category known up front, they just group objects that are similar between them and dissimilar from objects in the other groups. Classification is a type of predictive model, while clustering is more a type of descriptive model.

10.1.2 Binary Classification

There are two different types of classification: binary and multiclass. Here is a quick explanation of the difference:

- **Binary classification**
  This is a type of classification model that allows you to predict targets with exactly two categories: yes or no, will buy or won't buy, etc.

- **Multiclass (or multinomial) classification**
  This is a type of classification model that allows you to predict targets with more than two categories (prediction of a color, etc.).

Smart predict only handles binary classification models; multiclass classification models aren't supported. In practice, most of the questions you need to answer using a classification model in a business context are questions addressed by binary classification models.

When working with binary classification models, one of the two target categories is usually considered more important than the other. When predicting which customers will end a subscription, there are two possible answers: "will end subscription" and "won't end subscription." But we're usually making predictions with a goal in mind, such as performing retention actions. These retention actions will only be targeted to customers who are likely to end subscriptions. If you had to express what you want to predict, you would probably insist on one of the two values rather than the other: "I want to predict which customers will end their subscription in the coming six months."

This specific value of the target that is more important than the other is called the *positive target category*. The other value is called the *negative target category*. Alternatively, when the values to be predicted correspond to events—such as predicting customer attrition—the terms *positive event* and *negative event* can be used instead.

10.1.3   Predicted Category and Probability

We've defined the classification model as a model that predicts one categorical value, called the predicted category, among several possible categorical values. But most classification models can provide a more subtle prediction. They don't directly predict a category of the target; instead, they predict the probability of the target value to be the positive target. Such a classification model would predict the likelihood for a customer to buy shoes instead of just predictive "yes" or "no." In the same way, it would not predict if an employee will leave the company but would predict the risk that the employee will leave the company. As you'll see, this is more flexible than directly predicting a category of the target because it introduces a notion of certainty to the prediction.

The predicted category (sometimes called the *decision*) can be directly derived from the predicted probability. First, the observations are sorted by increasing the probability of belonging to the positive category: The observations predicted with the lowest probability first. Then, you must choose a probability threshold: The observations with a predicted probability lower than this threshold are predicted as belonging to the negative target category, and the observations with a predicted probability higher than or equal to the threshold are predicted as belonging to the positive target category. This value that separates the positive observations and the negative observations is called the *decision threshold.* Figure 10.2 illustrates this decision process for a classification model that predicts if customers will or won't buy shoes in the future using a decision threshold of 50% (this threshold is purely arbitrary for use in the example).

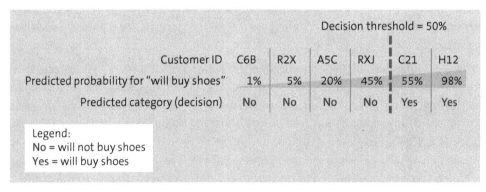

Figure 10.2 Converting the Predicted Probability to the Predicted Category

This decision threshold lets you specify the degree of certainty needed to predict an observation as positive. Higher decision thresholds limit the risk of wrongly predicting negative cases as being positive but increase the risk of missing some positive cases. Lower decision thresholds limit the risk of missing positive cases but increase the risk of wrongly predicting negative cases as positive. The usage of the decision threshold is explained in more detail in Chapter 13, Section 13.5.

> **Note**
>
> If you're only interested in sorting the observations according to their probability of being positive, you don't even need to calculate the predicted category.

10.2   What Is Regression?

First, let's explain what a regression model can be used for. We'll introduce a few important concepts to give you a better understanding of how regression models work in smart predict.

10.2.1   Key Terms and Concepts

A *regression model* is a type of predictive model that allows you to predict the values of a numeric variable for an object of interest, based on other variables associated with this object. A *regression algorithm* models relationships between the numeric variable that needs to be predicted (this variable is sometimes referred to as the dependent variable or target variable) and the other variables related to the object (these variables are sometimes referred to as independent or input variables). In formal terms, a regression model corresponds to a function $f(x_1, ..., x_n) = y$, where $(x_1, ..., x_n)$ are input variables describing specific aspects of the object of interest, and y is the variable that we want to predict that relates to the same object. Figure 10.3 illustrates the principle of a regression model that predicts the sale price of a secondhand car based on the car's characteristics.

Extracting the relationships that exist between the numeric variable to be predicted and the other variables is called the *predictive model training*. During training, the regression model learns from past examples where the variable value to be predicted is known. This type of learning is called *supervised learning*.

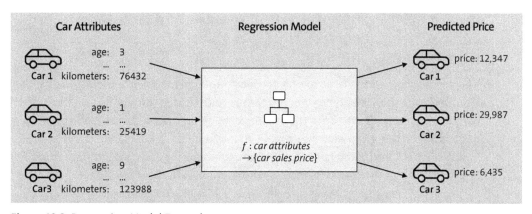

Figure 10.3 Regression Model Example

In a business environment, you'll often need to predict the future value of a numeric variable for a given object of interest. You might have faced business questions like these:

- What is the expected sales price for a secondhand car currently for sale?
- What is the expected delay for an invoice to be paid?
- What is the commercial value I can expect from my customer next year?

Let's consider the business question, "What is the expected sales price for secondhand car currently for sale?" Answering this question requires predicting the possible sales price for each car based on the car's attributes.

In this example, the car is considered the *object of interest*, and the car's sales price is the variable to be predicted, which is called the *target*.

One specific occurrence of the object of interest, for instance, a given car with the corresponding car variables, is called an *observation*. The overall observation set—in our example, all the secondhand cars that are currently for sale—is called the *population*.

Finally, the *regression algorithm* creates a regression model by learning from past data. We'll cover this in more detail in Section 10.4.

Regression versus Time Series Forecasting

Regression can be mistaken for time series forecasting because both lead to the prediction of numeric values. Both predictive techniques rely on different algorithms and answer different business questions. With *regression*, you want to predict the values of a target variable based on a set of input variables. *Time series forecasting*, however, is predicting the values of a target variable over time.

The way input variables are handled is also quite different. In its most basic form, time series forecasting only needs a target variable evolving over a period of time, while regression requires one or more input variables to be present in the data source. In data science terms, regression is about value interpolation, while time series forecasting is about value extrapolation.

10.2.2   Predictions

As previously mentioned, the main goal of a regression model is to predict the value of a numeric variable. This type of prediction is called the **Predicted Value** in the smart predict user interface. On top of the predicted value, you can generate **Prediction Explanations**. Prediction explanations provide you with a detailed explanation on how each input variable contributed to the final predictive value for each observation. Examples of such outcomes generated from a regression model are shown in Figure 10.4.

Chapter 12 provides you with a full walk-through example where you'll create, assess, and use a regression model.

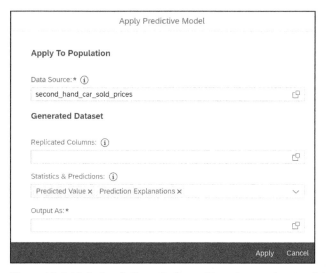

Figure 10.4 Main Predictions Delivered by a Regression Model

10.3   Data Sources for Classification Models and Regression Models

Smart predict uses a dataset as the data source for classification models and regression models. In this section, we first introduce the different roles a dataset can play in a classification or regression model, and then we cover the expected dataset structure for these roles.

10.3.1   Data Sources

Classification models and regression models use SAP Analytics Cloud datasets as their data source. Both acquired and live datasets are supported. Classification predictive scenarios don't support analytic and planning models as data sources. Classification models and regression models are trained using data stored in a dataset, and the predictions are written to another dataset.

When working with classification models and regression models, three datasets must be considered:

- **Training dataset**
  This is the dataset the smart predict algorithm will use to train a classification or a regression model.

- **Application dataset**
  This is the dataset that will be provided as input for the predictive model to generate predictions.

- **Predictions dataset**
  This is the dataset generated by the predictive model that contains the predictions.

209

Smart predict enforces data source consistency between these three datasets for a given predictive model based on the type of dataset used:

- **Acquired dataset**
  When a predictive model is created using an acquired training dataset, both the application and the predictions dataset must be acquired datasets.

- **Live dataset**
  When a predictive model is created using a live training dataset, both the application and the predictions dataset must be live datasets. In addition, both datasets must be available in the same data repository (meaning they are all stored in the same SAP HANA instance).

The data source consistency is enforced only in the context of the predictive model. A predictive scenario can contain predictive models trained and applied both with live and acquired datasets, or predictive models trained and applied using different data repositories (meaning possibly different SAP HANA instances).

10.3.2 Basic Data Preparation for Datasets

Training datasets for classification models and regression models must have a specific structure. The structure is identical for both types of models. Training datasets for classification models and regression models only differ by the nature of the target column, as shown in Table 10.1 and Table 10.2.

Unique Identifier	Object of Interest Attributes			Target
	Attribute 1	**...**	**Attribute N**	
ID. 1	Attribute 1.value 1	...	Attribute n.value 1	Positive target category
ID. 2	Attribute 1.value 2	...	Attribute n.value 2	Negative target category
...	...	...	...	...
ID. n	Attribute 1.value n	...	Attribute n.value n	Negative target category

Table 10.1 Structure of a Training Dataset for Classification

Unique Identifier	Object of Interest Variables			Target
	Variable 1	**...**	**Variable N**	
ID. 1	Variable 1.value 1	...	Variable n.value 1	Target.value 1
ID. 2	Variable 1.value 2	...	Variable n.value 2	Target.value 2
...	...	...	...	...
ID. n	Variable 1.value n	...	Variable n.value n	Target.value n

Table 10.2 Structure of a Training Dataset for Regression

Each row of the dataset is an observation, that is, a specific example or instance of the object of interest. If the object of interest is the customer, then each row represents a specific customer. We'll walk through the components of this dataset in the following sections.

Identifier Columns

A training dataset for classification or regression must contain one or more identifier columns. The identifier columns allow you to identify uniquely each individual observation in the training dataset. This could be an employee number or a product ID depending on the use case. While these columns aren't strictly mandatory for a predictive purpose, they represent the only way to distinguish between two individuals when building stories based on the predictions.

Target Column

A training dataset for classification or regression must contain one column that we call the *target*. The target represents what you want to predict. The structure of the application dataset is identical to the structure of the training dataset. But the target column is optional because the classification model's purpose is to predict the target's value. Let's compare the target for classification models versus regression models:

- **Target for classification models**

  The target column for classification must have exactly two distinct values: the positive target category and the negative target category.

  In smart predict, you don't need to specify which target category is the positive category. The rarest event is always considered the positive event, which corresponds to most use cases. Note that this mainly affects how the modeling reports must be interpreted. The predicted category isn't affected.

- **Target for regression models**

  The target column for a regression model must contain numeric values representing the value to be predicted.

Object of Interest Attributes

A training dataset for classification or regression must contain a set of columns that are attributes describing the object of interest for which predictions will be produced. The predictive model will process these attributes to find how they relate to the target. The term "attribute" is used in a very wide sense here. The attributes can be any information that can be associated with an object of interest in the dataset and would be directly or indirectly in relation to the predicted behavior. Considering an employee attrition prediction example, it can go from the employee's age to the number of human resources (HR) tickets the employee has raised during the past six months.

Table 10.3 shows some examples of attributes that could be used to predict the turn-over.

Employee Number	Employee Characteristics (December 31, 2021)				Turnover (between January 1, 2022, and December 31, 2022)
	Age	Job Role	. . .	Education	
2015	42	Manager	. . .	4	Yes
3546	37	Sales Executive	. . .	2	No
. . .	. . .	. . .	. . .	. . .	. . .
512	45	Research Director	. . .	3	No

Table 10.3 Example of Training Dataset for Classification

The attributes of the object of interest aren't to be confused with the influencers of the model (introduced in Chapter 11, Section 11.3.4). The columns representing the attributes of the object of interest will be processed by the classification algorithm during the training phase. Only if the attributes are selected by the algorithm will they become influencers of the classification model (also known as predictors).

Dataset Editor

The dataset editor (see Chapter 2, Section 2.3.1) provides some capabilities that can be used for the following purposes:

- **Data type and statistical type edition**
  The data type is the characteristic of a column that lets SAP Analytics Cloud know if the column values should be interpreted as integers, numbers, dates, or plain strings. The statistical type is a characteristic of the column that lets smart predict know what type of calculation can be applied to the values. Can the values be ordered or summed, or are they just labels? For convenience, it's also possible to edit these properties directly in smart predict. Data type and statistical type are discussed in further detail in Chapter 11, Section 11.3.2.

- **Data cleaning**
  You can use the dataset editor to replace missing values, to group categories, or to rename categories.

- **Feature engineering**
  Feature engineering is the process of extracting or creating attribute columns. You can derive new columns from the existing ones using string manipulation operations such as concatenation, value splitting, value replacement, and so on.

However, beside these generic capabilities, the dataset editor doesn't provide capabilities specific to the creation of training and application datasets for classification or regression purposes. Specifically, capabilities such as merging datasets, numeric calculation, or aggregation aren't available in the dataset editor. We recommend you create the data tables corresponding to the training dataset and to the application dataset outside of SAP Analytics Cloud and import them as SAP Analytics Cloud training and application datasets.

10.4   End-to-End Workflow

Figure 10.5 illustrates the end-to-end workflow for creating stories using predictions generated by either a classification model or a regression model. Let's walk through the key steps in this workflow:

1. Identify the data sources that will be used to create the story and train the predictive model. At this step, you must also prepare the data so it can be used for predictive purposes (Section 10.3.1).
2. Enable SAP Analytics Cloud to consume this data by creating acquired or live datasets.
3. Train classification or regression models in a predictive scenario.
4. Using the trained classification or regression models, produce predictions in a dataset.
5. Consume the predictions dataset in a story.

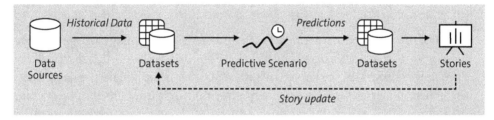

Figure 10.5 End-to-End Workflow

Figure 10.6 details the different datasets involved in a predictive workflow. This workflow works identically to time series forecasting models.

A training dataset and various user settings are provided to the classification or regression algorithm. The classification or regression algorithm then processes the training data to produce a classification or regression model. Finally, predictions are generated by applying the classification or regression model to an application dataset. For each row in the application dataset, the classification or regression model calculates a prediction using the attributes of the object of interest.

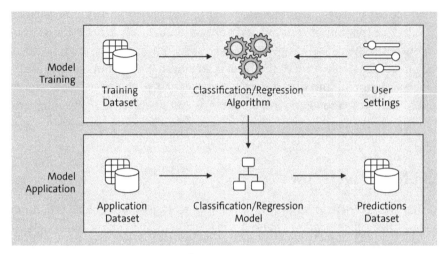

Figure 10.6 Predictive Model Workflow

Your business is evolving, and the predictions you've produced based on the reality of last month may not correspond to the reality of today. Maybe you've acquired new customers, or some attributes of the existing customers have changed over time. You must update the story periodically with new predictions. To do so, some of the steps mentioned previously must be repeated:

1. If you're working with acquired datasets, then the training and the application dataset must be updated by reimporting data. If you're working with live datasets, you must recreate the training and the application datasets in SAP Analytics Cloud if their structure has changed. If the structure of your live datasets hasn't changed, then you can move to the second step.

2. The behavior you're trying to predict with a predictive model may change over time. Relationships that once existed and have been learned by the predictive model may have been replaced by new relationships. You must train a new classification or regression model that will learn these new relationships from the updated training dataset.

3. Using the refreshed predictive model, you can now generate new predictions for the predictions dataset.

4. If you've overwritten the data of an existing predictions dataset, you don't need to update the story.

10.5   Summary

In this chapter, we've introduced concepts that enable you to understand what classification models and regression models are and what they can be used for. We've explained the main principles of binary classification and of regression. Then, we explained how classification models and regression models can be used with the data sources available in SAP Analytics Cloud. Finally, we detailed the different steps involved in the creation of stories based on predictions.

With this foundation in place, we'll explain step-by-step how to use classification models in stories in the next chapter.

10

Chapter 11

Creating Classification Insights to Enrich Stories

Classification models can be used to predict a large variety of events in multiple business domains: Which customers will buy certain products? Which employees will leave the company this year? These use cases are available in SAP Analytics Cloud thanks to smart predict.

In this chapter, we'll introduce a turnover prediction business scenario in Section 11.1 that will serve as an illustration throughout the chapter. Using that business scenario, you'll learn how to create a training dataset for classification (Section 11.2) and use it to create your first classification model (Section 11.3). Then, you'll learn how to use the modeling reports to understand and improve your classification model in Section 11.4 and Section 11.5, respectively. Finally, this chapter will teach you how to generate predictions in Section 11.6 and use them in a story in Section 11.7.

11.1 Business Scenario

You're working as a human resources (HR) manager in a large company. Losing an employee is disruptive for the activity they were responsible for, and hiring a new employee also comes with a cost. Employee turnover has been costly for your company in recent years. To reduce the turnover rate, you've been granted a budget for employee retention actions. But there is one major problem: By the time you know that an employee will leave the company, usually when the employee has submitted their resignation letter, it's already too late to try to retain them. To apply targeted retention actions, you need to know in advance which employees are the most likely to leave the company. For your activity, it makes sense to predict who will resign over a full year. Additionally, you want to understand in detail the reasons for the turnover at a global and at an individual level, so you can take the right actions. Predicting the turnover will also help you plan the replacement needs in advance. You would be able to build stories that show the replacement needs in the next 12 months by geographic area, service, or contract type.

This can be summarized into one business question: Among my employees, who hasn't resigned yet but will in the coming 12 months? This is a classification problem because we want to distinguish between two categories of employees: those who will quit and those who won't.

In this chapter, you'll learn in detail how to use the classification predictive scenarios to answer this business question. Then, you'll learn how you can use predictions in a story.

The comma-separated values (CSV) files to create the SAP Analytics Cloud datasets to support this scenario are available at *https://sap-press.com/5771*.

11.2   Using Datasets with Classification Models

This section will walk you through the three datasets used in a classification scenario:

- Training dataset
- Application dataset
- Predictions dataset

11.2.1   Training Dataset

The training dataset provided in the *turnover-training-dataset.csv* file contains 2,934 employees described by the 31 variables in Table 11.1.

To upload the training data as an SAP Analytics Cloud dataset, follow the steps described in Chapter 2, Section 2.3.1.

Variable Name	What Does the Variable Correspond To?
EmployeeNumber	Unique identifier of each employee.
Turnover	True if the employee has left the company during the year, but false otherwise. This is the variable we want to predict.
Age	Age in years of the employee.
AgeSegment	Range of age the employee belongs to: [20, 30[, [30, 40[, etc.
AgeCategory	HR age category: early talent, teammate, etc.
ContractStatus	Status of the employee contract.
BusinessTravel	How often the employee travels for business reasons.
Department	The department of the company the employee belongs to.
DistanceFromHome	The distance in miles from the employee's home to the office.
Education	Education level of the employee.

Table 11.1 Variables of the Training Dataset

Variable Name	What Does the Variable Correspond To?
EducationField	Label describing the education field of the employee.
Gender	Employee's gender: male or female.
JobInvolvement	Involvement rating from 1 to 4.
JobLevel	Level from 1 to 5.
JobRole	Label describing the employee's job nature.
JobSatisfaction	Satisfaction rating from 1 to 4.
MaritalStatus	Marital status: single, married, or divorced.
MonthlyIncome	Monthly salary in US dollars.
NumCompaniesWorked	The number of companies the employee has worked for previously.
OverTime	Whether the employee works overtime.
PerformanceRating	Employee's last performance rating.
StockOptionLevel	Stock option level from 0 to 3.
TotalWorkingYear	Number of years since the employee started working (in any company).
TrainingTimeLastYear	Number of trainings attended last year.
WorkLifeBalance	Work life balance rating from 1 to 4 (the higher the better).
YearsAtCompany	Number of years since the employee started working in the company.
YearsInCurrentRole	Number of years in the current role.
YearsSinceLastPromotion	Number of years since the last promotion.
YearsWithCurrManager	Number of years working with the current manager.
HireYear	The year the employee was hired in the company.
Country	Country the employee is working in.

Table 11.1 Variables of the Training Dataset (Cont.)

Let's relate the columns in Table 11.1 to the training dataset structure we introduced in Chapter 10, Section 10.3.2 (refer to Table 10.1):

- EmployeeNumber is the unique identifier column.
- Turnover is the target.
- All the other columns are attributes of the employee (the object of interest).

Population Snapshot

The training dataset described in the previous section is ready to be used to train a classification model without any modification. But this dataset is the result of a specific data preparation necessary to get meaningful predictive results. This section explains how the training dataset was prepared so you can create training datasets for your own use cases.

In our turnover scenario, we're predicting an event that corresponds to a change of state of an employee. There is an implicit relation to the time that must be considered when creating the training dataset. The relation of John Smith with the company has probably evolved over time. Possibly he didn't think about quitting a few weeks ago but does now because he wasn't promoted. Both the Turnover column (target) and the YearsSinceLastPromotion column (attribute) are affected by this time dependency. The training dataset is a snapshot of a situation at a specific date in the past before the event to be predicted occurred. We call this specific date the *reference date*:

- For the target, the reference date stands for the date at which we start observing the occurrence of the event to be predicted. Has the employee resigned during the 12-month period that has started at the reference date? The 12-month period is called the *observation period*.

- For the attributes, the reference date stands for the date at which they are calculated. At the reference date, what was the employee's tenure? What was his salary?

Fixing the snapshot in the past, before the event to be predicted has happened, allows the classification model to properly learn to detect information that is available before the occurrence of the event.

Figure 11.1 illustrates how these temporal considerations apply to the training dataset for turnover prediction. The note "Now (January 15, 2024)" indicates that we're at the very beginning of 2024. Considering the monthly data granularity, December 2023 is the most recent date with available data. Given that we want to predict if the employee will resign in the coming 12 months, we've determined an observation period ending on December 31, 2023 (most recent available data) and starting on January 2023 (12 months before). Only the employees who had not resigned yet in January 2023 are included in the training datasets. If an employee has resigned between January 2023 and December 2023, then the target value is "yes"; otherwise, it's "no". The attributes of the employees are calculated using January 2023 as the reference date because we want to train the classification model considering what was known before the employees resigned.

The exact list of observations considered in the training dataset is also affected by the reference date. You need to be sure to filter out employees that appear in your database but had already left or weren't yet in the company workforce at the reference date.

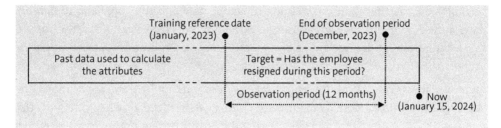

Figure 11.1 Training Dataset for Turnover Prediction Timeline

How would you determine the training reference date and the size of the observation period? The length of the observation period depends on your business requirements. If you want to predict the turnover 12 months ahead, you need the observation period to be 12 months long. The length of the observation period also depends on the frequency of occurrence of the event to be predicted. You want a significant number of positive events to exist in the training dataset. You'd probably need to check the number of resignations per month to determine a size for the observation period that would allow you to catch a significant number of resignations.

Note that you probably don't want the observation period to be too large either. The larger the observation period, the more certain the positive event.

The classification model can learn from the most recent behavior, so you usually want the end of the observation period to be as close as possible to the present time.

11.2.2   Application Dataset

The application dataset provided in the *turnover-application-dataset.csv* file contains 2,517 employees still working for the company at the end of 2023, described with the same 30 characteristics listed in Table 11.1. The Turnover column is missing from the variable list as this is what we want to predict.

To upload the training data as an SAP Analytics Cloud dataset, follow the steps described in Chapter 2, Section 2.3.1.

The application dataset provides information the classification model needs to generate the predictions:

- Which entities do you want to get predictions for?
- What is the current state of these entities?

Like the training dataset, the application dataset is a snapshot of the population you're interested in. The main difference is that instead of considering the state of the population in the past, you're considering the state of the population as it was based on the most recent available data (which can never be exactly "now" but should be as close as possible). Because between the training reference date and the application reference date, some employees have left and some new employees have been hired, the population of the training dataset and the population of the application dataset aren't the same.

Figure 11.2 illustrates how these temporal considerations apply to the application dataset for turnover prediction. At the time of writing, we're at the very beginning of 2024 (January 15, 2024, precisely) and considering the monthly data granularity, December 2023 is the most recent date with available data. We'll use December 2023 as the reference date to create an application dataset. Only the employees who had not resigned at that date are included in the dataset. The attributes of the employees are calculated using December 2023 as the reference date because we want the classification model to predict the resignation based on the states of the employees at that date.

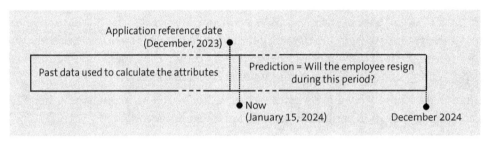

Figure 11.2 Application Dataset Timeline

11.2.3   Predictions Dataset

The *predictions dataset* is the generated dataset that will receive the predictions calculated by the classification model. The columns written to the predictions dataset depend on the options you choose when applying the model (we'll cover this in Section 11.7.1 and Section 11.7.2).

When predicting an event, the prediction horizon is defined by the length of the observation period for the training dataset: If the turnover was observed for 12 months in the training dataset, then the model will predict the turnover in the 12 months following the reference date of the application dataset.

11.3   Creating Classification Models

In this section, we'll explain how to create a classification model. We'll provide an extensive overview of the settings and how they can be used to get the insights you need.

11.3.1 Create a Predictive Scenario

Without further ado, let's create our first predictive scenario. Follow these steps:

1. Click the **Predictive Scenarios** icon 👓 in the left navigation bar of the user interface (UI). The **Predictive Scenarios** button may be hidden in the **More** menu ⋯ in the navigation bar depending on the space available on the screen. The **Predictive Scenarios** button is also available under the **Create** menu ➕∨. If you can't find the **Predictive Scenarios** button, make sure you've been granted the proper privileges.

2. Click the **Classification** button under **Create New**, as shown in Figure 11.3.

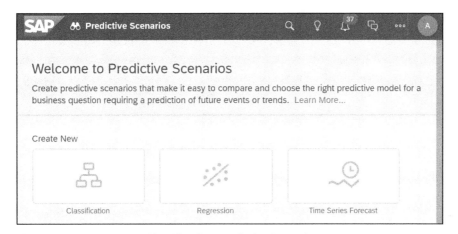

Figure 11.3 Create a New Classification Predictive Scenario

3. The **New Predictive Scenario** dialog box appears to let you save the newly created predictive scenario. In the **Name** field, enter "turnover prediction", and click **Save**. The predictive scenario will be saved in your private user folder.

4. The predictive scenario interface is displayed, and a first classification model is automatically created. You can see the settings for this model in the **Settings** panel to the right of the screen. For now, the settings are empty.

The next sections explain the different model settings.

11.3.2 General Settings

Now, let's get started with the different model settings. The **General** section of the predictive model settings is shown in Figure 11.4.

Figure 11.4 General Settings of a Classification Model

Predictive Model Description

Description is a free-form text field that allows you to describe the intent of a specific predictive model. While it's optional, it's a best practice to provide a meaningful description for your classification models. For more information, see Chapter 5, Section 5.3.2.

For our example, we'll enter "Baseline turnover prediction".

Training Data Source

Training Data Source is a mandatory setting that allows you to select the data you want to use to train a classification model. When working with classification predictive scenarios, you're only allowed to use acquired datasets or live datasets as training data sources. Analytic and planning models aren't supported in classification predictive scenarios. In our example, we've entered "turnover-training-dataset".

The **Edit Columns Details** icon allows you to edit some metadata for the columns of the training dataset, as shown in Figure 11.5.

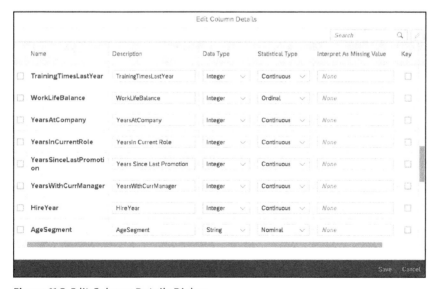

Figure 11.5 Edit Column Details Dialog

It's important to review the columns' metadata and make it as accurate as possible before training a model as it may have an impact on the modeling results. The metadata provides hints to smart predict so it can handle the data correctly and apply the most relevant processing to the data.

For each column, you can edit the following properties:

- **Description**

  This property lets you provide a viewer-friendly column name. When available, the description is shown in place of the column name in the modeling reports. In our example, we could use the description to improve the readability of column names by adding spaces: Monthly Income instead of MonthlyIncome, Distance from Home instead of DistanceFromHome, and so on.

- **Data Type**

  This property tells smart predict how to read the values in the column. Currently, only **String**, **Integer**, **Number**, **Boolean**, **Date**, and **Date & Time** can be used in smart predict.

- **Statistical Type**

  This property tells smart predict the type of processing that can be applied to the values in the column. Currently, only **Nominal**, **Continuous**, and **Ordinal** can be used. A definition of the statistical types is provided in Table 11.2.

Statistical Type	Description
Nominal	Nominal variables (also called categorical variable) are variables whose values define categories. No intrinsic ordering exists between the values of a nominal variable. MaritalStatus is an example of a nominal variable.
Continuous	Continuous variables represent numeric quantities and can be used to perform calculations. MonthlyIncome is an example of a continuous variable.
Ordinal	Ordinal variables are variables whose values define ordered categories. Each category represents a position on a scale. In smart predict, only integers can be used as values for an ordinal variable, so the order can be inferred. JobLevel is an example of an ordinal variable.

Table 11.2 Statistical Types

In our example, we change the statistical type of all the variables representing a level (Education, JobLevel, JobInvolvement, etc.) from continuous to ordinal as they represent a position on a qualitative scale.

- **Interpret As Missing Value**

  This property tells smart predict if a value in the column must be interpreted as missing. This can be useful when a specific value is used to code for "missing" or "unknown." For instance, it may happen that by convention, in the imported dataset, the value -99 is used when the age of a person is unknown. It's important in such cases to let smart predict know about this convention to get good results. There can be only one value used as the missing value.

- **Key**
  This property allows you to define a set of columns whose values identify uniquely an observation in the dataset. When you use the predictions generated by the classification model, you must be able to associate them with a specific item of the population. Smart predict needs to know what the identifier columns are so their existence and their consistency is always enforced. In our example, we select EmployeeNumber as key.

Note that if you need to set the same data type, statistical type, or missing value for several columns, it's possible to do so by selecting the relevant columns and using the **Edit Selected Columns Details** icon [✎].

11.3.3   Predictive Goal

The only setting to be selected in this section is the **Target**. The target is the column that represents what you want to predict. Only columns with a nominal statistical type can be used as targets in a classification model.

Figure 11.6 shows the **Predictive Goal** section with the target setting. In our example, we've selected the **Turnover** variable as target.

Figure 11.6 Target Setting

11.3.4   Influencers

The **Influencers** section of the model settings is shown in Figure 11.7. We'll discuss these settings in more detail in the following sections.

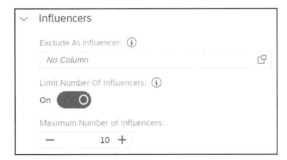

Figure 11.7 Influencers Section of the Classification Model Settings

Exclude As Influencer

The influencers are the columns of your dataset that are correlated to the target and whose values are used for predicting the target. Usually, it's the data scientist's job to select the influencers (referred to as "features" or "predictors" in the data science literature). The data scientist would first talk with the business owner to identify the columns available that may be correlated to the target. Then, they would use their data science knowledge to find the columns that are actually correlated to the target and can be used to explain it.

In smart predict, the influencer selection step is automated. You don't have to know up front what columns explain the target. Instead, you're encouraged to put in your dataset all the columns that are related to the underlying business question, and smart predict will automatically use the columns that are useful to predict the target.

That's why, by default, all the columns available in the training dataset are selected as influencers. More accurately, they are selected as "candidate" or "potential" influencers and may become actual influencers if they explain the target. Most of the time, you don't have to change this default, but there are cases where you'll need to use the **Exclude As Influencer** selector to force smart predict to ignore some columns. In Figure 11.8, the columns visible in the text field are excluded as influencers and won't be processed by the classification algorithm. In our example, we've excluded **ContractStatus** because it's a leak variable (refer to Section 11.5 for details about the leak variables).

Figure 11.8 Columns Selected Get Ignored by the Classification Model

There are mainly three cases where you would want to exclude some columns:

- **The column is a leak variable.**
  Refer to Section 11.5 for details about the leak variables.

- **The column is redundant with another column.**
  Refer to Section 11.5 for details about redundant columns.

- **The column isn't a reliable influencer.**
  Sometimes smart predict may detect accidental correlations. From a statistical standpoint, the columns and target seem correlated, but this is purely accidental. There is no business reason to explain this correlation. This can happen when the training dataset wasn't created from predictive purpose in the first place and contains many unrelated columns. It's usually wise to keep in the training dataset only columns that you think could legitimately be related to the target. A column that conveys some information it's not expected to convey is another type of not reliable influencer. For instance, if the unique identifier (ID) for your employee is a simple integer incremented for each new employee, the employee ID is directly related to

the employee start date, to the employee tenure, and to some extent to their age. But the ID column isn't meant to be a proxy for the age nor the tenure and can't be used reliably as an influencer. As a rule of thumb, always exclude the columns that are part of the observation key from the model.

Limit Number of Influencers

The **Limit Number Of Influencers** setting allows you to limit the number of influencers used by the classification model. By default, this option is disabled. When enabled, you must choose the **Maximum Number of Influencers**. The classification model will keep the most contributing influencers.

There are several reasons why you would want to limit the number of influencers used by the classification model:

- Predictive models with fewer influencers are easier to interpret.
- Predictive models with fewer influencers will tend to be more robust (refer to Chapter 13).
- Predictive models with fewer influencers have a lower total cost of ownership (TCO): Every time you'll want to generate predictions with the model, you'll need to provide columns corresponding to the influencers in the apply-in dataset.

11.4   Understanding Classification Models

Smart predict is an automated tool that creates good models by default without requiring any data science knowledge. So, you could use the classification model you've just created to immediately generate predictions, right? Well, you could, but there are a few things you may want to check first: What about the model accuracy? What factors explain the occurrence of the event you want to predict? Smart predict provides some modeling reports about your classification model that help you understand how good your model is and how it works, which we'll discuss next.

11.4.1   Assessing Model Performance

Let's be very direct: The predictive model you just created isn't perfect. No predictive model is. The reality is complex, and a model is meant to be a simplification of this reality. That means that sometimes the classification model will fail to detect that an employee is about to leave, or sometimes it will suggest an employee is likely to leave when that's not true. As a stakeholder in a predictive project, knowing how accurate the prediction will be is probably your main concern.

Data Partition

In the smart predict modeling reports you'll certainly come across the terms *data partition*, *training*, and *validation*. What do they refer to? To validate the classification model, smart predict splits the training dataset into a training set and a validation set. Each set is called a data partition in the smart predict modeling reports. The training dataset is used to train the predictive model, while the validation set is used only to calculate performance indicators. Smart predict enables you to see the statistics and performance indicators calculated on both sets. But for most users, it's sufficient to consider only the statistics and performance indicators calculated on the validation set.

If you want to understand the data partition in more detail, you can refer to Chapter 13, Section 13.3 and Section 13.4.2.

Once the model is trained or when you open a model that was previously trained, the modeling reports are displayed automatically. You can navigate between the different reports using the provided tabs. You may have to scroll down the page to see the full content of some reports. Refer to Chapter 2, Section 2.1.2, for more details about using the smart predict UI.

In the following sections, we'll walk through the reports that are important for classification model performance.

Global Performance Indicators

In the **Overview** report, the first section is called **Global Performance Indicators**. There, you'll find the **Predictive Power** and the **Prediction Confidence**, two complementary indicators (Chapter 13, Section 13.4.4 explains how these performance indicators are calculated).

Predictive power represents the model quality. It measures the ability of your classification model to predict the values of the target variable using the influencers present in the training dataset.

Predictive power is a value from 0% to 100%. You would expect the predictive power of the model to be as close as possible to 100% without being equal to 100%. A predictive power of 0% denotes a purely random classification model with no predictive power where none of the influencers are correlated to the target. A predictive power of 100%, on the other hand, denotes a hypothetical perfect model where the available influencers are capable of accounting for 100% of the information in the target.

However, if the higher the predictive power the better, then why should it not be equal to 100%? In practice, a perfect model is suspicious. A predictive power of 100% is usually an indication that an influencer that is 100% correlated to the variable wasn't excluded from the training dataset. Such influencers are called leak variables. A good practice is to exclude this influencer when you define the settings of your classification model.

There is no absolute predictive power that separates a "good" performance from a "bad" performance. A classification model with a 30% predictive power, while far from perfect, is still better than no model at all. You should use the predictive power as a means to compare the accuracy of two classification models. The classification with the highest predictive power is better than the other one.

The *prediction confidence* is complementary to the predictive power. The prediction confidence represents the model robustness, also known as the ability to generalize. It measures the classification model's capacity to achieve the same performance on data not used to train it. Having a predictive model that performs well on the data it was trained on isn't enough; you also want to know if it will be able to deliver the same performance on the application dataset.

The prediction confidence is a value between 0% and 100%. This value should be as close as possible to 100%.

Figure 11.9 shows a classification model with a rather low predictive power (quality) and a good prediction confidence.

Figure 11.9 Predictive Power and Prediction Confidence

You should always use the predictive power and the prediction confidence together to evaluate the performance of a classification model. Table 11.3 will help you understand how you should interpret the two indicators in conjunction.

	Low Predictive Power	High Predictive Power
Low Prediction Confidence	The model accuracy could be better and isn't even expected to be comparable on new data.	The model is accurate, but the performance may not be the same on new data.
High Prediction Confidence	The model accuracy could be better, but comparable performance is expected on new data.	The model is accurate, and comparable performance is expected on new data.

Table 11.3 Predictive Power and Prediction Confidence

It may be a better idea to use a model with a lower predictive power but a high prediction confidence rather than a model with a higher predictive power but a low prediction confidence. In the first case, you have an idea of the performance you can expect on new data; in the second case, you don't.

As we'll see in Section 11.5, actions you take to increase the predictive power can have negative impacts on the prediction confidence, and actions you take to increase the prediction confidence can have negative impacts on the predictive power. It's important when improving a classification to ensure that these two indicators weren't degraded.

As part of the **Overview** report, you can also see some **Target Statistics** that show the distribution of the target (the percentage of positive cases versus the percentage of negative cases) over the training and validation data partitions. This is meant as a control screen to make sure the training and validation partitions have a similar data distribution when it comes to the target variable. Having different distributions over the training and validation data partition is the sign that the training dataset is too small. In Figure 11.10, the distributions are similar.

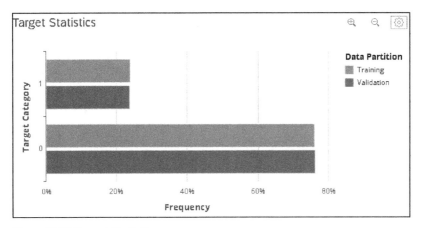

Figure 11.10 Target Statistics

Comparing Models

Getting the best possible classification model is an iterative process leading to the creation of several predictive models in the same predictive scenario. The **Predictive Models** table in the predictive scenario (see Chapter 2, Section 2.1.2) provides you with a means to easily compare the different models you've created and find the one that best suits your needs.

In this table, each row represents a predictive model, and each column is a piece of information about the predictive model. By default, some columns are hidden, but it's possible to customize which columns you want to see by using the **Select Columns** icon.

Besides the predictive power and the prediction confidence, several metrics are available:

- **Influencer count**
  The number of influencers actually used by the predictive model to generate a prediction—not to be confused with the number columns in the training dataset (candidate influencers).

- **Record count**
  The number of rows of the training dataset processed by the classification algorithm.

- **Area under the receiver operating characteristic (ROC) curve**
  The area under the ROC curve (also called the AUC) is a measure of the model performance. It measures the area under the ROC curve, which plots the true positive rate against the false positive rate. Details are provided in Chapter 13, Section 13.4.4.

- **Classification rate**
  The classification is the ratio of the number of correctly classified observations to the total number of observations in the training dataset. Details are provided in Section 11.4.3.

Performance Curves

The **Performance Curves** report provides a set of performance charts that allow you to get more details about the model performance. We encourage you to become familiar with all of them so you can choose the charts that make the most sense for you. Using one rather than the others is a matter of choosing the one that is best suited for your business case (and to some extent a matter of taste).

The **% Detected Target** chart (usually known as a "gain chart") shows the percentage of the positive cases detected by the model plotted against the percentage of the total population. We assume the population of the training dataset was ordered by decreasing the probability of belonging to the positive category of the target. The chart includes the following:

- The x-axis represents the "selected" percentage of this ordered population.
- The y-axis represents the percentage of positive cases reached for the corresponding population percentage.

The classification model you've trained, which is displayed as the **Validation** curve in the chart (see Chapter 13, Section 13.4.4), is compared to a **Random** model with no predictive power and a hypothetical **Perfect Model** that would make no error. With the random model, the positive cases are equally spread across the entire population; by selecting N% of the overall population, you would always get N% of the positive cases. With the perfect model, all the individuals with the highest probability of being positive are positive. The detected curve for the model you've trained is in between these two extremes. You'd want the **Validation** curve to be as close as possible to the **Perfect Model** curve. Usually, the **Validation** curve is very close to the **Perfect Model** curve for the first few percentages of the selected population.

The **% Detected Target** curve has also an operational purpose. Let's assume that you want to propose a retention incentive to the employees with a high risk of turnover. You would first determine the percentage of employees at risk you want to try to retain. Then, using the curve, you would determine the percentage of the employees with the highest probability of attrition to whom you would propose the retention incentive.

Example

You've built a classification to predict the employees with the highest risk of turnover, and you've determined that your budget allows you to propose retention actions for 20% of the employees.

Using the **% Detected Target** chart, as shown in Figure 11.11, you can determine the following for each model that is selecting 20% of the employee population:

- The smart predict classification model would reach 85% of the employees about to end their contract (positive population).
- A random model would reach only 20% of the employees about to end their contract (positive population).
- A perfect classification model would reach 100% of the employees about to end their contract (positive population).

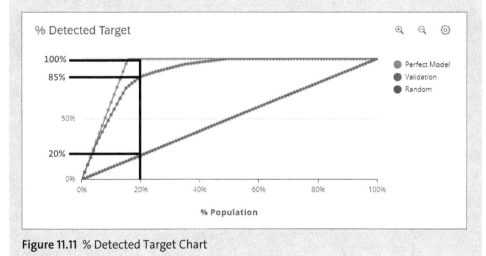

Figure 11.11 % Detected Target Chart

The **Lift** chart shows how much better a classification model is at detecting the positive cases compared to the random model (no model):

- The x-axis shows the percentage of the population sorted from highest probability to lowest probability.

- The y-axis shows how much better your model is compared to a random model. A hypothetical perfect model is represented for reference.

Example

You've built a classification to predict the employees with the highest risk of turnover. Using the **Lift** chart shown in Figure 11.12, you can see that selecting 12% of the employees with the highest predicted risk causes the following:

- Your classification model would detect 5.24 times more employees about to leave than a random classification model.

- A perfect classification model would detect 6.39 times more employees about to leave than a random classification model.

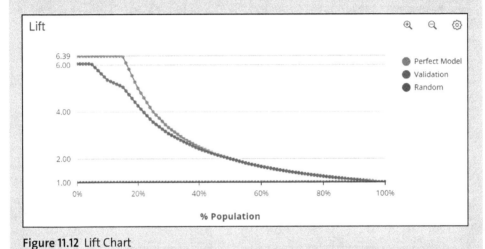

Figure 11.12 Lift Chart

The **Sensitivity** chart (also referred to as the ROC curve) tells you how well your classification model is balanced between sensitivity and specificity for any decision threshold:

- Each point on the chart corresponds to a specific decision threshold.

- The x-axis (**1-Specificity**) shows that the proportion of all the actual negative cases have been predicted positive (false positive rate).

- The y-axis shows the **Sensitivity**, that is, the proportion of actual positive cases that have been predicted positive (true positive targets).

You can find more details about the concepts used in the sensitivity chart in Section 11.4.3.

Example

You've built a classification to predict the employees with the highest risk of turnover. Using the **Sensitivity** chart shown in Figure 11.13, a false positive rate of 8% causes the following:

- Your classification model would detect 85% of the employees who are about to quit.

- A random classification model (i.e., no classification model) would detect 8% of the employees about to quit.

- A perfect classification model would detect 100% of the employees about to quit.

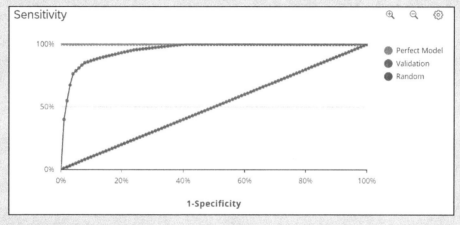

Figure 11.13 Sensitivity Chart

The **Lorenz** curve lets you display two different curves: the Lorenz "good" chart and the Lorenz "bad" chart (also referred to as a specificity chart) depending on the value you choose to display on the y-axis.

The **Lorenz** "good" chart can be displayed by choosing **1-Sensitivity** as the value for the y-axis. *1-sensitivity* is equivalent to the proportion of false negative, also called the miss rate. The Lorenz "good" chart shows the cumulative proportion of false negative predictions regarding the selected population threshold. The x-axis shows the percentage of the population ordered from the lowest to the highest probability. The y-axis shows **1-Sensitivity**, that is, *1-the proportion of positive targets classified as true positive*. The results are ordered from the lowest probability (on the left) to the highest probability (on the right).

The **Lorenz** "bad" chart (also referred to as a specificity chart) can be displayed by selecting **Specificity** as the value for the y-axis. It displays the cumulative proportion of actual negative targets that have been correctly predicted regarding the selected population threshold.

The x-axis shows the percentage of the population ordered from the lowest to the highest probability, while the y-axis shows the specificity.

Example

You've built a classification to predict the employees with the highest risk of turnover. Using the Lorenz curve visible in Figure 11.14, you can tell that selecting 70% of the population with the lowest risk causes the following:

- A random classification model would classify 70% of the employees who will actually quit as nonquitters (70% miss rate).
- A perfect classification model would classify 0% the employees who will actually quit as nonquitters (0% miss rate).
- The classification model created by smart predict (the validation curve) would classify 18% of the employees who will actually quit as nonquitters (18% miss rate).

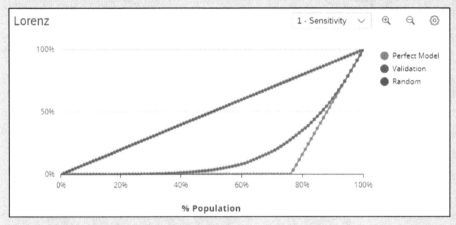

Figure 11.14 The Lorenz "Good" Chart

11.4.2   Influencer Contributions

So far, we've mainly discussed the performance of the classification model. But to understand the model, you also need to know how the model works and the global logic it uses to calculate the predictions. The **Influencer Contributions** report lets you drill into the details of your model's influencers so you can understand more about the model's internal logic and gain valuable business insights. We'll discuss some key visualizations available within the report in the next sections.

Influencer Contributions Table

The **Influencer Contributions** table provides a list of the model influencers ordered by decreasing contribution to the model. The contribution represents the relative weight or importance of an influencer in the model and quantifies how much the influencer explains the target. The most contributive influencers are those that best explain the target. The sum of the contributions always equals 100%.

Figure 11.15 shows that **OverTime** is the most important influencer, accounting for 28.02% of the target explanation.

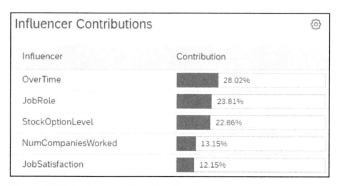

Figure 11.15 Influencer Contributions

Note that the classification model may decide that some of the columns of the training datasets aren't useful to generate the predictions. These columns aren't influencers, they aren't contributive, and therefore they aren't displayed in the table.

Correlation Doesn't Imply Causation

You must be careful of what you conclude from the list of influencers. A variable becomes an influencer when smart predict finds a strong enough correlation between this variable and the target. That's all the **Influencer Contribution** tables say. They don't say there is a relation of causality between the target and the influencer. There may be such a relation, but smart predict doesn't know it. The correlation may also be purely accidental: sometimes two variables can have the same "movement" just by chance.

Grouped Category Influence

Thanks to the **Influencer Contributions** table, you know the factors that have the most influence on the prediction. But this information alone isn't complete. The **Influencer Contributions** table tells you that the **EducationField** is an important influencer to predict if an employee will resign in the coming months. That's a relevant piece of information, but you'd probably want to know more precisely which education field leads to a higher probability of quitting and which education field leads to a lower probability of quitting. That's the exact purpose of the **Grouped Category Influence**, as shown in Figure 11.16.

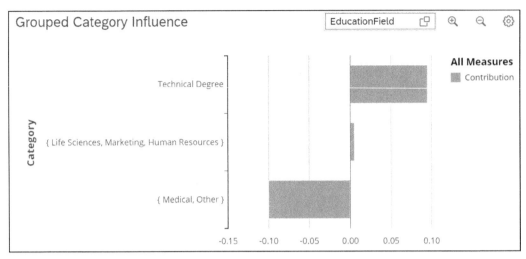

Figure 11.16 How the Education Field Influences the Risk of Leaving the Company for the Employees

Each bar of the **Grouped Category Influence** represents a category of the selected influencer. The value of the bar represents the influence of the category:

- The sign of the value gives the direction of the influence. If the bar's value is positive, the associated category increases the predicted probability of belonging to the positive target category. If the bar's value is negative, the associated category decreases the predicted probability of belonging to the positive target category.

- The absolute value associated with the category (i.e., the size of the bar) gives the strength of the influence. The bigger the bar, the stronger the influence of the category on the predicted probability.

- By default, the bars are ordered by descending influence, but this can be changed in the settings of the visualization.

In Figure 11.16, you'll notice that some bars correspond to several categories grouped inside of curly braces. These categories are grouped because they share the same relation to the target (statistically speaking). They can be considered as one category, which makes the chart more synthetic and easier to read. For instance, because the classification model has noticed that the behavior toward the target isn't significantly different, the employees belonging to the **Life Sciences**, **Marketing**, and **Human Resources** categories, it has grouped these categories into one.

Some categories of the influencer that existed in the training dataset but aren't statistically significant—usually happens when the category has very few occurrences—may be grouped into the **Other** category.

Example

Let's unpack our example shown in Figure 11.16:

- **The Technical Degree bar has a positive value and is large.**
  The employees with a technical degree have a much stronger probability of belonging to the positive value of the target (= will leave the company) compared to the other categories.
- **The {Life Sciences, Marketing, Human Resources} bar has a positive value but is rather small.**
  The employees who belong have slightly more chance to belong to the positive category of the target (= will leave the company) but not significantly.
- **The {Medical, Other} bar has a negative value and is large.**
  The employees who belong to that category have a much stronger probability of belonging to the negative value of the target (= will not leave the company) compared to the other categories.

Grouped Category Statistics

The **Grouped Category Statistics** chart shows statistics used to calculate the influence of the categories. It can be useful to understand in more detail why a certain category has a positive or negative influence. By default, it's displayed as a scatterplot in which the following is true for a selected influencer:

- Each point represents a category of the selected influencer.
- The x-axis displays the **Frequency of Positive Target** for the grouped category, that is, the percentage of rows where the target value was positive, considering only that grouped category (either for the training set or the validation set). *Frequency of positive target = P(positive_target_value | c)* where *c* is considered the grouped category.
- The y-axis shows the **Frequency** of the grouped category and the percentage of rows in the training dataset where it appeared. *Frequency = P(c)* where *c* is the considered category.

You can select the data partition to be displayed to compare the results obtained by the classification model on the training data partition and the one obtained on the validation data partition (refer to the "Data Partition" box in Section 11.4.1).

Figure 11.17 shows the grouped category statistics for the **OverTime** variable. You can see that the turnover rate (**Frequency of Positive Target**) is way higher among the employees who work overtime: 30% of the employees working overtime have resigned, while only 10% of the employees not working overtime have resigned. You can also see that about 28% of the employees work overtime.

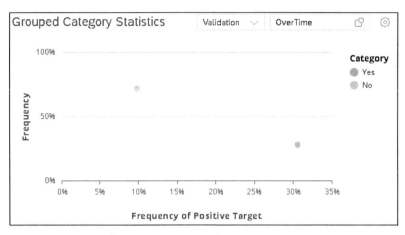

Figure 11.17 Grouped Category Statistics for OverTime

11.4.3   Confusion Matrix

This intimidating name hides a simple and powerful performance measurement tool. You can access the confusion matrix by clicking the **Confusion Matrix** tab in the reports area. The following sections explain why the confusion matrix is a powerful tool and how you can use it in smart predict.

Different Types of Error

The classification rate is the percentage of cases the model could classify in the right category: the number of times it was right divided by the total number of cases. It's usually the first indicator people have in mind when they think about the accuracy of a classification model. It's simple, but it doesn't tell the whole story and can even be misleading.

Let's forget about the employee turnover for a while and consider the following use case: You want to predict the persons who will develop a rare disease. Each year about 1% of the population gets that disease. A classification model would predict "true" for a person who will develop the disease and "false" for someone who would not. Now, let's assume a very simple model that would always predict "false." That model would simply fail to detect the disease. Still, it would achieve an outstanding 99% classification rate. The classification rate doesn't give the information you need.

With this use case, you need to drill into the detail of what type of error is made because all the types of errors aren't equivalent. For such a use case, what is most important is to not miss a positive case: You don't want the prediction for someone who will develop the disease to be missed by the screening. On the other hand, having some false alarms is probably acceptable: This may lead to additional medical assessment for some people who won't develop the disease, which is less of a problem.

For some other use cases, such as email spam detection, the expectations are quite the opposite: It's probably okay not to catch all the spam (miss), but it's certainly not okay to block an email if it wasn't really spam (false alarm).

The confusion matrix is meant to help you perform this detailed error analysis. As illustrated by Table 11.4, a confusion matrix is a simple 2 × 2 table that shows how many predictions can be expected to be correct and incorrect for each category of the target when applying the classification model. Table 11.4 also shows different wordings commonly used to refer to the different cells of the confusion matrix.

		Predicted Class	
		Positive	Negative
Actual Class	Positive	• Correctly predicted as positive • True positives (TP) • Hit	• Wrongly predicted as negative • False negatives (FN) • Miss
	Negative	• Wrongly predicted as positive • False positives (FP) • False alarm	• Correctly predicted as negative • True negatives (TN) • Correct rejection

Table 11.4 Confusion Matrix

The values shown in the confusion matrix in smart predict represent the percentage of each type of error that you can expect when applying the classification on a new dataset with a statistical distribution similar to the statistical distribution of the training dataset. Figure 11.18 shows an example **Confusion Matrix** in smart predict. Here, you can see that you can expect 15.78% of the observations to be classified as "yes" (positive target category) and the remaining 84.22% to be classified as "no". You can also see that you can expect 3.33% of the observations to be misclassified as "yes" while they should have been classified as "no".

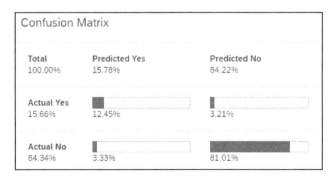

Confusion Matrix

Total 100.00%	Predicted Yes 15.78%	Predicted No 84.22%
Actual Yes 15.66%	12.45%	3.21%
Actual No 84.34%	3.33%	81.01%

Figure 11.18 Confusion Matrix in Smart Predict

Chapter 13, Section 13.3.1, explains in detail how the confusion matrix and other error estimations are calculated.

Decision Threshold

We already mentioned in Chapter 10, Section 10.1.3, that the predicted category is derived from the probability by applying a decision threshold. Depending on the threshold, the whole set of predictions will be different, so the errors made by the classification model will be different. As a result, the confusion matrix isn't unique for a given classification model. It's possible to calculate one confusion matrix for each threshold value.

The **Contacted Population** and the **Detected Target** threshold selectors at the top of the **Confusion Matrix** report (see Figure 11.19) allow you to select a specific decision threshold and see the corresponding confusion matrix. By moving these selectors, you can find the best decision threshold for your specific business case. As you move the threshold in one direction, you'll notice that some types of error will decrease and other types of error will increase. Finding the right threshold is always a trade-off between the different types of error and depends on what matters the most for your use case.

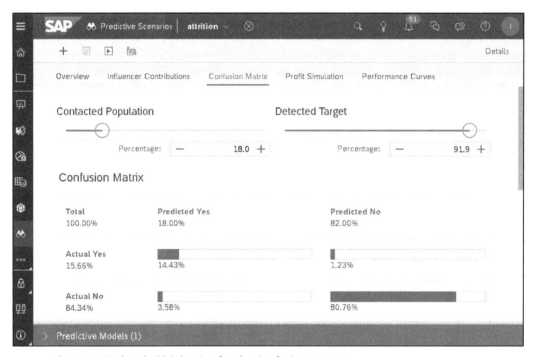

Figure 11.19 Threshold Selection for the Confusion Matrix

The **Contacted Population** threshold selector sets a decision threshold based on a percentage of the population with the highest probability of belonging to the positive target case that must be selected. You can use it if you have operational constraints on the number of positive cases you can handle. For instance, if you already know that you have enough budget to propose a retention plan to 5% of the employees, you can use the **Contacted Population** threshold selector to select 5% of the population and see the associated confusion matrix.

The **Detected Target** threshold selector allows you to set a decision threshold based on a percentage of the positive cases to be detected. You can use it if you have constraints on the minimum percentage of positive cases you need to detect. For instance, if you want to propose a retention package to 50% of the employees who will resign, you can set the **Detected Target** value to 50% and see the corresponding confusion matrix.

Derived Metrics

The confusion matrix provides a very detailed view of the errors. The **Metrics** section, at the bottom of the **Confusion Matrix** report, provides several synthetic metrics based on the values of the confusion matrix. Figure 11.20 shows the **Metrics** section of the **Confusion Matrix** report. Which metric you must use to evaluate your classification model depends on your business case.

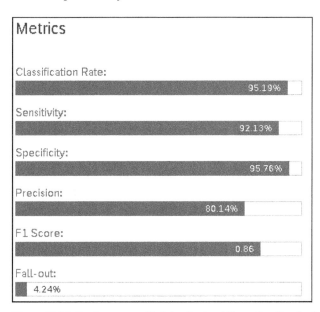

Figure 11.20 Performance Metrics Derived from the Confusion Matrix

Table 11.5 shows all the derived metrics available in smart predict.

Metric	Definition and Interpretation	Formula
Classification Rate	Percentage of correct answers.	$(TP + TN) \div (TP + TN + FN + FP)$
Sensitivity	Percentage of positive events that were predicted, which is also known as hit rate or recall. Is the model finding all the positive cases?	$TP \div (TP + FN)$
Specificity	Percentage of negative events that were predicted as negative. Is the model able to recognize a negative case properly?	$TN \div (TN + FP)$
Precision	Percentage of predicted positive events that are really positive. Is the model finding only what it's expected to find?	$TP \div (TP + FP)$
F1 Score	Synthetic accuracy metric that combines precision and recall.	$2 \times Precision \times Recall \div (Precision + Recall) = TP \div (TP + 0.5(FP + FN))$
Fall-out	Percentage of negative events that were predicted positive.	$FP \div (FP + TN)$

Table 11.5 Performance Metrics Derived from the Confusion Matrix

11.4.4   Profit Simulation

The **Profit Simulation** report, as shown in Figure 11.21, is another perspective on the confusion matrix that allows you to optimize the decision threshold based on operational constraints:

1. Enter a positive value in **Cost Per Predicted Positive**, found under **Unit Cost Vs. profit**. This represents the cost of conducting an action toward the individual predicted as positive. In our turnover example, this would be the estimated cost of the retention package.

2. Enter a positive value in **Profit Per Actual Positive**, found under **Unit Cost Vs. profit**. This represents the profit you expect for each positive individual successfully identified. In our turnover example, this would be the money you think can be saved by retaining an employee.

3. Click the **Maximize Profit** button.

Smart predict will calculate a decision threshold that optimizes the overall profit based on the provided unit profit and cost values. In the **Total Profit** you can compare the profit expected by using the classification model compared to the profit expected by using a random model.

Figure 11.21 Profit Simulation

11.5 Improving Classification Models

We encourage you to keep track of your experiments using the capabilities provided in the predictive scenarios:

1. Open the **Predictive Models** table at the bottom of the screen.
2. Open the context menu of a model you want to start from, and click **Duplicate**.
3. Select the copy of the model created at the previous step.
4. Change some settings. For instance, exclude an influencer.
5. In the predictive model **Description**, replace the default description to document your experiment: "excluded some influencers".
6. Train the model.

Repeat all of these steps for each test you do with the model settings.

You're now ready to make changes to the model settings while keeping track of your experiments. In the next sections, we'll provide guidance to improve your classification model.

11.5.1 Basic Checks

Smart predict does a lot of things automatically. However, there are still a few cases that require some human acuity and business knowledge to make the best decision. We'll discuss these basic checks to perform in the next sections.

Leak Variables

First, this is the right time to check for potential leak variables. A *leak variable* represents information not available at prediction time, so it can't be used to predict the target. The leak variables often represent a direct or indirect consequence of the event to be predicted. For instance, when predicting employees' turnover risk, the **Contract-Status** column must not be used as the influencer because its value immediately changes due to the resignation. Using **ContractStatus** would lead to a seemingly perfect model while it's of no use.

If the model performance is very high (the predictive power is suspiciously close to 100%) and one of the influencers has a very high contribution (greater than 90%), as shown in Figure 11.22, then this influencer is possibly a leak variable and may need to be excluded from the model. Note that these are just hints that the influencer may be a leak variable. You must use your knowledge of the business domain to decide if you've found a leak variable or a very good influencer.

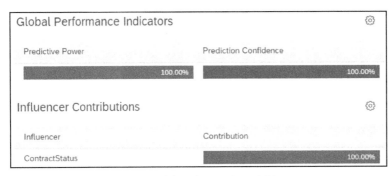

Figure 11.22 Classification Model with a Leak Variable

Redundant Influencers

Then, you can check for redundant influencers. The training dataset may contain several columns that are slightly different representations of each other. For instance, your training dataset may contain the employee's age but also some categorical representation of the employee's age coming from the HR system such as the "age group" or the "generation." Because these different representations aren't strictly identical, the classification model may find that each representation brings a little bit of additional information over the other representations. Keeping all of these redundant influencers makes the classification model more difficult to interpret and may have a negative impact on the robustness. When you find such influencers, keep only the one with the highest contribution, and exclude the other ones from the model.

11.5.2   Improving Model Accuracy

The main measure of the model accuracy is the predictive power. To improve the predictive power of your model, you can try adding more influencers to the training dataset. When more influencers are added to the training dataset, the smart predict classification algorithm can try finding correlations between the new influencers and the target that can explain more complex target behaviors.

There are mainly two ways to find new influencers:

- You can leverage new data sources. Are there other files or table in relation with what you're trying to predict that could be leveraged?

- You can derive new calculated columns from the existing columns (known as "feature engineering"). Often, it's possible to extract otherwise hidden information from the available data by calculating aggregates or just by transforming some existing columns. For instance, you could derive an employee's tenure from their starting date.

Ideally, the new influencers must bring some information that wasn't previously available to the model. Adding new influencers that are redundant with existing influencers will likely not improve the model accuracy and will possibly make the model more difficult to understand.

11.5.3   Improving Model Robustness

The main measure of the model robustness is the prediction confidence. To improve the prediction confidence, you can try adding more rows to your training dataset. Intuitively, by learning from more examples, the classification algorithm will learn more of the diversity available in real life and has more generalization capabilities.

For instance, if you've sampled the employees to reduce the training dataset size, try adding more employees to the training dataset. It's also possible to increase the number of rows by considering the customers state at different dates in the past (see our discussion of the population snapshot in Section 11.2.1).

To be robust, the classification must also have "seen" enough positive cases. If the frequency of the positive target category is very low, you can try to get more positive cases by increasing the length of the observation period (Section 11.2). For instance, you'll probably get more cases of resignations in your training dataset by observing the resignations over a 12-month period than over a 6-month period. However, keep in mind that when changing the length of the observation period, you also change your predictive goal: Instead of predicting who will leave the company in the coming 6 months, you're now predicting who will leave in the coming 12 months.

Finally, if the model has a lot of influencers (say more than 20), you can improve the model robustness by reducing the number of influencers in the model. Intuitively, we could say that by using many influencers, the model is lost in the details and has more difficulties generalizing what it learned to new data. The easiest way to reduce the number of influencers is to use the **Limit Number Of Influencers** option, as described in Section 11.3.4.

11.5.4 The Quality versus Robustness Trade-Off

Some model improvement advice may sound contradictory. You must add influencers to improve the model quality, but you must remove influencers to improve the robustness: improving the model quality may degrade the robustness and vice versa. Improving a model is always finding the right trade-off between the quality and the robustness. When improving one of these measures, you need to be careful not to impact the other one too negatively.

11.6 Applying Classification Models

Your classification model is now ready to generate some predictions. This process is called the *model application*. You must provide an application dataset as input for the model application. Refer to Section 11.2 for a detailed explanation of the application dataset.

The columns of the application dataset are a subset of the columns of the training dataset: The application dataset must contain the columns that have been defined as "key" columns in the training dataset metadata and all the columns corresponding to the influencer of the model. If one influencer is missing, then the application dataset isn't valid, and the application will fail. If the application dataset contains some columns that aren't influencers, they are just ignored silently during the model application. Thanks to that behavior, you can create your application dataset without having to know in advance what column will become an influencer. You can just create your application dataset with the same columns as the training dataset and let the classification model use what it needs to use.

Because the columns used in the application dataset always correspond to a subset of the columns in the training dataset, you don't need to provide metadata for the application dataset. The metadata of the training dataset is reused transparently for the application dataset.

During the model application, the predictions are written to the predictions dataset. The predictions dataset will contain one row with predictions for each row provided in the application dataset. It will always contain the columns that were described as keys in the training dataset and the predictions you've selected.

Follow these steps to apply your classification model:

1. In the **Predictive Models** table, select the model you want to use to generate the predictions.

2. Click the **Apply Predictive Model** icon [img] in the top toolbar. The **Apply Predictive Model** dialog appears, as shown in Figure 11.23.

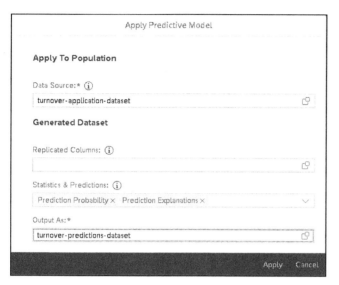

Figure 11.23 Application Dialog for Classification Models

3. Click the **Browse** icon of the **Data Source** field to select the application dataset.

4. In the **Statistics & Predictions** field, select **Prediction Probability** and **Prediction Explanations**. Table 11.6 lists the available predictions.

Application Options	Description
Prediction Probability	For each row in the application dataset, the **Prediction Probability** is the probability that the **Predicted Category** is the target value.
Predicted Category	For each row in the application dataset, the **Predicted Category** is the target category determined by the classification model.
	The **Predicted Category** is determined based on a default decision threshold. The default decision threshold is that the model predicts the same percentage of positive cases as found in the train set.
	Any change made by the user in the confusion matrix doesn't affect the **Predicted Category** in the generated dataset.
	An alternative way could be to generate the **Prediction Probability** instead of the **Predicted Category** and set a decision threshold in a story based on your business requirements.
Outlier Indicator	For each row in the application dataset, the **Outlier Indicator** is **1** if the row is an outlier with respect to the target; otherwise, it's **0**.
	An observation is considered an outlier when the prediction error is greater than three times the average prediction error found on similar observations.

Table 11.6 Application Options

Application Options	Description
Prediction Explanations	For each row of the application dataset, **Prediction Explanations** is a set of explanations for the prediction. What we mean by "explanation" is detailed in Section 11.7. This option is a bit specific because it's the only one that leads to a predictions dataset that contains more rows than the application dataset. That's why it's usually recommended to write the **Prediction Explanations** into a specific dataset and the other predictions into another dataset.
Apply Date	For each row of the application dataset, the **Apply Date** is the start date of the classification model application. The generated value is identical for each row.
Train Date	For each row of the application dataset, the **Train Date** is the start date of the classification model training. The generated value is identical for each row.
Replicated Columns	This allows you to write some columns of the application dataset to the predictions dataset. Only the columns in the training dataset can be written this way; the other columns are ignored. If the predictions are meant to be consumed in a story, it's recommended to use the blending capabilities instead of replicating data using this option.

Table 11.6 Application Options (Cont.)

5. Click the **Browse** icon of the **Output As** field to select the predictions dataset to be created.

6. Click the **Apply** button.

You can see the progression of the model application in the **Status** column of the **Predictive Model** table. The list of variables contained in the predictions dataset is provided in Table 11.7.

Variable Name	Variable Nature	What Does the Variable Correspond To?
EmployeeNumber	Dimension	This is a unique identifier of each employee.
Prediction Probability	Measure	This is the predicted probability of resignation for the employee.

Table 11.7 List of Variables in the Predictions Dataset

Variable Name	Variable Nature	What Does the Variable Correspond To?
Explanation Rank	Dimension	For each predicted price, the explanations are ranked according to their impact (absolute strength value) on the prediction. The lower the rank, the more important the impact of the specific explanation to the probability of resignation.
Explanation Influencer	Dimension	This variable contains the name of the influencer for the explanation.
Explanation Influencer Value	Dimension	This variable contains the value associated with the influencer for this prediction.
Explanation Strength	Measure	This variable represents a normalized contribution of the influencer for the predicted probability of resignation.

Table 11.7 List of Variables in the Predictions Dataset (Cont.)

Writing to an Existing Predictions Dataset

There are a few things you need to consider when writing new predictions to an existing dataset:

- Updating a dataset exactly means updating the data it contains. The dataset structure, that is, the columns of the dataset, can't be changed. It's not possible to add a column, nor is it possible to remove a column from the dataset.

- Consequently, when generating new predictions into an existing dataset, you must take care to select exactly the same output columns as you did when the dataset was initially created. Otherwise, the model application will fail.

- When writing to an existing dataset, the data that exists in the dataset is replaced by the new predictions (the old dataset content is deleted before the predictions are written).

11.7   Enriching Stories with Classification Insights

Now you know how to create a classification model and how to apply it to generate predictions. This section provides step-by-step examples that teach you how to use the generated predictions to enrich a story.

11.7.1   Prediction Probability

Prediction probability can be leveraged in stories in a few ways. We'll discuss them next.

Estimation of the Number of Resignations

You don't always need a binary prediction when working with a classification. If you want to display the number of predicted positive cases in a story, you can simply calculate the sum of the probability over the entire population, which is considered a good estimation of the number of positive cases. In a story, working with probability also allows more flexibility: You can play with the decision threshold and compare the results for different values.

Let's create a chart that shows the estimated number of customers who will end their subscription in the coming three months. Follow these steps:

1. We assume you've already created a predictions dataset containing the prediction probability. If not, follow the steps in Section 11.6.

2. Create a new story by clicking the **Stories** icon ⊞ in the SAP Analytics Cloud navigation bar.

3. Choose the type of layout you want for your story. You can choose either **Responsive** or **Canvas**.

4. You'll be prompted to choose a **Design Mode Type**. Select **Optimized Design Experience** (default choice).

5. Click the **Insert · Chart** button in the top toolbar.

6. You'll be prompted for the selection of a data source. Select your predictions dataset.

7. The **Builder** panel is opened to the right of the screen. In the **Currently Select Chart** dropdown, select **Numeric Point**.

8. Click the **At least 1 Measure is required** link under **Measures · Primary Values**, and then click **Add Calculation** in the dropdown menu.

9. The **Calculation Editor** will open. In the **Type** dropdown list, select **Aggregation**.

10. To sum up the probability of all the customers, under **Properties**, in the **Operation** field, select **SUM**. In the **Measure** field, select **Prediction Probability**. Finally, in the **Aggregation Dimensions** field, select **EmployeeNumber**. Figure 11.24 shows the configuration of the calculation.

11. Provide a name for your new calculated column in the **Name** field. For instance, call it "turnover estimation". Click **OK** to create the calculated column.

    The visualization should now be configured as shown in Figure 11.25.

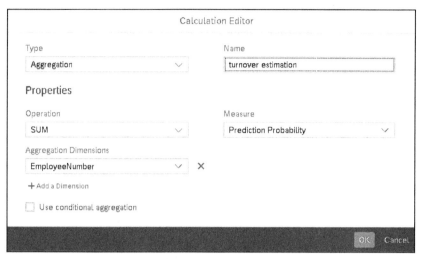

Figure 11.24 Summing the Probabilities

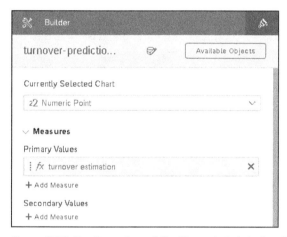

Figure 11.25 Configuration of the Numeric Point Visualization

12. By default, the displayed value is a decimal number because the summed value (**Prediction Probability**) is a decimal number. In the **turnover estimation** token, open the context menu ⸽•••⸽, and click **Format**.

13. In the **Formatting** popup, enter "0" in the **Decimal Places** field. Click **OK**.

14. The chart displays an estimation of the number of employees who may leave the company during the next 12 months.

Your story should display a chart similar to Figure 11.26 (the exact displayed value may differ).

Figure 11.26 Turnover Estimation

Employee List Ordered by Decreasing Probability of Turnover

The probability is also convenient for some more operational uses cases. Let's assume that for your retention campaign, you need to call the customers you want to retain. You have a limited amount of time, say two weeks, for this campaign, and you have no idea how many customers you can reach during this period. One way to handle that is to generate the probability of turnover and display it on a table ordered by decreasing probability of attrition. You can then contact the customers with the highest attrition probability first and stop either when you run out of time or when you've reached your objective of contact.

Let's build that contact table:

1. Click the **Insert · Table** button in the top toolbar. The **Builder** panel is opened to the right of the screen.
2. We want one row per customer, so let's click **Rows · Add Dimensions** link, and check **EmployeeNumber** in the **DIMENSIONS** section.
3. Click the **Manage Filters** button in the **Columns · Measures** token.
4. Select **Prediction Probability**, and make sure everything else is deselected.
5. Click **OK**.
6. In the table, right-click the **Prediction Probability** column, and select **Sort Options · Highest to Lowest**.

The table is now sorted by decreasing probability of turnover, as shown in Figure 11.27.

Figure 11.27 Employees Sorted by Probability of Turnover

This is a starting point, and there are many ways you can improve your story from here. For instance, you may use the blending (join operation) and linked analysis capabilities of the stories to use the table as a selector and display information about the selected customer.

11.7.2   Prediction Explanations

Knowing the risk of resignation of an employee is important. But you can get the best of this information only if you understand the reasons behind the prediction. The prediction explanations allow you to understand the factors that increased or decreased the predicted probability for a specific employee. In this section, we explain how the prediction explanations can be displayed in a story.

Understanding the Explanations

For each predicted row, the prediction explanations explain how the classification model came to the specific predicted probability. There are mainly two reasons you would want these explanations:

- **Explanations help build trust**
  When people are provided with data that has a predictive origin, there is often suspicion and even sometimes distrust. This lack of confidence usually comes from the fact that the consumers of the predictions don't know the logic used by the model to calculate the prediction. By providing the explanations along with the predicted probability, you allow the consumers of the predictions to see that the explanations for the prediction make sense to them.

- **Explanations are complementary to the predictions**
  For some use cases, you may want to use the prediction to perform some targeted actions. For instance, you may want to use the predictions to perform retention actions on the employees with the highest probability of turnover. Thanks to the prediction explanations, you can adapt your retention actions reasons to why the employee was predicted with a high risk of turnover.

Local Model Interpretation

Explainable artificial intelligence (AI; or explainable machine learning) is a set of tools and methods that aim at making the machine learning models interpretable by humans. There are mainly two levels of explainable AI:

- Global interpretability (or global explainable AI) that aims at explaining the global logic of the model. The modeling reports enable global interpretability of the classification models.
- Local interpretability (or local explainable AI) that aims at explaining the reasons for a specific individual prediction. The prediction explanations enable local interpretability of the classification models.

Table 11.8 shows the structure of the prediction dataset when the **Prediction Explanation** output is enabled in the model application settings (refer to instructions in Section 11.6).

Identifier	Explanation Rank	Explanation Influencer	Explanation Influencer Value	Explanation Strength
...	...	...	...	...
ID i	1	WorkLifeBalance	3	-0.25
ID i	2	MonthlyIncome	5,993	0.89
...	...	...	...	...
ID i	9	EducationField	Life Sciences	0.15
...	...	...	...	...

Table 11.8 Structure of a Dataset with Prediction Explanations for Employee Turnover

The following explains what each column of the predictions dataset corresponds to:

- **Identifier**
  Depending on the number of influencers in the classification model, each observation identifier can appear between 1 and 10 times in the dataset.

- **Explanation rank**
  This column can be used to order the explanations by decreasing absolute strength.

- **Explanation influencer**
  This is the name of an influencer.

- **Explanation influencer value**
  This is the value of the influencer in the application dataset.

- **Explanation strength**
  This is the measure of the contribution of the influencer.

For convenience, we'll refer to the triplet (Explanation Influencer, Influencer Value, Explanation Strength) as an "explanation" of the prediction.

You can use the prediction dataset to display visualizations in a story, like the example shown in Figure 11.28. We'll explain how to create this visualization at the end of this section.

This representation is centered on one observation: The whole chart represents a set of explanations for the predicted probability for the employee selected in the table to the left (**1926**, in this case). Each bar represents an influencer and its value in the application dataset. The size of the bar represents the contribution of the influencer to the prediction (stored in the **Explanation Strength** column).

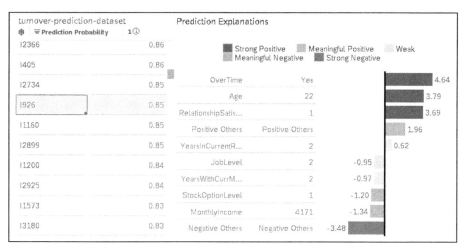

Figure 11.28 Explanations of the Predicted Probability for Employee I926

Larger bars represent a greater contribution to the prediction. The contribution can be either positive or negative:

- When the contribution is positive, the predicted probability is increased.
- When the contribution is negative, the predicted probability is decreased.

In Figure 11.28, you can see the reason that most increases the probability of employee I926 leaving is that he works overtime. His age also significantly increases his probability to leave. Other factors, such as his rather high monthly income and his stock option plan, tend to decrease the predicted probability to leave.

As you may have noticed, the prediction explanations are very similar to the grouped category influence: Both provide the same information, locally (to a specific prediction) for the prediction explanations and globally (to the whole classification model) for the grouped category influence.

The "strength" is a normalized measure of the contribution and hence must not be interpreted as a probability (when summed, the strengths for a prediction aren't equal to the predicted probability).

Discretizing the Strength

The strength is a continuous value in a range that isn't easy to interpret. Consumers of the explanation will usually prefer interpreting the value more qualitatively using discrete categories. These categories can be associated with some color coding for a better visual impact.

Table 11.9 show the recommended ranges of value to discretize the strength. Note that this is only a recommendation, and you may adapt these ranges based on your needs. For instance, you may want to differentiate between positive and negative in the]-1;-1[range.

Range	Interpretation of the Explanation Contribution on the Prediction
[3; +∞[	Strong positive contribution
[1; 3[	Medium positive contribution
]-1; 1[	Low contribution (not significant)
]-3; -1]	Medium negative contribution
]-∞; -3]	Strong negative contribution

Table 11.9 Recommended Discretization Ranges for Strength

Positive Others and Negative Others

It may be difficult to have a synthetic view of what influenced the prediction if too much information is provided. More explanations lead to more data points, which may be more difficult to read and interpret. So, the choice was made to limit the number of generated explanations to 10 per prediction.

However, a classification model can obviously use more than 10 influencers. So, to comply with the 10 explanations limit while keeping the provided information "complete," we've introduced the Positive Others and Negative Others influencers.

There is always a maximum of 10 explanations in total, including the Positive Others and Negative Others generated influencers. Depending on how the positive and negative explanations are balanced, Positive Others and Negative Others may exist alone.

Because they are aggregating several individual explanations, the strength of Positive Others and Negative Others can be significant while the aggregated individual strengths may be small.

Using the Explanations in a Story

Following are the step-by-step instructions to create a visualization similar to Figure 11.28.

First, create a table listing the employees ordered by decreasing probability of turnover. You can follow the instructions in Section 11.7.1 (specifically, the employee list ordered by decreasing probability).

Then, you want to configure the table to act as an employee selector by following these steps:

1. In the table context menu ⊡, click the **Linked Analysis • Settings** menu item.
2. In the **Linked Analysis** panel, as shown in Figure 11.29, select **All Widgets on the Page** under **Interactions apply to**, and then select **Filter on Data Point Selection** under **Settings**.
3. Click **Apply** to confirm your choices.

Figure 11.29 Configuration of the Linked Analysis Panel

Next, you'll create the visualization that will display the explanations:

1. Click **Insert · Chart** ▣ in the top toolbar.
2. In the **Builder** panel, configure the chart as follows (see Figure 11.30):
    – Keep **Bar/Column** as **Currently Selected Chart**, and keep **Horizontal** as **Chart Orientation**.
    – Set **Explanation Strength** for **Measures**.
    – Set **Explanation Influencer** and **Explanation Influencer Value** for **Dimensions**.

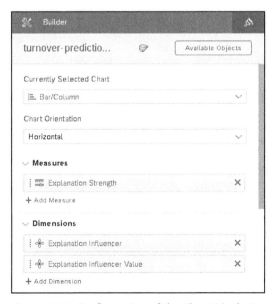

Figure 11.30 Configuration of the Chart Displaying the Explanations

For more convenient reading, order the bars by decreasing the influencer strength. First select a row in the left-hand table then right-click the bar chart, and select **Sort** · **Explanation Strength** · **Highest to Lowest** in the context menu.

The explanations are easier to understand when using discrete categories such as "Strongly Positive" or "Weakly Negative", as explained in the earlier section on discretizing the strength. For even more convenience, we'll use color coding to represent these categories. You'll now discretize the strength using the recommended ranges (as listed earlier in Table 11.9) and configure the color coding:

1. Right-click the bar chart, and click **Add** · **Threshold** in the context menu **More Options.**

2. Select **Explanation Strength** for **Measure** in the **Thresholds** panel.

3. Using the **Add Range** link, create and configure five ranges, as shown in Figure 11.31.

4. Click **Apply** to close the **Thresholds** panel.

5. If the color coding doesn't appear in the chart, click the **Threshold Options** icon that is visible in the **Explanation Strength** measure. Then select the option **Show Threshold** · **Story Defined.**

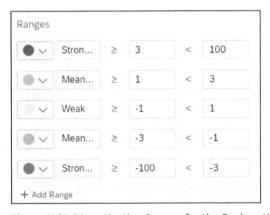

Figure 11.31 Discretization Ranges for the Explanations

11.8   Summary

In this chapter, we walked you through automated classification models. You've learned what datasets they use and generate, as well as how to understand and improve them. Finally, you've seen different examples of how predictions can be consumed into stories.

In the next chapter, we'll provide a step-by-step explanation of how to use regression models in stories.

Chapter 12

Creating Regression Insights to Enrich Stories

Regression models can be used to predict a large variety of events in multiple business domains: What is the price I can expect to sell a given product for? What is the commercial value I can expect from my customer next year? These use cases are available in SAP Analytics Cloud thanks to smart predict.

This chapter opens with a new business scenario for our discussion of regression models in Section 12.1. Section 12.2 discusses the datasets used with regression models, and then Section 12.3 teaches you to create regression models. You'll then learn how to assess them (Section 12.4), improve them (Section 12.5), and apply them (Section 12.6). Finally, we'll explain how to use regression model predictions in SAP Analytics Cloud stories in Section 12.7.

12.1 Business Scenario

You're working as a car dealer selling secondhand cars. You need a quick and reliable price estimation for each secondhand car you currently have for sale. You can use your sales history to predict the prices of used cars on sale.

Your business question is the following: "What is a realistic price for each of my secondhand cars?" This is a regression problem because you want to predict a numerical value (the price) based on car characteristics. In this chapter, you'll learn in detail how to create and use a regression model to answer your business question.

First, you'll create a regression model based on historical sales prices. The regression model will capture the relationships between the used car characteristics and the corresponding prices. Then, you'll generate a price estimation for all secondhand cars that are currently on sale. Finally, you'll create a story. The story can display the cars currently on sale, their characteristics, and their estimated prices. You can use this story to best negotiate with your interested customers.

Note

You can find the files supporting this business scenario here: *https://sap-press.com/5771.*

12.2   Using Datasets with Regression Models

This section will walk you through the three datasets used in a regression scenario:

- Training dataset
- Application dataset
- Predictions dataset

12.2.1   Training Dataset

The training dataset provided in the *second_hand_car_sold_prices.csv* file contains 111,000 sold secondhand cars described by the 36 variables listed in Table 12.1.

Variable Name	Corresponds To
Offer ID	Unique identifier for each car offer
Sales Channel	Whether the car was sold via e-shop or car dealer
Price	Price that the car was sold for, which is the variable we want to predict
Car Type	Car type, for example, limousine or sport
Gearbox	Flags whether the gearbox is automatic or manual
Horsepower	Horsepower of the car
Car Model	Model of the car
Kilometers	Mileage of the car in kilometers
Fuel Type	Fuel type of the car
Unrepaired Damage	Flag if the car has unrepaired damage or not
Postal Code	Postal code of the car dealer, which is empty if the car is sold via e-shop
stylePackagePremiumLine	Flag whether the car design is "Premium Line" or not
stylePackageSportsLine	Flag whether the car design is "Sports Line" or not

Table 12.1 List of Variables (Training Dataset)

Variable Name	Corresponds To
Backup Camera	Flag whether the car has a backup camera or not
GPS	Flag whether a GPS system is included or not
Voice Control	Flag whether the car has voice control or not
Sport Steering Wheel	Flag whether the car has a sport steering wheel or not
Air Condition	Flag whether the car has air conditioning or not
Sport Seats	Flag whether the car has sport seats or not
Adjustable Steering Wheel	Flag whether the car has an adjustable steering wheel or not
Keyless Go	Flag whether the car has keyless go or not
Rear Seat Heating	Flag whether the car has rear seat heating or not
Warranty	Flag whether the car is sold with warranty or not
Effect Paint 2	Flag whether the car has this certain kind of effect paint or not
Heatable Mirrors	Flag whether the car has heated mirrors or not
stylePackage1	Flag whether the car has this certain kind of style package or not
stylePackage2	Flag whether the car has this certain kind of style package or not
Leather Seats	Flag whether the car has leather seats or not
Interior Premium	Flag whether the car has the premium package for the interior design or not
Interior Sport	Flag whether the car has the sports package for the interior design or not
Peculiarity Drive Assistant Systems	Describes which peculiar drive assistant systems the car has from 0 to 5, where the higher the number the more extensive the drive assistant systems are
Effect Paint 1	Flag whether the car has this certain kind of effect paint or not
Business Package	Flag whether the business package is included or not
Heatable Steering Wheel	Flag whether the car has a heated steering wheel or not
Peculiarity Interior	Describes which peculiar interior design the car has from 0 to 5, where the higher the number the more exclusive the design is
Age	Age of car

Table 12.1 List of Variables (Training Dataset) (Cont.)

To upload the training data as an SAP Analytics Cloud dataset, follow these steps:

1. Open the **Datasets** area using the left-side bar of the application.

2. Click on **Create New** and then **From a CSV or Excel File**, as shown in Figure 12.1.

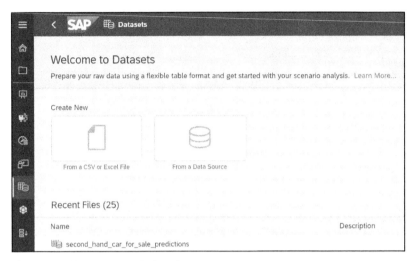

Figure 12.1 Create a New Dataset

3. Click **Select Source File**, and select the *second_hand_car_sold_prices.csv* source file on your local system. Click **Import**, and then select the location where you want the dataset to be created. Finally, click **OK** and wait for the data upload to proceed.

4. You don't need to change anything on the dataset itself. Just make sure to click the **File/Save** button. Your training dataset will appear, as shown in Figure 12.2.

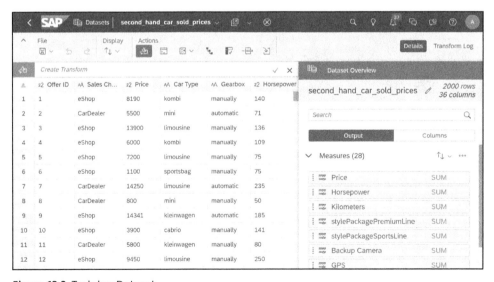

Figure 12.2 Training Dataset

12.2.2   Application Dataset

The application dataset provided in the *second_hand_car_for_sale.csv* file contains 658 secondhand cars for sale described with the same 35 characteristics just shown in Table 12.1. The price is missing from the variable list as this is what we want to predict.

To upload the application data as an SAP Analytics Cloud dataset, follow similar steps that you performed for the training data. Instead of selecting the *second_hand_car_sold_prices.csv* file, you need to select the *second_hand_car_for_sale* file. Your application dataset will appear, as shown in Figure 12.3.

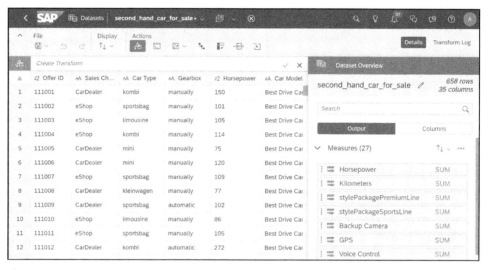

Figure 12.3 Application Dataset

12.2.3   Predictions Dataset

The predictions dataset is the one we'll get at the end of the process, when we'll be able to apply the regression model to the application dataset. The variables contained in the predictions dataset is listed in Table 12.2.

Variable Name	Variable Nature	Corresponds To
Offer ID	Dimension	Unique identifier for each car offered for sale.
Predicted Value	Measure	The predicted price for the car sale.
Explanation Rank	Dimension	For each predicted price, the explanations are ranked according to their impact (absolute strength value) on the prediction. The lower the rank, the more important the impact of the specific explanation to the predicted price.

Table 12.2 List of Variables (Predictions Dataset)

Variable Name	Variable Nature	Corresponds To
Explanation Strength	Measure	This variable represents a normalized contribution of the influencer for the predicted price. In the context of regression models, the Explanation Contribution variable is easier to understand and more useful.
Explanation Contribution	Measure	This variable is the absolute contribution of the influencer for the predicted price. It's expressed with the same unit as the price.
Explanation Influencer	Dimension	This variable contains the name of the influencer for the explanation.
Explanation Influencer Value	Dimension	This variable contains the value associated with the influencer for this prediction.

Table 12.2 List of Variables (Predictions Dataset) (Cont.)

12.3   Creating Regression Models

In this section, we'll explain how to create a regression model. We'll provide an extensive overview of the regression model settings and how they can be used to get the insights you need.

12.3.1   Create a Predictive Scenario

Regression models are created as part of regression predictive scenarios. To create a regression predictive scenario, follow these steps:

1. Click on **Predictive Scenarios** on the left side panel.
2. Under **Create New**, click the **Regression** option, as shown in Figure 12.4.

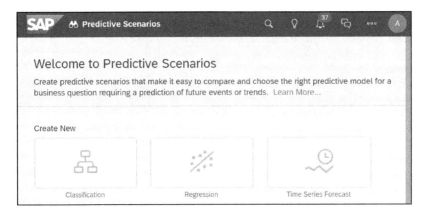

Figure 12.4 Create a New Regression Scenario

3. In the **New Predictive Scenario** dialog box that opens, when prompted to give a **Name** to your scenario, enter "Predicting Sale Prices".

Your predictive scenario is now created and contains a predictive model with empty settings (see Figure 12.5).

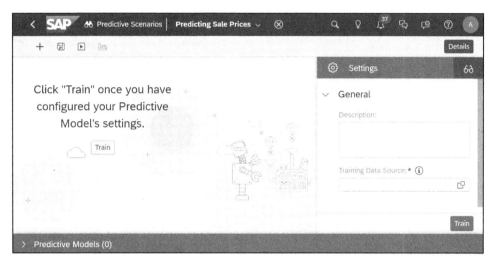

Figure 12.5 Predictive Model Is Created

The next section explains the different model settings.

12.3.2 General Settings

The general settings contain the following fields:

- **Name**
  This is created by the application. The first model in the scenario is named Model 1. When the end user creates new models, they will be named Model 2, Model 3, and so on.

- **Type**
  This shows the **Regression** value as we created a regression model.

- **Description**
  As we did when creating the scenario, you can optionally enter a description to document what each model is about. In practice, it's highly recommended that you take the time to enter precise descriptions as they will help you remember what each model you created is about. Enter the following description: "This model predicts car sale prices."

- **Training Data Source**
  Select your training dataset, **second_hand_car_sold_prices**, as the data source.

- **Edit Column Details**

  You can edit different properties of the variables that are part of the training dataset. It's important to note that any updates you're making to the dataset are permanent and can impact other files that depend upon this dataset. The options are as follows:

  - **Description**: The name of the variable as part of the dataset.

  - **Data Type**: The variable data type.

  - **Statistical Type**: The variable statistical type. Typical statistical types include continuous, nominal, and ordinal. Continuous variable values are numerical, continuous, and sortable, for example, car price. Nominal variable values are label data, for example, car type. Ordinal variables are discrete numeric columns where the relative order matters, for example, school grades.

  - **Interpret As Missing**: If missing values use a special encoding, for example, #missing, you can specify the corresponding value here.

  - **Key**: You can check this property if your training dataset contains one or several columns that uniquely describe each observation of the dataset. In our business scenario, this nicely applies to the variable *offer ID*.

Now it's your turn! In the **Training Data Source** field, make sure you select the dataset **second_hand_car_sold_prices**. Then, click on **Edit Column Details**, and check the **Key** field on variable Offer ID. Your settings should now look like Figure 12.6.

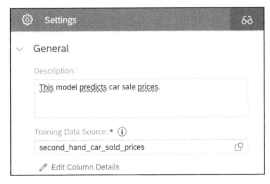

Figure 12.6 General Settings

12.3.3   Predictive Goal

The **Predictive Goal** contains one single field: **Target**. In this field, you specify the variable of your dataset containing the data that needs to be predicted. Only numeric and continuous variables are listed in this field. If the variable you want to select doesn't appear, it might have the data or statistical type incorrectly set. For our business scenario, the target will be the variable **Price**. The **Target** variable for a regression model must contain only numerical values.

In our example, we'll set the **Target** with the **Price** variable.

12.3.4 Influencers

The **Influencers** section contains two fields: **Exclude as Influencer** and **Limit Number of Influencers**. By default, all variables that aren't the target in the dataset are considered potential influencers of the target and can become part of the regression model. You might want to exclude certain influencers if they are directly correlated with the output variable. If you would keep them, your regression model would not be so helpful. Let's consider an example here. Imagine you have a variable that is named *price times 2*. If you wouldn't exclude this variable, then your regression model will likely consist of a single input variable (*price times 2*) explaining the target (*price*), which is a tautology.

The **Limit Number of Influencers** option makes it possible to limit the maximum number of input variables that can be part of the regression model. Using this setting can be helpful if you want to have a more compact and robust model, limiting the number of influencers.

In our business scenario, you won't be using these options. Now that you've filled in all the settings, as shown in Figure 12.7, you can click on the **Train** button so that your regression model gets trained.

Figure 12.7 Regression Model Settings

12.4   Understanding Regression Models

This section will help you understand regression models in more detail. First, you'll learn how to assess your model performance and then understand how the different influencers contribute to the model at various levels.

12.4.1   Assessing Model Performance

The first thing you'll notice once your regression model has been trained are the two main performance indicators found under the **Global Performance Indicators** section of the **Overview** report: **RMSE** (root mean square error) and **Prediction Confidence**. It's important that you understand these two performance indicators in detail as they evaluate the accuracy and the robustness of your regression model, respectively.

RMSE calculates the square root of the average of squared errors. Errors are defined as the difference between the values predicted by a regression model and the actual values. **RMSE** estimates how accurate the predictive model is when predicting the target value. The lower the value of **RMSE**, the more accurate the regression model is. In a regression model that perfectly predicts the expected values in every case, the **RMSE** equals 0.

The **RMSE** is expressed in the same unit of measure as the predicted value. It's then very easy to interpret and compare to the target variable. As an example, if you try to predict the sales price of secondhand cars in US dollars, then the RMSE can also be interpreted as the average amount of error that the regression model is having, also expressed in US dollars.

Prediction Confidence evaluates the capacity of the regression model to achieve a similar performance when it's applied on a new dataset if the new dataset has equivalent data characteristics as the training dataset. **Prediction Confidence** can take values between 0% and 100%. A robust regression model has a prediction confidence value closer to 100%, while a less robust regression model will have a prediction confidence value closer to 0%.

Table 12.3 explains how you should interpret the two indicators in conjunction.

	Low RMSE	High RMSE
Low Prediction Confidence	The model is accurate, but prediction accuracy won't be consistent on new data.	The model isn't accurate, and prediction accuracy won't be consistent on new data.
High Prediction Confidence	The model is accurate, and prediction accuracy will be consistent on new data.	The model isn't accurate, yet prediction accuracy will be consistent on new data.

Table 12.3 RMSE and Prediction Confidence

As an example, in Figure 12.8, in our business scenario, **RMSE** is close to 2,601 while **Prediction Confidence** equals 99.63%. The performance of the predictive model will be consistent on new data, meaning **RMSE** will be the same when applying the predictive model to new data, but the predictive model accuracy (as measured by the RMSE) can be further improved if we want to minimize the price prediction error.

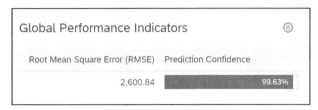

Figure 12.8 Global Performance Indicators

In Section 12.5, we'll explain in detail how to improve the model accuracy and the model confidence to get an accurate and trusted regression model.

As part of the **Overview** report, you can also notice some **Target Statistics** that show the distribution of the target (in this example, the sales car price) over the training and validation data partitions. This is meant as a control screen to make sure the training and validation partitions have similar data distributions when it comes to the target variable. This is the case in our example as **Minimum** and **Maximum** values are identical, while **Mean** and **Standard Deviation** are close. If the distributions are too different, it might be useful to check if your dataset contains enough observations. Figure 12.9 shows the **Target Statistics** for the regression model.

Target Statistics				
Data Partition	Minimum	Maximum	Mean	Standard Deviation
Training	300	44,000	8,598.88	7,007.47
Validation	300	44,000	8,655.78	6,961.41

Figure 12.9 Target Statistics

Finally, the **Predicted vs Actual** chart represents different curves:

- **Validation – Actual**
  This curve shows the actual target values (on the validation partition) on the y-axis as a function of the predicted values on the x-axis.

- **Perfect Model**
  This curve corresponds to the ideal yet hypothetical case of a predictive model that would get all the predictions right when compared to actuals. In this case, the values on the x-axis and the values on the y-axis are identical and correspond to the actual target values (on the validation partition).

- **Validation – Error Min** and **Validation – Error Max**
  These curves correspond to the error ranges for the predictions. The area between the two curves is the confidence interval of the predictions.

The chart makes it possible to analyze the fine grain of the model's accuracy. If the **Validation – Actual** and **Perfect Model** curves don't match, the predictive model isn't accurate, which you can also see from the main indicators. If they match closely, it's a sign that your model is accurate. Finally, it could be that certain parts of the curve don't match, which typically indicates difficulties to predict locally.

In Figure 12.10, we first notice that most of the curves are matching but at the beginning, when we predict very low sales prices, the cars typically sell for a higher price. We can zoom and further refine this analysis as shown in Figure 12.11.

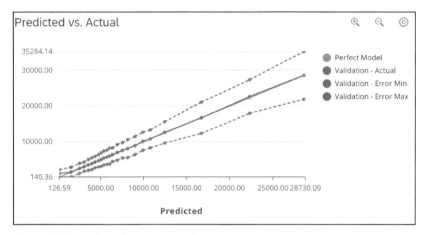

Figure 12.10 Predicted versus Actual

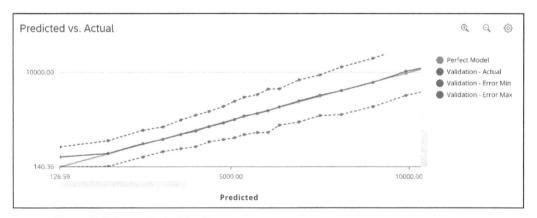

Figure 12.11 Lower End of the Curve

12.4.2   Influencer Contributions

The **Influencer Contributions** report shows the relative importance of each influencer used in the predictive model. It allows you to understand the specific contribution of each influencer to the predictive model. The most contributive influencers are the ones that best explain the target, in relationship with others.

Only the contributive influencers are displayed in this report; the variables that aren't contributing to the model aren't displayed. The sum of the influencers contributions equals 100%.

In our example shown in Figure 12.12 we can see that the most contributing influencers are **Horsepower**, **Age**, **Kilometers**, **Car Type**, and **Car Model**. The **Overview** tab displays only the five most contributive influencers, while the **Influencer Contributions** page shows all of them. Out of the 36 variables in our dataset, only 9 are contributive influencers.

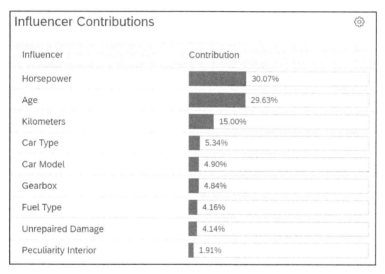

Figure 12.12 Influencer Contributions

Grouped Category Influence

The **Grouped Category Influence** report helps you dig into the influence of specific influencer categories to the predicted result. Positive values lead to increasing the value predicted by the model, while negative values lead to decreasing the value predicted by the model. The higher the absolute value of the influence category is, the higher the influence on the predicted will be. In Figure 12.13, you can see that the more recent the vehicle, the higher the predicted sales price.

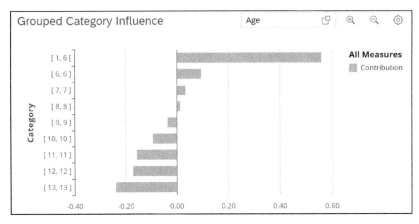

Figure 12.13 Grouped Category Influence

Grouped Category Statistics

The **Grouped Category Statistics** chart shows statistics used to calculate the influence of the categories. It can be useful to understand in more detail why a certain category has a positive or negative influence. By default, it's displayed as a scatterplot for a selected influencer with the following characteristics:

- Each point represents a category of the selected influencer.
- The x-axis displays the **Target Mean** for the grouped category, that is, in the validation data partition dataset, the mean of the target variable, considering only the grouped category.
- The y-axis shows the **Frequency** of the grouped category, that is, the percentage of rows in the validation data partition where it appeared.

In our example shown in Figure 12.14, you can see the frequency of vehicles with fewer than 6 years is the highest. This category also corresponds to the highest sale prices.

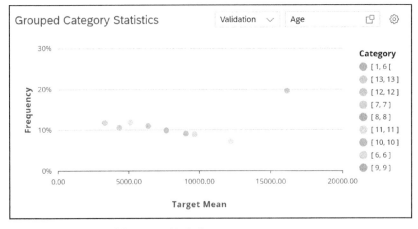

Figure 12.14 Grouped Category Statistics

12.5 Improving Regression Models

To improve a regression model, you should investigate similar strategies to those we described in Chapter 11, Section 11.5. First, you need to check that your regression model isn't too perfect. This could be caused by a leak variable. Then, if the RMSE is too high and/or the prediction confidence of your model is too low, you'll need to improve them.

Table 12.4 summarizes your possible next steps.

	Low RMSE	High RMSE
Low Prediction Confidence	You need to add more rows to the source dataset.	You need to add explanatory variables and more rows to the source dataset.
High Prediction Confidence	The model is safe for use and doesn't need to be improved.	You need to add explanatory variables into the source dataset.

Table 12.4 Guidance to Improve a Regression Model

The following sections will quickly walk you through steps you can take to improve your regression model whether for accuracy or robustness.

12.5.1 Improving Model Accuracy

The model accuracy is measured by the RMSE. If you consider the RMSE of the model as too high, you'll need to find additional input variables that can explain the variation of the target variable. So, you need to identify additional, relevant variables in the source dataset and make sure they will be considered influential in the regression model. This task is what data scientists typically define as feature engineering. You can try to leverage additional data sources and derive calculated columns from existing columns. These new variables must bring additional information compared to the variables that already exist in the dataset; avoid introducing redundant information in this process.

12.5.2 Improving Model Robustness

A low prediction confidence in most cases is caused by a small number of rows in the training dataset. If you consider the prediction confidence of your regression model as being too low, you'll need to add more rows to the training dataset. This provides more data points to learn from and increases the model's robustness. In our business scenario, the prediction confidence is very high as the dataset contains enough rows for the model to be trained on. In other cases, more rows might be needed.

Finally, if the model has a lot of influencers (say, more than 20), you can improve the model robustness by reducing the number of influencers in the model. Intuitively, when using too many influencers, the model is lost in the details and has difficulties generalizing what it learned to new data. The easiest way to reduce the number of influencers is to use the **Limit Number Of Influencers** option.

12.5.3   The Quality versus Robustness Trade-Off

Some of the model improvement advice may sound contradictory. You must add variables to improve the model quality, whereas you must remove influencers to improve the robustness. In other words, improving the model quality may degrade the robustness and vice versa. Improving a model is about finding the best possible trade-off between the model accuracy and the model robustness. When improving one of these measures significantly, you should be careful not to impact the other one negatively.

12.6   Applying Regression Models

Once you've created and improved your regression model, you're ready to use it to generate predictions. In the toolbar of the predictive model, click on the factory-like icon **Apply Predictive Model**. A dialog will open, as shown in Figure 12.15.

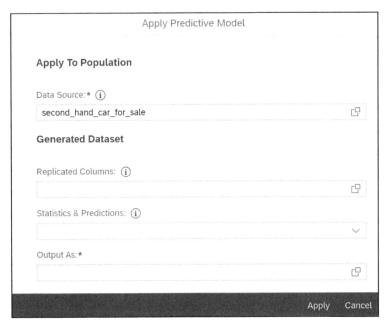

Figure 12.15 Apply the Regression Model

The dialog includes two main parts, **Apply To Population** and **Generated Dataset**.

The **Apply To Population** part is about selecting the application dataset. We trained the regression model based on historical car sales. We now want to apply the model to our cars that are currently for sale (see Section 12.2). Therefore, we select the dataset **second_hand_car_for_sale**.

The **Generated Dataset** part is where we specify the content of the dataset that will contain the predictions. In this book, we chose to call it the predictions dataset.

First, you can choose to replicate some columns of the application dataset into the predictions dataset. Here, you don't need this. As you previously checked the **Key** field of the **Offer_ID** column, it will be automatically replicated. So, you should leave the **Replicated Columns** field empty.

In the **Statistics & Predictions** field, you can select several types of statistics or predictions that will be included in the predictions dataset. The most relevant ones include the following:

- **Apply Date**
  The date when the model was applied.

- **Train Date**
  The date when the model was last trained.

- **Outlier Indicator**
  For each row of the application dataset, **Outlier Indicator** will be equal to **1** if the row is considered an outlier with respect to the target; otherwise, it will be equal to **0**. An observation is considered an outlier when the prediction error is greater than three times the average prediction error found on similar observations.

- **Predicted Value**
  For each row of the application dataset, **Predicted Value** has been predicted for the target that will be part of the predictions dataset.

- **Prediction Explanations**
  For each row of the application dataset, **Prediction Explanations** is a set of explanations for the prediction that will be part of the predictions dataset. **Predictions Explanations** provide reasons for individual predictions. We'll come back to this in more detail in Section 12.7.

In most cases, you want to select **Predicted Value** as this is the most desirable outcome of a regression model. In addition, if you want to have more details and reasons around individual predictions, select **Prediction Explanations.** The other options can also be useful but are more specific.

Finally, filling in the **Output As** field opens a dialog (see Figure 12.16) that makes it possible to save the predictions dataset.

Once you click **Apply**, the dataset *second_hand_car_for_sale_predictions* will be created, which you can open right away (see Figure 12.17). Table 12.5 explains the list of variables that are part of the predictions dataset.

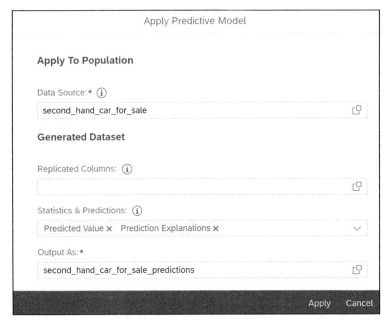

Figure 12.16 Predictive Model Ready to Be Applied

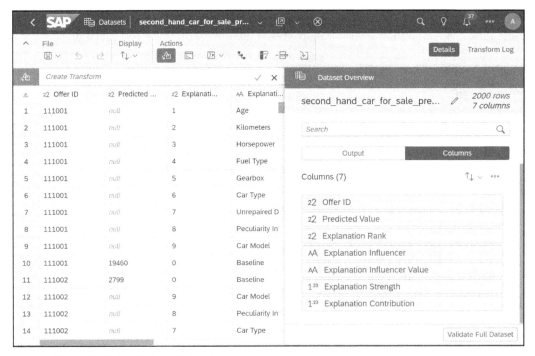

Figure 12.17 Predictions Dataset

Variable Name	Variable Nature	Corresponds To
Offer ID	Dimension	Unique identifier for each car offered for sale.
Predicted Value	Measure	Predicted price for the car sale.
Explanation Rank	Dimension	For each predicted price, the explanations are ranked according to their impact (absolute strength value) on the prediction. The lower the rank, the more important the impact of the specific explanation to the predicted price.
Explanation Strength	Measure	This variable represents a normalized contribution of the influencer for the predicted price. In the context of regression models, Explanation Contribution is easier to understand and more useful.
Explanation Contribution	Measure	This variable is the absolute contribution of the influencer for the predicted price. It's expressed with the same unit as the price.
Explanation Influencer	Dimension	This variable contains the name of the influencer for the explanation.
Explanation Influencer Value	Dimension	This variable contains the value associated with the influencer for this prediction.

Table 12.5 List of Variables (Predictions Dataset)

12.7   Enriching Stories with Regression Insights

Once you've created your dataset containing predictions, you can start including insights in your stories. The top insights you can derive from a regression model are the predicted value and the prediction explanations. We're going to examine both in detail and see how to practically include them in stories.

12.7.1   Predicted Value

As we explained, the **Predicted Value** statistic provides the values predicted for each row. Here, it corresponds to the predicted price for each car for sale. Using this information is easy as you can report on the entities of interest (car offers) and the predicted value as a measure.

Let's create a table that shows the predicted price for each car for sale. Follow these steps:

1. Create a new story by clicking the **Stories** icon 🔲 in the SAP Analytics Cloud navigation bar.

2. Choose the type of layout you want for your story, selecting **Canvas** under **Create New**.

3. You'll be prompted to select a **Design Mode Type**. Keep the **Optimized Design Experience** choice selected (default choice).

4. Click the **Insert · Table** 🔲 icon in the top toolbar.

5. You'll be prompted for the selection of a data source. Select your prediction dataset **second_hand_car_for_sale_predictions**.

6. The **Builder** panel is opened to the right of the screen. Under **Filters**, click **Measures (1)**, and set the value to **Predicted Value** instead of **Explanation Contribution**.

7. Click **Add Dimensions** under **Rows**, and select **Offer ID**.

8. In the header or your table, click the ⬜ icon, click **Edit Drill Limitation**, and set the drill limitation to **Unlimited**.

9. Resize your table to make sure the various fields are visible. Your table should now look like the one presented in Figure 12.18. Don't forget to save your story.

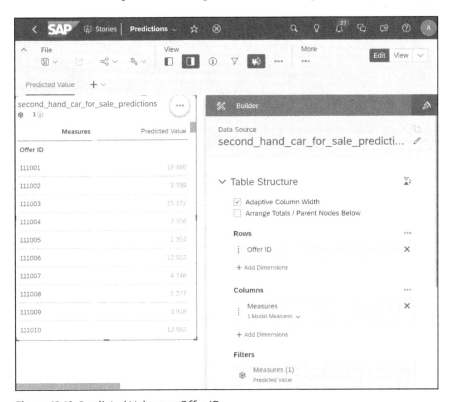

Figure 12.18 Predicted Value per Offer ID

12.7.2 Prediction Explanations

Prediction explanations can provide detailed explanations for each predicted value. The simplest way to expose prediction explanations in a story is to create a waterfall chart side to the table we just created for predicted value. Then, using the **Linked Analysis** feature, clicking on each **Offer ID** in a table will provide additional details to the explanations underneath the predicted value.

Let's walk through the step-by-step instructions:

1. Create two calculated dimensions, *rank* and *explanation*. To create both calculated dimensions, you'll first need to click **Add Dimensions** and then click the **Create Calculated Dimension** entry in the **Builder**, as shown in Figure 12.19.

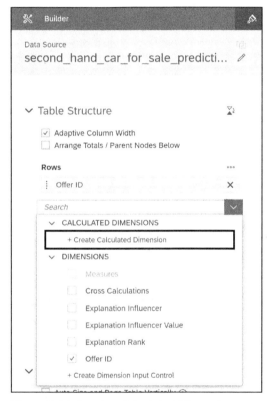

Figure 12.19 Create a Calculated Dimension

2. Set the dialog to create the calculated dimension **rank**, as shown in Figure 12.20. The rank calculated dimension will help us properly order the rows as part of the waterfall chart. This is the formula that can be used to create the calculated dimension *rank*:

   IF(LENGTH(ToText([d/"second_hand_car_for_sale_predictions":Explanation_Rank])) = 1; CONCAT("0";ToText([d/"second_hand_car_for_sale_predictions":Explanation_Rank])); ToText([d/"second_hand_car_for_sale_predictions":Explanation_Rank]))

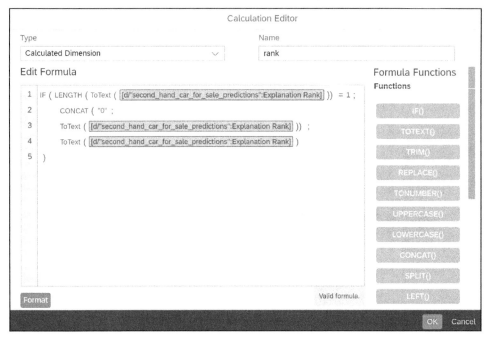

Figure 12.20 Calculated Dimension Rank

3. In a similar way, create the calculated dimension **explanation**, as shown in Figure 12.21. The **explanation** calculated dimension will help us have easy-to-understand labels for each row. The **explanation** dimension concatenates the rank text, the influencer name, and the influencer value into a single text.

   This is the formula that can be used to create the calculated dimension *explanation*:

   CONCAT([d/"rank"].[p/ID]; CONCAT(" - "; CONCAT([d/"second_hand_car_for_sale_ predictions":Explanation_Influencer].[p/Explanation_Influencer]; CONCAT(" = "; [d/"second_hand_car_for_sale_predictions":Explanation_Influencer_Value].[p/ Explanation_Influencer_Value]))))

4. Once you're done with the creation of the calculated dimensions, don't forget to remove them from under the **Rows** section of the table as they won't be needed in the table.

5. Next, you'll add a waterfall chart. Click the **Insert · Chart** icon ⊟ in the top story toolbar.

6. Set the chart options in the following way, as shown in Figure 12.22:

   – In the **Currently Selected Chart** dropdown, select **Waterfall**.

   – Set **Explanation Contribution** as the measure.

   – Set **Offer ID** and **explanation** as dimensions.

   – Change the color palette to green, pink, and black.

Figure 12.21 Calculated Dimension Explanation

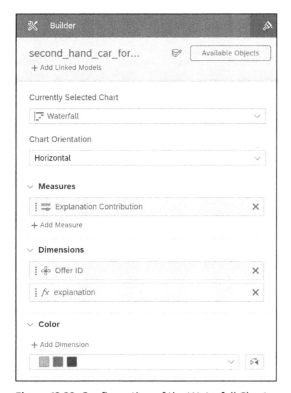

Figure 12.22 Configuration of the Waterfall Chart

7. You'll now take advantage of the **Linked Analysis** feature so that when you click a row in the table, the **Offer ID** displayed in the waterfall chart will change.

8. Right-click on the table, and select **Linked Analysis • Settings** in the menu.

9. Configure the **Linked Analysis** panel by choosing **All Widgets on the Page** and selecting the **Filter on Data Point Selection** checkbox, as shown in Figure 12.23.

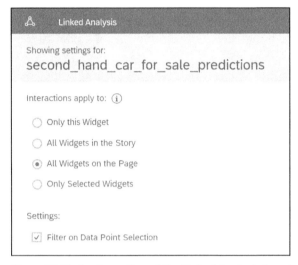

Figure 12.23 Configuration of the Linked Analysis Panel

10. Set the number styling format values in the **Number Format** section, as shown in Figure 12.24. In particular, select the **Unformatted** option under **Scale** and set the value of **Decimal Places** to 0.

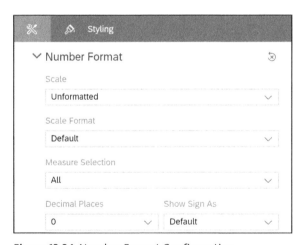

Figure 12.24 Number Format Configuration

11. To present the final result in the story, choose the concrete example of **Offer ID 111001**, as shown in Figure 12.25.

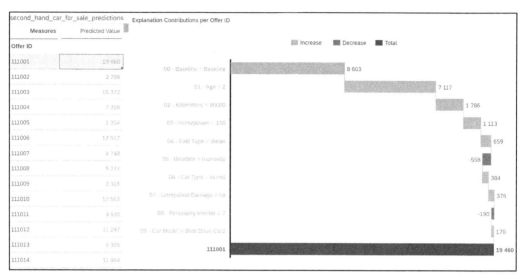

Figure 12.25 Using Prediction Explanations in Stories

We first notice the **Baseline** entry. Independent of the use case and dataset you may use, the explanations for a specific prediction will always contain a baseline generated influencer associated with the rank 0. This is the base value for any prediction. The baseline is simply the average of the target (in our case, the average car sales prices) as seen in the training dataset.

The other bars of the waterfall chart represent influencers of the dataset, and the associated value is an increase or a decrease that can be interpreted in the unit of the car sales price.

Using the example **Offer ID 111001**, we can see the following:

- The average price is 8,603. This is the basis for the prediction.
- The influencer with the highest impact is the car age. It increases the predicted price by 7,117 as the car is newer.
- The second most impacting influencer is the number of kilometers. It increases the predicted price by 1,786.
- You can also see that the car has a manual gearbox, which decreases the predicted price by 558.
- The final predicted price is equal to 19,460.

12.8   Summary

In this chapter, we walked you through automated regression models, including which datasets they use and how to create, understand, and improve them if needed. Finally, you've seen how to apply them to get predicted values and prediction explanations that can be consumed in stories.

In the next chapter, we'll examine the underlying data science behind classification and regression models.

Chapter 13
The Data Science behind Classification Models and Regression Models

We hope the preceding chapters have sparked an interest in learning about the machine learning techniques used behind the scenes. Or, if you're already well versed in the machine learning domain, here's your opportunity to compare smart predict to the techniques you know.

This chapter unveils the cover on the automated data science techniques used to generate classification and regression models. We'll start with the fundamentals of fitting a model function in Section 13.1, and then we'll establish some prerequisites that enable machine learning algorithm fitting such functions in Section 13.2. We'll provide an overview of the principles that underlie the evaluation of a classification model in Section 13.3, and then we'll provide some details about how it's implemented in smart predict in Section 13.4. Finally, we'll provide more details about how some of the classification outputs are generated in Section 13.5.

Note that Section 13.1 to Section 13.3 provide general information about machine learning. The concepts explained here aren't specific to smart predict.

> **Classification versus Regression**
>
> Most of the explanations provided in this chapter apply both to classification and regression models.

13.1 Fitting a Predictive Function

Classification and regression models are primarily functions $f(x_1, ..., x_n) = y$, where $x_1, ..., x_n$ represents the characteristics of an observation, and y is the predicted value. "Predicted value" is meant here in a broad sense; that is, it can be the predicted numeric value for a regression model, the probability of belonging to the positive target category, or even the predicted category for a classification model. Similarly, the function must be understood as a process that takes inputs and returns a value: the model doesn't necessarily hold an explicit representation of a mathematical function. Figure 13.1 illustrates a classification model that would predict attrition for customers based on the tenure and subscription price of a customer.

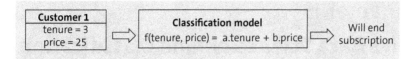

Figure 13.1 Predictive Function Example

Training a classification or regression model is fitting the f function, that is, finding the parameters for f (a and b in the Figure 13.1 example) that allows for minimizing the error made by the model. This is done by minimizing the value of another function, called the *loss function* (or cost function), that measures the amount of error made by the model. The loss function is chosen before training the model depending on the nature of the model (classification or regression) and many criteria such as the ability of the function to handle outliers, the need to penalize the model larger errors, and the need to take the error sign into account (is a positive error equivalent to a negative error?). There are many state-of-the-art loss functions to choose from.

Many algorithms exist to fit the predictive function. Here are a few of the most famous classification/regression algorithms: logistic regression, naïve Bayes, k-nearest neighbors, decision tree, random forest, support vector machine, neural networks, and so on.

You may think that the goal of a good classification or regression algorithm is to find a function that perfectly separates the observations of the training dataset. But reality can be complex, and fitting a complex reality may require a complex function. A complex function can lead to what is called *overfitting*, while, on the other hand, overly simple functions can lead to *underfitting*. Let's take a closer look at what these terms mean:

- **Overfitting**
  Overfitting occurs when the predictive model learned patterns are too specific to the training dataset. The model is very good on the training data but isn't able to generalize what it has learned to new observations. The model isn't robust; it's performance on observations that don't belong to the training dataset is bad. In Figure 13.2, the overfitting model is using a complex function that perfectly separates the positive and the negative cases on the training dataset, but it's unlikely to perform well on new observations close to the "border."

- **Underfitting**
  Underfitting occurs when the model has failed to learn patterns from the training data. The model performs poorly on the observations of the training dataset and on the new observations. Underfitting can occur because the data doesn't allow the model to learn properly (not the right variables, not enough observations, etc.) or, as illustrated by the underfitting model in Figure 13.2, because the function used by the model is too simple. In this example, the behavior to be predicted is too complex to be modeled by a linear function.

A good model must not overfit or underfit. The robust model shown in Figure 13.2 is a middle ground between overfitting and underfitting. Unlike the underfitting model, it's complex enough to consider the major patterns of the training dataset, but unlike the overfitting model, it remains simple enough to have the chance to generalize well on new data. Section 13.3.3 explains in further detail how the robustness of the model is evaluated.

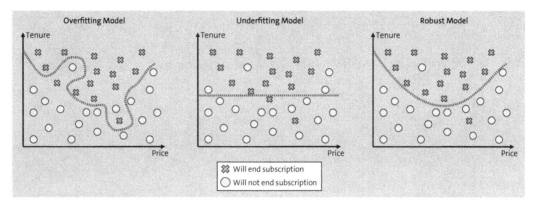

Figure 13.2 Overfitting, Underfitting, and Robust Models

The size of the training dataset impacts the performance of the model in the following ways:

- When provided with more observations, the predictive model can discover relationships between the target and the other variables it may have missed otherwise.

- By learning from more observations, the model is better able to generalize and is less likely to overfit.

- By learning from more examples, chances increase to encounter outliers and observation with data quality issues, which can have a negative impact on model performance.

These considerations lead to the following recommendations:

- When possible, favor a larger dataset (dataset with more observations) when training a model. The more complex the predictive model, the more observations are needed. One of the most important parameters impacting the model complexity, besides the selected classification or regression algorithm itself, is the number of variables used in the training dataset. The most popular rule to estimate the minimum number of observations in a training dataset is the 10 times rule: You need at least 10 times more observations than variables in the training dataset. You must consider this a strict minimum—the more observations, the better.

- Identify and exclude low-quality observations. Examples of low-quality observations are observations with missing values, observations with some values that are

289

obviously out of range (e.g., age can't be a negative value), or, generally speaking, any observation that contains values that you know don't reflect reality.

However, it's not possible to create a perfect model just by adding more rows to the training dataset. Given a classification or regression algorithm and a set of variables, there is a limit to the amount of information that can be extracted. Increasing the training dataset size will only help approach this limit, as shown in Figure 13.3.

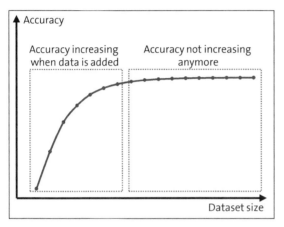

Figure 13.3 Evolution of the Model Accuracy Compared to the Training Dataset Size

13.2   Prerequisites to Generating a Model

Machine learning requires careful selection and preparation of the dataset before generating a model. Here are the main prerequisites to generating a model:

- **Basic data preparation**
  Classification algorithms usually consume a single dataset in tabular format, with one row per observation, meaning that if you have multiple data sources (possibly multiple tables or CSV files), they must first be merged into a single dataset. Then, you would probably want to calculate additional variables that can be used by the classification model to find relationships with the target (feature engineering).

- **Data cleaning**
  With machine learning, the results are only as good as the data. To get acceptable results, you need to provide properly cleaned data. Data cleaning encompasses many data modifications such as replacing the missing values, fixing labels errors, and so on.

- **Data encoding**
  Machine learning algorithms need the values of the variables to comply with some specific representation. The exact requirements depend on the exact algorithm. The process of transforming the raw values into values the algorithm can use is called

data encoding. Most algorithms require the categorical values to be encoded into numeric values. Different methods exist for that. Some algorithms also require the numeric values to be *scaled* so they are in a comparable range, and a variable such as salary isn't considered as more important than age just because the values are higher.

- **Have enough observations**
  A classification model requires a lot of data to be accurate and robust. This is explained in more detail in Section 13.1.

- **Have enough variables**
  As explained in Section 13.1, a classification or regression model learns relationships between the target and the other variables in the training dataset. The more columns in the training dataset, the more chances for the model to find these relationships. But keep in mind that accidental correlations exist and that a model has no way to distinguish a legitimate correlation from an accidental one. If you feed a model with thousands of variables, it will certainly find correlation, but most of them will be purely accidental. The rule of thumb here is to use your business knowledge to evaluate if it makes sense to include a certain variable in the training dataset.

13.3   Evaluating the Model Performance

When you create a classification or regression model, you obviously want to know how good it is. Evaluating the model's performance is one of the most important steps of a predictive project. While it looks simple compared to the creation of the model, this task can prove tricky. In this section, we'll first introduce some standard performance indicators, and then we'll discuss how the future performance of a predictive model can be evaluated using the hold-out technique.

13.3.1   Performance Indicators for Classification Models

First, to measure the error, we need a reference dataset where the actual value of the target is known, such as the training dataset. We can apply the model on this reference dataset and, for each observation, compare the prediction to the actual value for the corresponding observation. We count one error every time the predicted category is different from the actual category. This method is illustrated by Figure 13.4. Note that to be able to reason on the predicted category (as opposed to reasoning on the predicted probability), we've ordered the observations by increasing predicted probability and have applied a decision threshold (0.5, in this example).

Now that we can identify classification errors, the classification rate (or accuracy) is certainly the first performance metric most people would calculate. The accuracy answers the question, "What is the proportion of observations that are classified correctly?" It's simply the number of observations correctly classified divided by the total number of observations.

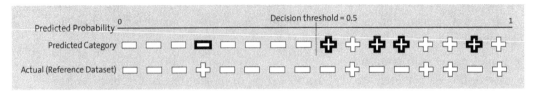

Figure 13.4 Predicted versus Actual

But the classification rate can be misleading. Think about a fraud detection scenario where transactions must be classified as fraudulent or nonfraudulent. Fraud is relatively rare, and 99% of the transactions are nonfraudulent. A naïve model that would always predict that the transactions are nonfraudulent, would never detect any fraudulent transaction. Such a model would be useless in practice. Yet, the classification rate for this model would be 99%. The classification rate isn't the right way to evaluate the performance of the model. We're more interested in the sensitivity indicator, which tells us the proportion of all the fraudulent transactions that have been detected. Like many other performance indicators, it can be derived from the confusion matrix.

As a reminder a confusion matrix (see Table 13.1) is a simple 2 × 2 table that shows how many predictions are correct and incorrect for each category of the target.

		Predicted Class	
		Positive	**Negative**
Actual Class	**Positive**	■ Correctly predicted as positive ■ True positives (TP) ■ Hit	■ Wrongly predicted as negative ■ False negatives (FN) ■ Miss
	Negative	■ Wrongly predicted as positive ■ False positives (FP) ■ False alarm	■ Correctly predicted as negative ■ True negatives (TN) ■ Correct rejection

Table 13.1 Confusion Matrix

A large variety of performance metrics can be derived from the confusion matrix. Each metric is relevant for different purposes. Which one you should use depends on the specific requirement of your predictive use case. Table 13.2 shows the most common performance metrics and explains when they should be used.

Metric	Definition and Interpretation	Formula
Classification rate	Percentage of correct answers. Use it when false negatives and false positive are equally important.	$(TP + TN) \div (TP + TN + FN + FP)$
Sensitivity (aka recall or hit rate)	Percentage of positive events that were predicted. Use it when identifying a maximum of positive cases is the main objective. False alarms (FP) are preferred over misses (FN). For instance, you may want to optimize the sensitivity, when trying to detect a medical condition that would cause short-term death. In such cases, you don't want to miss positive cases. When optimizing the sensitivity, be sure that the specificity and the precision always remain within an acceptable range.	$TP \div (TP + FN)$
Specificity	Percentage of negative events that were predicted as negative. Use it when you want to minimize the number of negative cases incorrectly classified. For instance, you may want to optimize the specificity when trying to detect a medical condition and avoid proposing potentially harmful treatment to healthy individuals. In such cases, it's more important to correctly identify the negative cases than the positive cases. When optimizing the specificity, be sure that the sensitivity and the precision always remain within an acceptable range.	$TN \div (TN + FP)$
Precision	The percentage of predicted positive that are really positive. Use it when you need to be confident that the cases classified as positive are positive. False alarms aren't acceptable. For instance, when identifying spam emails, you usually want to optimize the precision, so you don't direct legitimate emails to the spam folder. When optimizing precision, be sure that the sensitivity and the specificity always remain within an acceptable range.	$TP \div (TP + FP)$

Table 13.2 Performance Metrics Derived from the Confusion Matrix

Metric	Definition and Interpretation	Formula
F1 score	Synthetic accuracy metric that combines precision and sensitivity. Use it when you consider that false positives and false negatives are equally important.	$2 \times Precision \times Sensitivity \div (Precision + Sensitivity) = TP \div (TP + 0.5(FP + FN))$
Fall-out	Percentage of negative events that were predicted positive. Use it as a complement to sensitivity and precision when you need to avoid false alarms. For instance, when predicting spam emails, the fall-out represents the proportion of legitimate emails that are wrongly detected as spam.	$FP \div (FP + TN)$

Table 13.2 Performance Metrics Derived from the Confusion Matrix (Cont.)

All the performance indicators we've mentioned so far depend on a specific decision threshold, but some global performance indicators also exist. The most widely used one is the *area under the ROC curve* (AUC). As stated in the name, the AUC measures the area under a curve called *receiver operating characteristic* (ROC). The ROC curve is a chart showing *sensitivity* (or *true positive rate*), plotted against the *fall-out* (or *false positive rate*), for several values of the decision threshold. This represents the trade-off between the true positive (hits) and the false positive (false alarms). In Figure 13.5, you can see that model 1 is better than model 2: The AUC for model 1 (the area under the **Model 1** curve) is greater than the AUC for model 2 (the area under the **Model 2** curve).

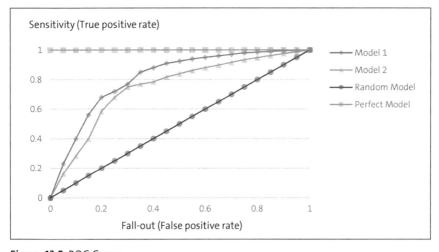

Figure 13.5 ROC Curve

The AUC is in the range [0 ; 1]. An AUC of 0 denotes a model that misclassified all the observations. An AUC of 1 denotes a model that classified all the observations correctly.

Performance Reference

What is the minimum sensitivity, accuracy, or AUC value your model must reach to be considered good enough? Some absolute performance references exist (though not for all the performance indicators), but the model performance indicators are usually used for model comparison. It's not possible to tell if a sensitivity of 0.6 is good or bad. But, if the model sensitivity is what matters to you, you can tell that a model with a sensitivity of 0.6 is better than one with a sensitivity of 0.5. The performance indicators can also be used to check if the model meets some business requirements; for instance, the stakeholder may decide on a maximum percentage of false alarms that must not be exceeded.

13.3.2   Performance Indicators for Regression Models

For a regression model, the prediction error made for one observation is the difference between the actual value of the target for the observation (as available in the training dataset) and the predicted value for the observation. This is summarized by the following expression, where e_i is the prediction error for the observation i, y_i is the actual target value for the observation I, and $\hat{y}_i$ is the predicted target value for the observation i:

$$e_i = y_i - \hat{y}_i$$

Note that as the predicted value can be greater or lower than the actual, the error can be either positive or negative.

Based on the prediction error made for each observation, it's possible to calculate various performance indicators to summarize the overall error made by the regression model. Smart predict provides several standard performance indicators for regression as follows (where e_i is the prediction error for the observation i, and n is the number of observations):

- **Root mean squared error (RMSE)**
  The RMSE is the square root of the mean of squared differences between the predicted and the actual values. The RMSE is expressed in the same unit as the predicted value. The formula is as follows:

$$RMSE = \sqrt{\frac{1}{n}\sum_{i=1}^{n}(e_i)^2}$$

The lower the RMSE, the better the performance of the time series forecasting model. A RMSE of 0 denotes a perfect model.

Squaring the error gives more weight to larger errors while preventing positive errors to be compensated by negative errors as only positive terms are summed.

- **Maximum error (LINF)**
  The maximum error is the highest absolute prediction error across all the observations. It tells you the largest error made by the regression model regardless of the sign of the error. The formula is as follows:

  $Maximum\ error = max_{i=1}^{n}(|e_i|)$

- **Error mean**
  The error mean is the average of the prediction error across all the observations. The formula is as follows:

$$Error\ mean = \frac{1}{n}\sum_{i=1}^{n} e_i$$

When using the error mean, you must keep in mind that both negative and positive errors are summed and therefore can compensate mutually. An error mean equal to 0 doesn't imply a perfect model.

13.3.3   Evaluating the Future Performance of the Model

As mentioned in Section 13.3.1, we need a reference dataset to measure the model's performance. So far, we've assumed that the training dataset would be this reference dataset. Using the training dataset as a reference tells us how well the model explains the data used to train it. This is what we call the model quality, and it's reflected by the **Predictive Power** in smart predict (Section 13.4.4).

Unfortunately, this tells us nothing about the model robustness; that is, its ability to provide good results on new observations. If the performance on the training data reflects the performance you can expect on new data, it's too optimistic. This can be illustrated by considering an extreme case of overfitting (Section 13.1). The model likely would perform poorly on new data, but because we're testing our model only on observations that have been used to train it, the performance metric would tell us that the model is very good.

There are plenty of techniques to evaluate the future performance of a classification model. The most common of these techniques and arguably the simplest is called *hold-out*. The hold-out technique consists of splitting the training data into two sets:

- A major part of the data is assigned to a set usually referred to as the *train set*. The train set is used to effectively train the predictive model.

- The remaining data is assigned to a set usually referred to as the *test set*. The test set is used to evaluate the performance of the predictive model (or "test" it).

Commonly, 70% to 80% of the training data is used to effectively train the model and the remaining 20% to 30% is kept for the performance evaluation. Typically, the observations are assigned to each partition randomly, but more advanced techniques also exist. It may be tempting to use a very small test set to get more data to train the model. But, if the test dataset isn't large enough, the estimated performance can be too optimistic.

The performance of the model on the test dataset is a good estimation of the future performance of the model under the assumption that the behavior to be predicted hasn't changed between the moment the model was trained and the moment the model was used.

Some classification algorithms have *hyperparameters*, that is, parameters to configure the algorithm itself. Hyperparameters are typically used to configure the complexity of the function to be used to fit the data. Determining the best values for the hyperparameters is empirical: The performance must be tested for different values of the hyperparameters. Using the test set both to optimize the hyperparameters and test the resulting model may lead to a biased evaluation of the performance. The final model must be tested on data that hasn't been used to tweak the hyperparameters. This is why, in addition to the test set, a *validation set* is introduced to evaluate performance during the tuning of the hyperparameters.

It's up to the data scientist to use their knowledge to choose a validation technique and a specific setup for this technique (size of the test set, method of selection of the observation, etc.) depending on the specificities of the data at hand.

13.4   End-to-End Automated Modeling

In the previous section, we discussed some foundations of data science for classification and regression. This is only scratching the surface, but we can already sense the complexity of creating a proper classification model and all the time-consuming work it involves. Next, we'll explain how smart predict hides most of this complexity from its users.

13.4.1   Automated Data Encoding

Machine learning algorithms usually have specific requirements about how data values are represented. Transforming the raw values into values that can be processed by a specific algorithm is called *data encoding*. This section explains how the smart predict regression algorithm automatically handles the data encoding phase.

Categorical Variables

Predictive algorithms can't process categorical values directly. Such values require to be transformed into a numeric value through a process called *data encoding*.

Smart predict uses an encoding technique for the categorical variables called *label encoding*. The values of the variable are sorted alphabetically, and each value is assigned to a numeric value corresponding to its rank. Table 13.3 illustrates the label encoding method for the marital-status variables.

Raw Category	Encoded Category
Divorced	0
Married	1
Never Married	2

Table 13.3 Category Encoding for the Variable Marital-Status

Numeric Variables

The classification algorithm of smart predict is based on the gradient boosting technique (Section 13.4.3), which relies on decision trees. Decision trees don't require numeric values to be scaled so they are in comparable ranges. The numeric values in smart predict are processed without specific transformation.

13.4.2   Data Partitions

With smart predict you don't have to take care of the model validation. smart predict automatically assesses the model performance using a hold-out technique. The training dataset is automatically partitioned into a train (75%) and a validation set (25%).

So that more data is available for the train set, smart predict creates only a validation set and no test set. Because only one hyperparameter is tweaked by smart predict, the impact of the model remains limited. Therefore, the performance on the validation set is a good estimation of the performance on the test set.

13.4.3   Gradient Boosting

The classification and regression algorithms of smart predict are based on the *gradient boosting* technique. Gradient boosting belongs to the family of *ensemble methods* and more specifically to the subfamily of *boosting methods*. Ensemble methods combine multiple simple models called weak learners. The intuition behind this is that combining a multitude of simple models will provide more accurate and robust predictions than one "strong" and complex model. A weak learner is a model that alone is just a bit better than a random model. Boosting methods are a subset of the ensemble methods where the weak learners are created sequentially to compensate the weakness of the previous weak leaners.

When using the gradient boosting technique, the weak learners are decision tree models. Before going any further in the explanation of the gradient boosting technique, let's understand what decision trees are. Decision trees are models that provide predictions by iteratively splitting the data based on the values of the variables in a dataset. A decision tree can be represented as a tree where each nonleaf node is a variable of the training dataset, each leaf node is a prediction, and each branch is a decision about the value of the variable in the parent node. A prediction is calculated by following a path in the tree until a leaf is reached. Decision trees can be used both for classification and regression.

Figure 13.6 shows an example of a decision tree for an attrition use case where only the customer tenure and the subscription price variables are available. With this tree, the prediction will be "will end subscription" for a customer where tenure = 3 and subscription price = 6.

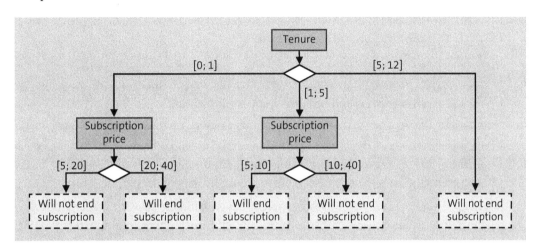

Figure 13.6 Decision Tree Example

As a boosting technique, gradient boosting trains several decision tree models sequentially and combines them to produce a prediction. Let's explain that process in detail:

1. **Bootstrap model**
   A first weak learner is created. This first weak learner is specific as it's not even a decision tree. It's a naïve model that predicts a constant value. This value is the target average for a regression and the probability of the positive target class for a classification. Obviously, this first model makes a lot of errors, but more weak learners will be created to compensate.

2. **Calculating the pseudo residuals**
   For all the observations, *pseudo residuals* are calculated. A pseudo residual is simply the difference between the value predicted by the model and the actual value. For a classification model, the predicted probability is compared to a probability corresponding to the actual category: 0 for the negative category and 1 for the positive category.

3. **Decision tree weak learner**
   A decision tree model is trained using the pseudo residuals as the target: The second weak learner and all the subsequent weak learners predict the remaining error, not

the original target. In other words, this model predicts corrections of the previous prediction.

4. **Prediction**

   The bootstrap model and the decision tree model are combined by summing the predictions of both models.

Using the combined model, pseudo residuals are calculated, and a new weak learner is trained on these residuals. This process is repeated until the error becomes negligible or the maximum number of trees is reached.

The prediction at a given iteration is the sum of the prediction at the previous iteration with the prediction of the new decision tree created on the residual of the previous iteration. This can be summarized as follows:

$$f_i(x) = f_{i-1}(x) + \mu \times h_i(x)$$

Here, $f_i(x)$ is the prediction at the iteration i, $h_i(x)$ is the prediction of the decision tree trained on the residuals at iteration i, and μ is the *learning rate*.

The learning rate reduces the contribution of the added tree to the prediction. This helps reduce the risk of overfitting. The learning rate ranges between 0 and 1. A smaller learning rate increases the processing time because more trees are needed to fit the data correctly but is usually preferable to reduce the risk of overfitting.

The processes of creating a classification or a regression model with gradient boosting are identical. The only difference is the loss function: usually mean squared error (MSE) for a regression and log-likelihood for a classification.

Gradient boosting has several parameters whose purpose is to avoid overfitting:

- **Number of iterations (= number of trees) limit**
  Having too many trees in the model can lead to overfitting. Setting a maximum number of trees allows for stopping the learning process before too many trees have been created.

- **Trees depth limit**
  Deeper trees have more complex decision rules, which can be compared to a complex fitting function. Trees that are too deep may overfit.

- **Shrinkage**
  The learning rate limits the risk of overfitting by reducing the contribution of the decision trees created on the residuals.

- **Minimum number of observations in leaves**
  Each leaf of the tree (node corresponding to a prediction) corresponds to a specific number of observations in the training dataset. A leaf node with few observations corresponds intuitively to a decision rule that applies to few observations and is possibly too specific. Overfitting can be reduced by ignoring splits that lead to nodes with fewer observations than the provided threshold.

- **Minimum loss improvement threshold**
  The goal of this threshold is to reduce a tree's complexity. The tree is pruned by removing branches that don't reduce loss by at least the specified threshold.

The values for these parameters are determined automatically and aren't exposed in smart predict.

13.4.4 Model Performance Evaluation

Smart predict provides many performance indicators for the classification or regression models. Most of them are standard indicators that we've already detailed in Section 13.3. In this section, we'll explain two performance indicators that are specific to smart predict, *predictive power* and *prediction confidence*. These performance indicators don't depend on a specific decision threshold, similarly to AUC.

The *predictive power* is a measure of the model quality, that is, of how well it explains the data of the training dataset by comparing it to a hypothetical perfect model. This comparison is performed using a gain chart, as illustrated in Figure 13.7. The surface between the validation curve and the random curve is divided by the surface between the perfect model curve and the random curve:

Predictive power = C ÷ (A + B + C)

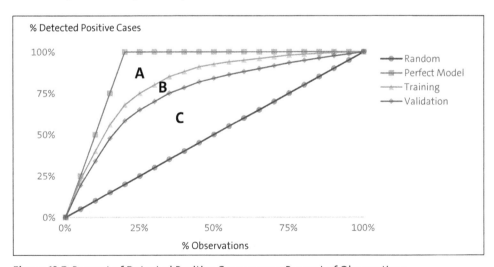

Figure 13.7 Percent of Detected Positive Cases versus Percent of Observations

The value of the predictive power is between 0 and 1:

- A predictive power value close to 0 denotes a model that didn't perform better than a random model on the validation set. The **Validation** curve for such a model is close to the **Random** curve, leading to a surface C close to 0 and a predictive power close to 0.

- A predictive power value close to 1 denotes a model that performed almost as well as a perfect model on the validation set. The validation curve for such a model is very close to the **Perfect Model** curve, meaning that the surface C is almost equal to the surface (A + B + C). As a result, the predictive power is close to 0. A perfect or almost perfect model should be considered with caution. A predictive power very close to 1 may be the sign that a leak variable is used by the model.

The prediction confidence measures the model's robustness, that is, the likelihood that the model will be as accurate on new data as it was on the training data, by measuring how far the **Validation** curve is from the **Training** curve in Figure 13.7. The prediction confidence is calculated using the following formula:

Prediction confidence = 1 – B ÷ (A + B + C)

The value of the prediction confidence is between 0 and 1. The predictive power should be as close as possible to 1. The prediction confidence can be increased by adding more rows to the training dataset.

13.5   Generating Predictive Insights

This section provides details about how smart predict generates predictive insights for classification or regression. We'll cover both the predicted category and the prediction explanations options.

13.5.1   Predicted Category

The classification models generated by smart predict don't predict a category directly. Instead, they predict the probability that the observation belongs to the positive category of the target. The predicted category is derived from the predicted probability. Internally, the observations of the application dataset are sorted by increasing the predicted probability, and a decision threshold is applied. The observations with a probability higher or equal to the threshold are predicted as belonging to the positive category of the target, and the observation with a probability lower than the threshold are predicted as belonging to the negative category of the target. Figure 13.8 and Figure 13.9 illustrate these methods with different thresholds.

While having to choose a decision threshold can be perceived as a constraint, it's in fact a lever that allows you to fine-tune the predictions for your specific business requirements. As explained in Section 13.3.1, different decision thresholds correspond to different confusion matrixes: It's possible to choose a threshold to favor the model sensitivity or the model specificity, for instance.

Let's look at the results with a lower and higher threshold. Figure 13.8 and Table 13.4 show the results for a lower threshold. With this threshold, the sensitivity is equal to 1.

Overall the model has detected all the positive cases of the reference dataset. But this comes with a cost: The model has wrongly predicted positive for eight negative cases.

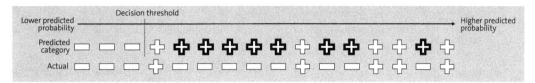

Figure 13.8 Low Decision Threshold

Accuracy = 0.5		Predicted Class	
		Positive	Negative
Actual Class	Positive	True Positive = 5	False Negative = 0
	Negative	False Positive = 8	True Negative = 3

Table 13.4 Confusion Matrix for Figure 13.8

Figure 13.9 and Table 13.5 show the results for a higher and more selective threshold. There are fewer false alarms, but it's at the expense of sensitivity: Two positive cases have been missed.

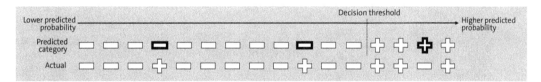

Figure 13.9 High Decision Threshold

Accuracy = 0.8		Predicted Class	
		Positive	Negative
Actual Class	Positive	True Positive = 3	False Negative = 2
	Negative	False Positive = 1	True Negative = 10

Table 13.5 Confusion Matrix for Figure 13.9

For a disease screening scenario, you would probably prefer the lower decision threshold that allows for catching more positive cases. For a spam detection scenario, on the other hand, you would probably prefer the higher decision threshold that reduces the risk of false alarms.

13.5.2   Prediction Explanations

The measure of the impact of the prediction explanations is called the *strength*. It's calculated as follows:

$$strength_i = \frac{contribution_i}{\sigma}$$

Here, *strength*$_i$ is the strength of the influencer, *contribution*$_i$ is the contribution of the influencer *i* for the considered prediction, and σ is the standard deviation of the contributions of all the influencers used by the classification model over the validation dataset.

The strength is a normalized measure of the contribution and hence can't be interpreted as a probability (when summed, the strengths for a prediction aren't equal to the predicted probability) when working with classification models.

Thanks to the *1/σ* factor, the strength can be interpreted as the distance to the average expressed in number of standard deviations. A contribution that is 1 standard deviation lower than the average contribution leads to a strength value of -1, a contribution that is 2 standard deviations higher than the average contribution leads to a strength of 2, and so on.

In statistics, it's usual to measure the distance to and from the average using the standard deviation as the distance unit. Referring to Figure 13.10, we can see that for a normal distribution, most values (68.2%) would be at less than 1 deviation from the average.

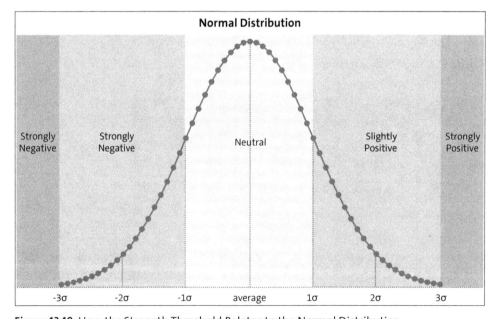

Figure 13.10 How the Strength Threshold Relates to the Normal Distribution

These values aren't significantly different from the average, and a strength between -1 and 1 can be regarded as neutral as the impact is neither significantly positive nor significantly negative. On the other hand, only a few values are expected to lie further than 3 standard deviations (0.4% of the values), so a strength higher than 3 and lower than -3 can be regarded as strong.

Therefore, we recommend using -3, -1, 1, and 3 as the default threshold values when discretizing the strength. But this is only an all-purpose default recommendation. It may make sense for your specific use case to differentiate neutral positive and neutral negative, to add one more threshold at -2 and 2, and so on.

13.6 Summary

In this chapter, we unveiled the data science behind the classification and regression models. First, we touched on the foundational idea that training a model fits a function and mentioned some resulting prerequisites. Then, you learned how the performance of a classification is evaluated. Finally, we explained some specific aspects of the smart predict implementation of the classification and regression algorithms.

We've reached the end of our exploration of predictive analytics in SAP Analytics Cloud. We'll wrap up in the next chapter with a look back on what we've learned.

13

Chapter 14
Conclusion

Now that we're at the end of our predictive analytics journey, let's take a quick moment to summarize what you've learned from this book, what the future of predictive scenarios in SAP Analytics Cloud could look like, and where you can go from here, armed with your new knowledge.

14.1 Lessons Learned

In Part I of this book, you learned about the predictive analytics capabilities offered by SAP Analytics Cloud (the predictive scenarios) and how to successfully implement a predictive analytics project. Our goal was to make sure that you get an initial view of the possibilities offered by SAP Analytics Cloud.

In Part II, you then learned everything you need to know about time series forecasting models. You learned what they are, how to use them in the context of enterprise planning processes, and how to automate them. You then deepened your knowledge to the specific use of time series forecasting models on top of datasets to the overall best practices, hints, and tips you need to be aware of when using time series forecasting models. Finally, you discovered the automated data science that makes the creation of time series forecasting models possible.

In Part III, you learned more about classification and regression models. You discovered how insights from classification models, such as the predicted probability of a specific event, can be used to enrich stories. You then discovered regression models and the type of outcomes you can use to enrich stories with predicted values, for instance. You were introduced to the automated data science that makes the creation of classification and regression models possible.

All throughout the book, our main goal was to introduce you to all the important aspects of predictive analytics capabilities so that you can feel at ease and empowered when it's your turn to put them into practice.

14.2 The Future of Predictive Scenarios in SAP Analytics Cloud

This book describes the predictive scenario capabilities as they are in the first quarter of 2024. Yet, remember that SAP Analytics Cloud is a software as a service (SaaS) product and continuously evolves through four annual deliveries. By the end of 2024, the solution will be quite different from the one we know today.

Therefore, we highly recommend that you can keep an eye to the future product road map: *http://s-prs.co/v577123*. You can be part of the future of SAP Analytics Cloud predictive capabilities. You can refer to and vote on existing product enhancement requests at *http://s-prs.co/v577124* or create new ones via *http://s-prs.co/v577125*.

You can also stay informed on SAP Community at *http://s-prs.co/v577126*. In addition, you can refer to this central blog that lists all resources on the go: *http://s-prs.co/v577127*.

14.3   Your Next Steps

Now it's time for you to start or continue using the solution by yourself. Start your first experiments with the sample data we've provided in this book or try your own! The best way to learn is to select business questions with corresponding data and to put the predictive capabilities in action. You can, for instance, leverage known websites such as *www.kaggle.com/*, *https://ourworldindata.org/*, or *https://datasetsearch.research.google.com/* to pick a few interesting datasets to get started.

Now, at the end of this book, we wish you success with your predictive projects in SAP Analytics Cloud. Happy predicting!

The Authors

Antoine Chabert is a product manager for SAP Analytics Cloud. He joined SAP more than 16 years ago and developed his expertise in SAP Analytics products, including SAP BusinessObjects, SAP Lumira, SAP Predictive Analytics, and SAP Analytics Cloud, in various functional roles. He helps SAP Analytics Cloud customers get the most out of the product and he works with SAP Engineering to create exciting innovations, connecting predictive analytics, business intelligence, and planning. Antoine holds a master's degree in computer science engineering. Outside of the office, he loves reading, playing badminton, and spending time with his family.

David Serre is the product owner of the smart predict capability in SAP Analytics Cloud. He works closely with the product management team to convert customer needs into the features delivered in smart predict. David holds a master's degree in computer science and data exploration. In 2007, he started working as a software developer and later became a product owner for KXEN, an editor of predictive solutions. David joined SAP in 2014 and has worked as product owner for predictive analytics and smart predict since then.

Index

- Your all-in-one guide to SAP Analytics Cloud

- Connect to data sources and create stories, visualizations, and dashboards

- Develop planning models, predictive models, and analytical applications

Abassin Sidiq

SAP Analytics Cloud

Discover the next generation of BI with this guide to SAP Analytics Cloud! Get your data into the system and see which data models to use in which situations. Next, learn about stories—how to create visualizations for them, publish them, and enhance them. With expanded information on the analytics designer, analytics catalog, and planning models, this fully updated edition is your one-stop shop for all your SAP Analytics Clouds needs!

421 pages, 3rd edition, pub. 02/2024
E-Book: $74.99 | **Print:** $79.95 | **Bundle:** $89.99

www.sap-press.com/5753

- Optimize the performance of SAP Analytics Cloud applications and dashboards

- Build efficient models and make improvements to the story builder and analytics designer apps

- Learn to measure, test, and monitor performance

Bertram, Dannenhauer, Holzapfel, Loop, Range

SAP Analytics Cloud Performance Optimization Guide

Frustrated with slow performance in SAP Analytics Cloud? This guide is your answer! Learn the basics of solution performance and optimization and then start making your adjustments: get the story builder and analytics designer apps running smoothly, fine-tune your backend settings, and follow best practices for viewing dashboards. With detailed examples of performance improvements throughout, this book has everything you need for an optimal SAP Analytics Cloud experience!

344 pages, pub. 08/2023
E-Book: $84.99 | **Print:** $89.95 | **Bundle:** $99.99

www.sap-press.com/5669

- Master financial planning, budgeting, and forecasting in SAP Analytics Cloud with step-by-step instructions

- Connect to source systems and model financial planning data

- Run automatic planning logic, simulations, and what-if analysis for your organization

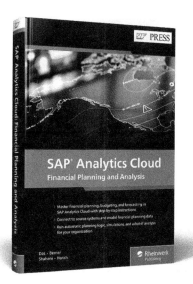

Das, Berner, Shahani, Harish

SAP Analytics Cloud: Financial Planning and Analysis

FP&A is now in the cloud! In this comprehensive guide, begin by provisioning your data for financial planning and analysis in SAP Analytics Cloud. Then follow step-by-step instructions to set up the planning process and use SAP Analytics Cloud's automated planning logic to calculate key metrics. Learn how to perform simulations to model what-if scenarios, streamline your planning workflow, and share results with stakeholders. With details on implementation best practices, this is your all-in-one resource!

468 pages, pub. 06/2022

E-Book: $84.99 | **Print:** $89.95 | **Bundle:** $99.99

www.sap-press.com/5486

- Learn to design and develop interactive dashboards with SAP Analytics Cloud for consumption and integration

- Build dashboards with acquired data, live SAP BW data, SAP S/4HANA Cloud data, and more

- Use R scripts and the analytics designer to create complex dashboards

Bertram, Charlton, Hollender, Holzapfel, Licht, Paduraru

Designing Dashboards with SAP Analytics Cloud

SAP Analytics Cloud is overflowing with visualization options. Charts, tables, drilldowns, geomaps—if you can dream it, you can design and build it. Learn how to create a dashboard for any use case, from acquired data dashboards and responsive mobile dashboards to procurement dashboards using SAP S/4HANA Cloud data. Follow step-by-step instructions to structure your data, choose the relevant features, and then implement them. Contains custom-designed dashboards for each chapter!

344 pages, pub. 07/2021
E-Book: $84.99 | **Print:** $89.95 | **Bundle:** $99.99

www.sap-press.com/5235

Interested in reading more?

Please visit our website for all new book
and e-book releases from SAP PRESS.

www.sap-press.com

Made in the USA
San Bernardino, CA
30 November 2019

6067505SR00069

Additional Notes:

Additional Notes:

Additional Notes:

Additional Notes:

Additional Notes:

Dr. Jylla Moore Tearte
20th International Grand Basileus
Centennial Commission Chair

Soror Denise Marie Snow
Centennial Passport Chair

Soror Sheila Bowers
Compilation of Photos

Soror Doris McAdams Stokes
Compilation of Quotes

100

DATE: ----------------------------------

EVENT: ---------------------------------

MOMENT TO REMEMBER: ----------

AFFIX STAMP HERE

PASSPORT *the Journey to Centennial*

CELEBRATING ONE CENTURY · OF SERVICE
ZΦB
1920 2020

DATE:

EVENT:

MOMENT TO REMEMBER:

AFFIX STAMP HERE

the Journey to Centennial

ΖΦΒ
CELEBRATING ONE CENTURY · OF SERVICE
1920
2020

the Journey to Centennial PASSPORT

LEGACY

ZETA

<<<<<< ZETA PHI BETA SORORITY, INC.

DATE: _____

EVENT: _____

MOMENT TO REMEMBER: _____

AFFIX STAMP HERE

PASSPORT

the Journey to Centennial

ZΦB

CELEBRATING ONE CENTURY · OF SERVICE ·
1920 2020

>>
ZETA PHI BETA SORORITY, INC. <<<<<<

DATE: _____

EVENT: _____

MOMENT TO REMEMBER: _____

AFFIX STAMP HERE

the Journey to Centennial

PASSPORT

ZΦB
CELEBRATING ONE CENTURY · OF SERVICE ·
1920   2020

>>>
<<<<<< ZETA PHI BETA SORORITY, INC. >>>>>>

DATE: _____

EVENT: _____

MOMENT TO REMEMBER: _____

AFFIX STAMP HERE

PASSPORT
the Journey to Centennial

2 0 1 8

the Journey to Centennial **PASSPORT**

DATE: _____

EVENT: _____

MOMENT TO REMEMBER: _____

_____

_____

_____

_____

_____

AFFIX STAMP HERE

_____

_____

_____

_____

_____

_____

_____

_____

How will Zeta be a stronger organization because of my personal commitment to service, scholarship, sisterhood and finer Womanhood?

PASSPORT
the Journey to Centennial

ZΦB
CELEBRATING ONE CENTURY · OF SERVICE ·
1920 2020

DATE: _____

EVENT: _____

MOMENT TO REMEMBER: _____

AFFIX STAMP HERE

_____
_____
_____
_____
_____
_____
_____
_____
_____
_____
_____

>>
<<<<<< ZETA PHI BETA SORORITY, INC.

>>>
>>>>>> ZETA PHI BETA SORORITY, INC. <<<<<<

DATE: _____

EVENT: _____

MOMENT TO REMEMBER: _____

AFFIX STAMP HERE

the Journey to Centennial

PASSPORT

ZΦB

CELEBRATING ONE CENTURY · OF SERVICE ·

1920   2020

>>>
<<<<<< ZETA PHI BETA SORORITY, INC.

DATE:

EVENT:

MOMENT TO REMEMBER:

AFFIX STAMP HERE

PASSPORT *the Journey to Centennial*

ZΦB
CELEBRATING ONE CENTURY · OF SERVICE ·
1920 2020

>>
ZETA PHI BETA SORORITY, INC. <<<<<<

DATE: _____

EVENT: _____

MOMENT TO REMEMBER: _____

AFFIX STAMP HERE

the Journey to **Centennial**

PASSPORT

ZΦB
CELEBRATING ONE CENTURY · OF SERVICE
1920 2020

When will I experience my transformation as a next level community-conscious, action-oriented member?

PASSPORT

the Journey to
Centennial

ZΦB · CELEBRATING ONE CENTURY · OF SERVICE · 1920 · 2020

DATE: _____

EVENT: _____

MOMENT TO REMEMBER: _____

AFFIX STAMP HERE

>>
ZETA PHI BETA SORORITY, INC. <<<<<<

AFFIX STAMP HERE

DATE: _____

EVENT: _____

MOMENT TO REMEMBER: _____

PASSPORT

the Journey to Centennial

ZΦB

CELEBRATING ONE CENTURY · OF SERVICE

2020

1920

SERVICE · SIST

Founders Events

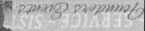

>>>>>>>>>>>>>>>>>>>>>>>>>>>>>>>>>>>>
<<<<< ZETA PHI BETA SORORITY, INC.

DATE:

EVENT:

MOMENT TO REMEMBER:

AFFIX STAMP HERE

PASSPORT *the Journey to Centennial*

ZΦB · CELEBRATING ONE CENTURY · OF SERVICE · 1920 · 2020

>>
>>>>>> ZETA PHI BETA SORORITY, INC. <<<<<<

DATE: --------------------------------

EVENT: -------------------------------

MOMENT TO REMEMBER: --------------------

AFFIX STAMP HERE

ZΦB

the Journey to Centennial

PASSPORT

CELEBRATING ONE CENTURY · OF SERVICE
1920 2020

>>>
<<<<<< ZETA PHI BETA SORORITY, INC.

DATE: _____

EVENT: _____

MOMENT TO REMEMBER: _____

AFFIX STAMP HERE

PASSPORT the Journey to Centennial

ZΦB
CELEBRATING ONE CENTURY · OF SERVICE
1920 2020

Who will I connect with as I travel the highways reflected in
"The House by the Side of the Road"?

>>>>>>>>>>>>>>>>>>>>>>>>>>>>>>>>>>>>>>>
>>>>>> ZETA PHI BETA SORORITY, INC. <<<<<<

AFFIX STAMP HERE

DATE: _____
EVENT: _____
MOMENT TO REMEMBER: _____

the Journey to Centennial PASSPORT

ZΦB
1920 2020
CELEBRATING ONE CENTURY OF SERVICE

GLOBAL YEAR OF SERVICE
2017
ZETA PHI BETA SORORITY, INCORPORATED
40 MILLION HOURS OF SERVICE

<<<<<< ZETA PHI BETA SORORITY, INC. <<<<<<

84

DATE:

EVENT:

MOMENT TO REMEMBER:

AFFIX STAMP HERE

PASSPORT

the Journey to Centennial

ZΦB

CELEBRATING ONE CENTURY · OF SERVICE ·
1920 · 2020

>>>>>>>>>>>>>>>>>>>>>>>>>>>>>>>>>>>>>>
<<<<<< ZETA PHI BETA SORORITY, INC. <<<<<<

DATE: ------------------------------

EVENT: ------------------------------

MOMENT TO REMEMBER: ------------------------------

AFFIX STAMP HERE

PASSPORT *the Journey to Centennial*

ZΦB — CELEBRATING ONE CENTURY · OF SERVICE

1920 2020

GLOBAL YEAR OF SERVICE

ZETA PHI BETA SORORITY, INCORPORATED · 2017

50 MILLION HOURS OF SERVICE

<<<<< ZETA PHI BETA SORORITY, INC.

DATE: _____

EVENT: _____

MOMENT TO REMEMBER: _____

AFFIX STAMP HERE

PASSPORT *the Journey to Centennial*

ZΦB
CELEBRATING ONE CENTURY · OF SERVICE
1920 2020

Where will I travel to capture and record memories of my journey?

>>>
ZETA PHI BETA SORORITY, INC. <<<<<<

81

AFFIX STAMP HERE

DATE:

EVENT:

MOMENT TO REMEMBER:

PASSPORT

the Journey to Centennial

ZΦB

CELEBRATING ONE CENTURY · OF SERVICE

2020

1920

#ZPHIB97

GLOBAL YEAR OF SERVICE

ZETA PHI BETA SORORITY, INCORPORATED

2017

30 MILLION HOURS OF SERVICE

>>>
>>>>>> ZETA PHI BETA SORORITY, INC. <<<<<<

DATE: _____

EVENT: _____

MOMENT TO REMEMBER: _____

AFFIX STAMP HERE

PASSPORT *the Journey to Centennial*

CELEBRATING ONE CENTURY · OF SERVICE · 2020 · 1920 · ZΦB

>>>>>>>>>>>>>>>>>>>>>>>>>>>>>>>>>>>>>>>
>>>>>> ZETA PHI BETA SORORITY, INC. <<<<<<

AFFIX STAMP HERE

DATE: _____

EVENT: _____

MOMENT TO REMEMBER: _____

the Journey to Centennial PASSPORT

ZΦB

CELEBRATING ONE CENTURY OF SERVICE

1920 2020

<<<<<< ZETA PHI BETA SORORITY, INC.

DATE: _____

EVENT: _____

MOMENT TO REMEMBER: _____

AFFIX STAMP HERE

PASSPORT *the Journey to* Centennial

ZΦB — CELEBRATING ONE CENTURY · OF SERVICE · 1920 2020

What will I do to "Be Finer in 2020"?

<<<<<<<<<<<<<<<<<<<<<<<<<<<<<<<<<<<<<<<<
ZETA PHI BETA SORORITY, INC. <<<<<<

DATE: _____

EVENT: _____

MOMENT TO REMEMBER: _____

AFFIX STAMP HERE

ZΦB
CELEBRATING ONE CENTURY · OF SERVICE
1920 2020

the Journey to Centennial PASSPORT

>>>
<<<<<< ZETA PHI BETA SORORITY, INC.

DATE: ------------------------------

EVENT: ------------------------------

MOMENT TO REMEMBER: ------------------------------

AFFIX STAMP HERE

PASSPORT *the Journey to Centennial*

>>>>>> ZETA PHI BETA SORORITY, INC. <<<<<<

AFFIX STAMP HERE

DATE: _____

EVENT: _____

MOMENT TO REMEMBER: _____

PASSPORT

the Journey to Centennial

ZΦB

CELEBRATING ONE CENTURY · OF SERVICE

1920 2020

GLOBAL YEAR OF SERVICE

ZETA PHI BETA SORORITY, INCORPORATED

2017

30 MILLION HOURS OF SERVICE

>>>>>>>>>>>>>>>>>>>>>>>>>>>>>>>>>>>>>>
<<<<<< ZETA PHI BETA SORORITY, INC. <<<<<<

PASSPORT
the Journey to Centennial

ZΦB
CELEBRATING ONE CENTURY · OF SERVICE
1920 2020

"Nothing is more powerful than an idea whose time has come. Such was the case nearly 100 years ago, when Brother Charles A. Taylor introduced to soror Arizona (Leaver Stemons) the idea of starting a new sisterhood predicated on the principles of sisterhood, scholarship, service and finer womanhood."

— Honorable Micheal E. Cristal,
International President, Phi Beta Sigma Fraternity, Inc.

DATE: _____

EVENT: _____

MOMENT TO REMEMBER: _____

AFFIX STAMP HERE

>>>
<<<<<<
ZETA PHI BETA SORORITY, INC. <<<<<<

AFFIX STAMP HERE

DATE: _____
EVENT: _____
MOMENT TO REMEMBER: _____

PASSPORT *the Journey to Centennial*

ZΦB
· CELEBRATING ONE CENTURY OF SERVICE ·
1920 2020

<<<<<< ZETA PHI BETA SORORITY, INC.

AFFIX STAMP HERE

MOMENT TO REMEMBER: -----------

EVENT: -----------------

DATE: ----------------

PASSPORT *the Journey to* *Centennial*

<<<<<<<
ZETA PHI BETA SORORITY, INC. <<<<<<

DATE: _____

EVENT: _____

MOMENT TO REMEMBER: _____

AFFIX STAMP HERE

PASSPORT

the Journey to
Centennial

ZΦB
CELEBRATING ONE CENTURY · OF SERVICE ·
1920   2020

GLOBAL YEAR OF SERVICE
2017
ZETA PHI BETA SORORITY, INCORPORATED
20 MILLION HOURS OF SERVICE

70

>>>
<<<<< ZETA PHI BETA SORORITY, INC.

DATE: _____

EVENT: _____

MOMENT TO REMEMBER: _____

AFFIX STAMP HERE

PASSPORT *the Journey to Centennial*

ZΦB
1920 · 2020
CELEBRATING ONE CENTURY · OF SERVICE

"The oath you took did not make you a Zeta, it made you a member,
but how you live that oath is what makes you a Zeta."
– Soror Mary Breaux Wright, 24th International Grand Basileus, 2012

the *Journey to Centennial* PASSPORT

DATE: _____

EVENT: _____

MOMENT TO REMEMBER: _____

_____

_____

_____

_____

_____

_____

_____

_____

_____

_____

_____

_____

_____

AFFIX STAMP HERE

ZETA PHI BETA SORORITY, INC. <<<<<<
<<<<<<<<<<<<<<<<<<<<<<<<<<<<<<<<<<<<<

69

>>>>>>>>>>>>>>>>>>>>>>>>>>>>>>>>>>>
<<<<<< ZETA PHI BETA SORORITY, INC.

DATE: _____

EVENT: _____

MOMENT TO REMEMBER: _____

_____

_____

_____

_____

_____

_____

_____

_____

_____

_____

_____

_____

_____

_____

_____

AFFIX STAMP HERE

PASSPORT *the Journey to Centennial*

ZΦB — CELEBRATING ONE CENTURY OF SERVICE — 1920 2020

>>>
>>>>>> ZETA PHI BETA SORORITY, INC. <<<<<<

AFFIX STAMP HERE

DATE: _____

EVENT: _____

MOMENT TO REMEMBER: _____

the Journey to Centennial

PASSPORT

ZΦB
CELEBRATING ONE CENTURY · OF SERVICE
1920 2020

GLOBAL YEAR OF SERVICE
ZETA PHI BETA SORORITY, INCORPORATED
2017
20 MILLION HOURS OF SERVICE

\>>>
\>>>>>> ZETA PHI BETA SORORITY, INC.

DATE: _____

EVENT: _____

MOMENT TO REMEMBER: _____

AFFIX STAMP HERE

PASSPORT

the Journey to Centennial

ZΦB

CELEBRATING ONE CENTURY · OF SERVICE ·
1920 2020

"I believe that it is important that one be passionate about the things that consume one's time, and I am passionate about Zeta...."

— Soror Sheryl P. Underwood, 23rd International Grand Basileus

the Journey to Centennial PASSPORT

DATE: _____

EVENT: _____

MOMENT TO REMEMBER: _____

_____

_____

_____

_____

_____

_____

_____

_____

_____

_____

_____

_____

_____

AFFIX STAMP HERE

>>
>>>>>> ZETA PHI BETA SORORITY, INC.

DATE: _____

EVENT: _____

MOMENT TO REMEMBER: _____

AFFIX STAMP HERE

PASSPORT

the Journey to Centennial

CELEBRATING ONE CENTURY · OF SERVICE ·
ZΦB
1920 2020

the *Journey to* **PASSPORT**
Centennial

DATE: _____

EVENT: _____

MOMENT TO REMEMBER: _____

_____

_____

_____

_____

_____

_____

AFFIX STAMP HERE

_____

_____

_____

_____

_____

_____

_____

_____

_____

ZETA PHI BETA SORORITY, INC. <<<<<<
<<<<<<<<<<<<<<<<<<<<<<<<<<<<<<<<<<<

63

> "Many chapters have implemented innovative and successful projects as part of the Z-Hope initiative, and we all ought to be extremely proud of the difference we are making in the lives of women, men, girls and boys in the communities we serve."
> – Soror Barbara C. Moore, 22nd International Grand Basileus

PASSPORT
the Journey to Centennial

CELEBRATING ONE CENTURY · OF SERVICE
1920 ZΦB 2020

AFFIX STAMP HERE

DATE: _____

EVENT: _____

MOMENT TO REMEMBER: _____

_____
_____
_____
_____
_____
_____
_____
_____
_____
_____
_____
_____
_____

<<<<<< ZETA PHI BETA SORORITY, INC.
<<<<<<<<<<<<<<<<<<<<<<<<<<<<<<<<<<

>>>>>>>>>>>>>>>>>>>>>>>>>>>>>>>>>>>>>>
<<<<<< ZETA PHI BETA SORORITY, INC. <<<<<

AFFIX STAMP HERE

DATE: _____

EVENT: _____

MOMENT TO REMEMBER: _____

ΖΦΒ

CELEBRATING ONE CENTURY · OF SERVICE
1920 · 2020

the Journey to Centennial

PASSPORT

Create A Museum
Ida

>>>>>>>>>>>>>>>>>>>>>>>>>>>>>>>>>>>>>
<<<<<< ZETA PHI BETA SORORITY, INC.

DATE: _____

EVENT: _____

MOMENT TO REMEMBER: _____

AFFIX STAMP HERE

PASSPORT
the Journey to Centennial

ZΦB — CELEBRATING ONE CENTURY · OF SERVICE — 1920 2020

<<<<<< ZETA PHI BETA SORORITY, INC. <<<<<<

AFFIX STAMP HERE

DATE: _____

EVENT: _____

MOMENT TO REMEMBER: _____

_____

_____

_____

_____

_____

_____

_____

_____

_____

_____

the Journey to Centennial

PASSPORT

> "While we build on the past, it is critical that we plan for a future for Zeta—one in which we will be recognized for the quality of work performed and the demonstration of a sincere commitment to a turbulent, struggling world...through service, technology, education and leadership."
> – Dr. Barbara West Carpenter, 21st International Grand Basileus, 1996

PASSPORT

the Journey to
Centennial

CELEBRATING ONE CENTURY
1920
ZΦB
2020
OF SERVICE

AFFIX STAMP HERE

DATE: _____

EVENT: _____

MOMENT TO REMEMBER: _____

_____

_____

_____

_____

_____

_____

_____

_____

_____

_____

_____

_____

_____

_____

_____

<<<<<< ZETA PHI BETA SORORITY, INC.
<<<<<<<<<<<<<<<<<<<<<<<<<<<<<<<<<<

>>>>>>>>>>>>>>>>>>>>>>>>>>>>>>>>>>>>>>
ZETA PHI BETA SORORITY, INC. <<<<<<

AFFIX STAMP HERE

DATE: _____

EVENT: _____

MOMENT TO REMEMBER: _____

ZΦB
1920 2020
CELEBRATING ONE CENTURY · OF SERVICE ·

the Journey to
Centennial

PASSPORT

>>
>>>>>> ZETA PHI BETA SORORITY, INC. >>>>>>

DATE: _____

EVENT: _____

MOMENT TO REMEMBER: _____

AFFIX STAMP HERE

PASSPORT *the Journey to Centennial*

ZΦB
CELEBRATING ONE CENTURY · OF SERVICE ·
1920 2020

55

ZETA PHI BETA SORORITY, INC. <<<<<<

AFFIX STAMP HERE

DATE:

EVENT:

MOMENT TO REMEMBER:

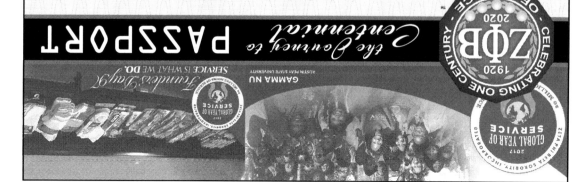

PASSPORT — the Journey to Centennial

ΖΦΒ

ΖΦΒ 2020 1920 CELEBRATING ONE CENTURY · OF SERVICE

GLOBAL YEAR OF SERVICE 2017 · ZETA PHI BETA SORORITY, INCORPORATED

GAMMA NU
AUSTIN PEAY STATE UNIVERSITY

SERVICE IS WHAT WE DO.

Founder's Day

"Soar on, Sweet Zeta! Ride the White Dove as it lifts its wings in its flight of love."
— Soror Nancy Shepard, 1996, 75th Anniversary Celebration

PASSPORT *the Journey to* *Centennial*

CELEBRATING ONE CENTURY
1920
ZΦB
2020
OF SERVICE

AFFIX STAMP HERE

DATE: _____

EVENT: _____

MOMENT TO REMEMBER: _____

_____

_____

_____

_____

_____

_____

_____

_____

_____

_____

_____

_____

_____

_____

AFFIX STAMP HERE

DATE: _____

EVENT: _____

MOMENT TO REMEMBER: _____

ΖΦΒ
1920 · 2020
CELEBRATING ONE CENTURY · OF SERVICE ·
TM

the Journey to Centennial

PASSPORT

"Zeta Phi Beta Sorority, Inc.: Phenomenal Women, Sisters, Girls and Friends...
Proclaiming a Legacy of World Class Service" – 1995, 75th Anniversary
– Dr. Jylla Moore Tearte, 20th International Grand Basileus

PASSPORT *the Journey to Centennial*

CELEBRATING ONE CENTURY
1920 ZΦB 2020
OF SERVICE

AFFIX STAMP HERE

DATE: ....

EVENT: ....

MOMENT TO REMEMBER: ....

....

....

....

....

....

....

....

....

....

....

....

....

....

<<<<<< ZETA PHI BETA SORORITY, INC.
<<<<<<<<<<<<<<<<<<<<<<<<<<<<<<<<<<<

>>>>>> ZETA PHI BETA SORORITY, INC. <<<<<<

DATE: _____

EVENT: _____

MOMENT TO REMEMBER: _____

_____

_____

_____

_____

_____

AFFIX STAMP HERE

PASSPORT *the Journey to Centennial*

ZΦB · CELEBRATING ONE CENTURY OF SERVICE · 1920 2020

>>>
>>>>>> ZETA PHI BETA SORORITY, INC. <<<<<<

AFFIX STAMP HERE

MOMENT TO REMEMBER: --------

EVENT: --------------------

DATE: ------------------------

PASSPORT *the Journey to Centennial*

>>>
ZETA PHI BETA SORORITY, INC. <<<<<<

DATE: _____

EVENT: _____

MOMENT TO REMEMBER: _____

AFFIX STAMP HERE

the Journey to **PASSPORT**
Centennial

ZΦB
CELEBRATING ONE CENTURY · OF SERVICE ·
1920 2020

"No other issue should be of more critical importance to each and every member of
the African American community than the crisis affecting our African American males."
– Dr. Eunice S. Thomas, 19th Grand Basileus, 1990

PASSPORT *the Journey to Centennial*

CELEBRATING ONE CENTURY
1920 ZΦB 2020
OF SERVICE

AFFIX STAMP HERE

DATE: _____

EVENT: _____

MOMENT TO REMEMBER: _____

_____
_____
_____
_____
_____
_____

_____
_____
_____
_____
_____
_____
_____
_____
_____
_____

<<<<<< ZETA PHI BETA SORORITY, INC.
<<<<<<<<<<<<<<<<<<<<<<<<<<<<<<<<

>>
<<<<<< ZETA PHI BETA SORORITY, INC. <<<<<<

DATE: _____

EVENT: _____

MOMENT TO REMEMBER: _____

AFFIX STAMP HERE

PASSPORT

the Journey to Centennial

ZΦB
1920 — 2020
CELEBRATING ONE CENTURY · OF SERVICE

Douglass School/
Arizona Cleaver Stemons
Park

<<<<<< ZETA PHI BETA SORORITY, INC.

DATE: _____

EVENT: _____

MOMENT TO REMEMBER: _____

AFFIX STAMP HERE

PASSPORT *the Journey to* *Centennial*

ZΦB

CELEBRATING ONE CENTURY · OF SERVICE ·
1920 2020

\|\|\|\|\|\|\|\|\|\|\|\|\|\|\|\|\| (barcode)

>>>>>>>>>>>>>>>>>>>>>>>>>>>>>>>>>>>>>>>
<<<<<< ZETA PHI BETA SORORITY, INC. <<<<<<

AFFIX STAMP HERE

DATE: _____

EVENT: _____

MOMENT TO REMEMBER: _____

PASSPORT

the Journey to Centennial

ZΦB
CELEBRATING ONE CENTURY · OF SERVICE ·
1920 2020

>>>>>>>>>>>>>>>>>>>>>>>>>>>>>>>>>>>>>
>>>>>> ZETA PHI BETA SORORITY, INC.

44

DATE: _____

EVENT: _____

MOMENT TO REMEMBER: _____

AFFIX STAMP HERE

PASSPORT
the Journey to Centennial

ΖΦΒ
CELEBRATING ONE CENTURY · OF SERVICE ·
1920 2020

"Zeta Phi Beta members are involved in a wide and impressive range of programs, projects, and activities that exemplify excellence in community outreach."
— Dr. Edith V. Francis, 18th Grand Basileus, circa 1980-1986

>>>>>> ZETA PHI BETA SORORITY, INC. <<<<<

DATE: _____

EVENT: _____

MOMENT TO REMEMBER: _____

AFFIX STAMP HERE

the Journey to *Centennial*

PASSPORT

ZΦB
CELEBRATING ONE CENTURY · OF SERVICE ·
1920 2020

>>>>>>>>>>>>>>>>>>>>>>>>>>>>>>>>>>>
<<<<<< ZETA PHI BETA SORORITY, INC.

DATE: _____

EVENT: _____

MOMENT TO REMEMBER: _____

AFFIX STAMP HERE

PASSPORT
the Journey to Centennial

the Journey to Centennial PASSPORT

ZΦB CELEBRATING ONE CENTURY OF SERVICE 1920 2020

DATE:_____

EVENT:_____

MOMENT TO REMEMBER:_____

_____

_____

_____

_____

_____

AFFIX STAMP HERE

_____

_____

_____

_____

_____

_____

_____

_____

>>
<<<<<< ZETA PHI BETA SORORITY, INC.

DATE: _____

EVENT: _____

MOMENT TO REMEMBER: _____

_____

_____

_____

_____

_____

_____

_____

_____

_____

_____

_____

_____

_____

AFFIX STAMP HERE

PASSPORT

the Journey to
Centennial

ΖΦΒ
CELEBRATING ONE CENTURY · OF SERVICE
1920 · 2020

"Zeta Phi Beta Sorority, Inc. ... a Community-Conscious, Action-Oriented Organization."
— Dr. Janice Gantt Kissner, 17th Grand Basileus, 1975

>>>>>>>>>>>>>>>>>>>>>>>>>>>>>>>>>>>>
<<<<<< ZETA PHI BETA SORORITY, INC. <<<<<<

AFFIX STAMP HERE

DATE: _____

EVENT: _____

MOMENT TO REMEMBER: _____

PASSPORT

the Journey to Centennial

SERVICE IS WHAT WE DO.

Founders' Day 1920

ZΦB
CELEBRATING ONE CENTURY · OF SERVICE
1920 2020

<<<<<< ZETA PHI BETA SORORITY, INC.

DATE: _____

EVENT: _____

MOMENT TO REMEMBER: _____

AFFIX STAMP HERE

PASSPORT

the Journey to Centennial

ZΦB — CELEBRATING ONE CENTURY · OF SERVICE · 1920 2020

36

>>
>>>>>> ZETA PHI BETA SORORITY, INC. <<<<<<

AFFIX STAMP HERE

DATE: _____

EVENT: _____

MOMENT TO REMEMBER: _____

PASSPORT
the Journey to Centennial

ZΦB
CELEBRATING ONE CENTURY · OF SERVICE ·
1920 2020

3F

DATE: _____

EVENT: _____

MOMENT TO REMEMBER: _____

AFFIX STAMP HERE

PASSPORT
the Journey to
Centennial

ZΦB
1920 2020
CELEBRATING ONE CENTURY · OF SERVICE

"Wherever I went and whatever I did, I was always aware that
consciously or unconsciously someone was saying, 'That's Zeta Phi Beta sorority.'"
— Soror Isabel Morgan Herson, 16th Grand Basileus, 1970

<<<<<< ZETA PHI BETA SORORITY, INC. <<<<<<

AFFIX STAMP HERE

DATE: _____

EVENT: _____

MOMENT TO REMEMBER: _____

PASSPORT

the Journey to Centennial

ΖΦΒ
CELEBRATING ONE CENTURY · OF SERVICE ·
1920   2020

DATE: _____

EVENT: _____

MOMENT TO REMEMBER: _____

AFFIX STAMP HERE

PASSPORT
the Journey to Centennial

ZΦB · CELEBRATING ONE CENTURY OF SERVICE · 1920 2020

"As we strive for perfection in Zeta, let it begin within each of us."
— Soror Mildred (Carter Bradham, 15th Grand Basileus, 1970, 50th Anniversary)

>>>>>>>>>>>>>>>>>>>>>>>>>>>>>>>>>>>>>>>
ZETA PHI BETA SORORITY, INC. <<<<<<

AFFIX STAMP HERE

DATE:

EVENT:

MOMENT TO REMEMBER:

PASSPORT

the Journey to
Centennial

ZΦB
1920 · 2020
CELEBRATING ONE CENTURY · OF SERVICE ·

35

On Soror Ida B. King, "She was a parliamentarian of rare talent,
an eloquent speaker, and a possessor of "une certaine de chapeaux."
– Soror Ola Adams, 1962

PASSPORT
the Journey to
Centennial

ZΦB
CELEBRATING ONE CENTURY · OF SERVICE ·
1920 2020

DATE: _____

EVENT: _____

MOMENT TO REMEMBER: _____

_____

_____

_____

_____

_____

_____

_____

_____

_____

_____

_____

_____

_____

_____

AFFIX STAMP HERE

>>>
<<<<<< ZETA PHI BETA SORORITY, INC. <<<<<<

AFFIX STAMP HERE

DATE: _____

EVENT: _____

MOMENT TO REMEMBER: _____

PASSPORT
the Journey to Centennial

ZΦB
CELEBRATING ONE CENTURY · OF SERVICE ·
1920 2020

DATE: _____

EVENT: _____

MOMENT TO REMEMBER: _____

_____

_____

_____

_____

_____

_____

_____

_____

_____

_____

_____

_____

_____

AFFIX STAMP HERE

PASSPORT

the Journey to Centennial

ZΦB 1920 2020 · CELEBRATING ONE CENTURY · OF SERVICE ·

ZETA PHI BETA SORORITY, INC. <<<<<<

AFFIX STAMP HERE

DATE: _____

EVENT: _____

MOMENT TO REMEMBER: _____

PASSPORT

the Journey to Centennial

ZΦB

CELEBRATING ONE CENTURY · OF SERVICE ·
1920 2020

SERVICE IS WHAT WE DO.

Founder's Day

2017 GLOBAL YEAR OF SERVICE

CENTENNIAL

Zeta Phi Beta

ZETA PHI BETA SORORITY INC.
The Journey To Centennial Launch Party
January 9, 2015 · Houston, Texas
"I WAS THERE"

"Those that don't got it, can't show it. Those that got it, can't hide it."
- Soror Zora Neale Hurston, 1903-1960

PASSPORT *the Journey to Centennial*

AFFIX STAMP HERE

DATE: _____

EVENT: _____

MOMENT TO REMEMBER: _____

_____

_____

_____

_____

_____

_____

_____

_____

_____

_____

_____

_____

_____

_____

_____

_____

<<<<<< ZETA PHI BETA SORORITY, INC.
<<<<<<<<<<<<<<<<<<<<<<<<<<<<<<<

>>>>>>>>>>>>>>>>>>>>>>>>>>>>>>>>>>>>>>
<<<<<<<
ZETA PHI BETA SORORITY, INC. <<<<<<

DATE: _____

EVENT: _____

MOMENT TO REMEMBER: _____

AFFIX STAMP HERE

PASSPORT

the Journey to Centennial

ZΦB
CELEBRATING ONE CENTURY · OF SERVICE · 2020 1920

Founders Day 9?

SERVICE IS WHAT WE DO.

>>>>>>>>>>>>>>>>>>>>>>>>>>>>>>>>>>>>>>
>>>>>> ZETA PHI BETA SORORITY, INC.

"It is that bond of sisterly love in Zeta women that unites us and makes us grow."

— Founder Myrtle Tyler Faithful, 1920

PASSPORT

the Journey to Centennial

ZΦB
CELEBRATING ONE CENTURY · OF SERVICE
1920 2020

DATE: _____

EVENT: _____

MOMENT TO REMEMBER: _____

_____

_____

_____

_____

_____

_____

_____

_____

_____

_____

_____

_____

_____

AFFIX STAMP HERE

>>>
ZETA PHI BETA SORORITY, INC. <<<<<<

AFFIX STAMP HERE

DATE: _____

EVENT: _____

MOMENT TO REMEMBER: _____

the Journey to Centennial

PASSPORT

ZΦB
CELEBRATING ONE CENTURY · OF SERVICE ·
1920 2020

SERVICE IS WHAT WE DO.

Founders Day

<<<<<< ZETA PHI BETA SORORITY, INC. <<<<<<

DATE: _____

EVENT: _____

MOMENT TO REMEMBER: _____

AFFIX STAMP HERE

PASSPORT

the Journey to Centennial

ZΦB · CELEBRATING ONE CENTURY · OF SERVICE · 1920 2020

DATE:

EVENT:

MOMENT TO REMEMBER:

AFFIX STAMP HERE

ZΦB
CELEBRATING ONE CENTURY · OF SERVICE ·
1920 2020

the Journey to Centennial

PASSPORT

22

>>
<<<<<< ZETA PHI BETA SORORITY, INC.

DATE: _____

EVENT: _____

MOMENT TO REMEMBER: _____

_____

_____

_____

_____

_____

_____

_____

_____

_____

_____

_____

_____

_____

_____

AFFIX STAMP HERE

PASSPORT

the Journey to Centennial

ZΦB
CELEBRATING ONE CENTURY · OF SERVICE
1920 2020

"We must accept the responsibilities that accompany this achievement, realizing that integration, like democracy, is a great social achievement, not a legacy; therefore, it may not simply be inherited."
— Dr. Deborah (Cannon) P. Wolfe, 14th Grand Basileus, 1955

>>>>>>>>>>>>>>>>>>>>>>>>>>>>>>>>>>>>>>>
ZETA PHI BETA SORORITY, INC. <<<<<<

AFFIX STAMP HERE

DATE: _____

EVENT: _____

MOMENT TO REMEMBER: _____

PASSPORT *the Journey to Centennial*

ZΦB
1920 2020
CELEBRATING ONE CENTURY · OF SERVICE

>>>>>>>>>>>>>>>>>>>>>>>>>>>>>>>>>>>>>>>
<<<<<< ZETA PHI BETA SORORITY, INC.

"I was honored to charter the first chapter in Monrovia on the West Coast of Africa
and Zeta became the first sorority to establish a chapter there."
— Dr. Nancy Bullock McGhee, 13th Grand Basileus, 1948

PASSPORT
the Journey to
Centennial

ZΦB — CELEBRATING ONE CENTURY · OF SERVICE · 1920 · 2020

DATE: _____

EVENT: _____

MOMENT TO REMEMBER: _____

AFFIX STAMP HERE

>>
>>>>>> ZETA PHI BETA SORORITY, INC. <<<<<<

AFFIX STAMP HERE

DATE: _____

EVENT: _____

MOMENT TO REMEMBER: _____

PASSPORT *the Journey to Centennial*

ZΦB
CELEBRATING ONE CENTURY · OF SERVICE ·
1920 2020

>>>>>>>>>>>>>>>>>>>>>>>>>>>>>>>>>>>>>>
>>>>> ZETA PHI BETA SORORITY, INC.

DATE: ----------------------------------

EVENT: ----------------------------------

MOMENT TO REMEMBER: ----------------

AFFIX STAMP HERE

PASSPORT *A Journey to the Centennial*

CELEBRATING ONE CENTURY · OF SERVICE · 1920 · 2020 · ZΦB

>>
ZETA PHI BETA SORORITY, INC. <<<<<<

AFFIX STAMP HERE

DATE:

EVENT:

MOMENT TO REMEMBER:

The Journey to Centennial

PASSPORT

ZΦB
1920 2020
CELEBRATING ONE CENTURY · OF SERVICE ·

"The lamp of learning is passed from hand to hand, the seed maturing
becomes the many seeds of future plantings."
— Founder Arizona (Leaver) Stemons, 1955

PASSPORT
the Journey to
Centennial

ZΦB
CELEBRATING ONE CENTURY · OF SERVICE ·
1920 2020

DATE:

EVENT:

MOMENT TO REMEMBER:

AFFIX STAMP HERE

>>
>>>>>> ZETA PHI BETA SORORITY, INC. <<<<<<

AFFIX STAMP HERE

MOMENT TO REMEMBER: ---------------------------------

EVENT: --

DATE: --

PASSPORT

the Journey to Centennial

ZΦB

CELEBRATING ONE CENTURY · OF SERVICE
1920   2020

Shades of Blue

Sister Circle

"Every soror is a torchbearer.... let us keep them (young people) ever mindful of the moral standards which make us appealing and which have characterized women through the ages."
– Soror Lullelia Walker Harrison, 12th Grand Basileus, 1945,

25th Anniversary

PASSPORT
the Journey to Centennial

ZΦB — CELEBRATING ONE CENTURY • OF SERVICE • 1920 2020

DATE: ----------------

EVENT: ----------------

MOMENT TO REMEMBER: ----------------

AFFIX STAMP HERE

>>
>>>>>> ZETA PHI BETA SORORITY, INC.

13

>>
ZETA PHI BETA SORORITY, INC. <<<<<<

AFFIX STAMP HERE

DATE: _____

EVENT: _____

MOMENT TO REMEMBER: _____

PASSPORT

the Journey to Centennial

ZΦB

CELEBRATING ONE CENTURY · OF SERVICE ·
1920 2020

25

>>>>>>>>>>>>>>>>>>>>>>>>>>>>>>>>>>>
<<<<<< ZETA PHI BETA SORORITY, INC.

DATE: _____

EVENT: _____

MOMENT TO REMEMBER: _____

AFFIX STAMP HERE

PASSPORT
the Journey to Centennial

ZΦB
1920 2020
· CELEBRATING ONE CENTURY · OF SERVICE ·

the Journey to Centennial PASSPORT

DATE: _____

EVENT: _____

MOMENT TO REMEMBER: _____

_____

_____

_____

_____

_____

_____

_____

_____

_____

_____

_____

_____

_____

AFFIX STAMP HERE

> "I, too, had a dream in the early 1920s of a group of the world's finest women to become sisters of Phi Beta Sigma fraternity. Thank God I have lived to see my dream come true."
> — Honorable Brother Charles Robert Taylor, 1930

PASSPORT *the Journey to Centennial*

CELEBRATING ONE CENTURY · 1920 ZΦB 2020 · OF SERVICE

AFFIX STAMP HERE

DATE: _____

EVENT: _____

MOMENT TO REMEMBER: _____

_____
_____
_____
_____
_____

_____
_____
_____
_____
_____
_____
_____
_____

10

<<<<<< ZETA PHI BETA SORORITY, INC.
<<<<<<<<<<<<<<<<<<<<<<<<<<<<<<<<<<

>>
ZETA PHI BETA SORORITY, INC. <<<<<<

DATE: _____

EVENT: _____

MOMENT TO REMEMBER: _____

AFFIX STAMP HERE

the Journey to Centennial
PASSPORT

ZΦB
CELEBRATING ONE CENTURY · OF SERVICE
1920 · 2020

>>
>>>>>> ZETA PHI BETA SORORITY, INC.

DATE: _____

EVENT: _____

MOMENT TO REMEMBER: _____

AFFIX STAMP HERE

PASSPORT
the Journey to Centennial

ZΦB
1920 2020
CELEBRATING ONE CENTURY · OF SERVICE

>>
<<<<<< ZETA PHI BETA SORORITY, INC. <<<<<<

AFFIX STAMP HERE

DATE: _____

EVENT: _____

MOMENT TO REMEMBER: _____

PASSPORT

the Journey to Centennial

ZΦB

CELEBRATING ONE CENTURY · OF SERVICE
1920 2020

PASSPORT

the Journey to
Centennial

DATE: _____

EVENT: _____

MOMENT TO REMEMBER: _____

AFFIX STAMP HERE

ΖΦΒ CELEBRATING ONE CENTURY · OF SERVICE · 1920 2020

"No Greek-letter organization has a greater movement than ours—'Finer Womanhood.'"
— Soror Venetia E. Nichols, 1920

5

>>>>>>>>>>>>>>>>>>>>>>>>>>>>>>>>>>>>
<<<<<< ZETA PHI BETA SORORITY, INC. <<<<<<

DATE:

EVENT:

MOMENT TO REMEMBER:

AFFIX STAMP HERE

PASSPORT

the Journey to
Centennial

ZΦB
CELEBRATING ONE CENTURY · OF SERVICE
1920 2020

4

>>>

<<<<<< ZETA PHI BETA SORORITY, INC.

DATE: _____

EVENT: _____

MOMENT TO REMEMBER: _____

AFFIX STAMP HERE

PASSPORT

the Journey to
Centennial

ZΦB · CELEBRATING ONE CENTURY · OF SERVICE · 1920 2020

"When Zeta calls, we'll answer one and all."

– Soror Anita Turpeau, 1924

3

AFFIX STAMP HERE

DATE:

EVENT:

MOMENT TO REMEMBER:

PASSPORT

the Journey to Centennial

ZΦB

CELEBRATING ONE CENTURY · OF SERVICE
1920   2020

SERVICE IS WHAT WE DO.

Founders Family

<<<<<< ZETA PHI BETA SORORITY, INC. <<<<<<<<<<<<<<<<<<<<<<<<<<<<<<<<<<<<<<<

DATE: _____

EVENT: _____

MOMENT TO REMEMBER: _____

AFFIX STAMP HERE

PASSPORT *the Journey to Centennial*

ZΦB

CELEBRATING ONE CENTURY · OF SERVICE ·
1920 2020

PASSPORT *the Journey to Centennial*

ZΦB
1920 · 2020 · CELEBRATING ONE CENTURY · OF SERVICE

DATE: _____

EVENT: _____

MOMENT TO REMEMBER: _____

AFFIX STAMP HERE

ZETA PHI BETA SORORITY, INC. <<<<<<
>>>

"A Zeta is a girl, regardless of race, creed or color, who has high standards and principles, a good scholarly average and an active interest in all things that she undertakes to accomplish."

Founder Viola Tyler Goings, circa 1920-1930

"I have a profound admiration and respect for those of you who have worked and built the fine structure upon the foundation laid in 1920: A structure whose fundamental principles are Sisterly Love, Service, Scholarship, and Finer Womanhood."

Founder Myrtle Tyler Faithful, 1960

WELCOME TO
"THE JOURNEY TO CENTENNIAL"

The Journey to Centennial officially launched on Friday, January 9, 2015 at the National Executive Board Meeting. Our journey concludes at the National Executive Board Meeting in January 2021.

There are poignant, pivotal and provocative questions that we must ask along this journey. THINK about:

- What will I do to "Be Finer in 2020"?
- Where will I travel to capture and record memories of my journey?
- Who will I connect with as I travel the highways reflected in "The House by the Side of the Road"?
- When will I experience my transformation as a next level community conscious, action-oriented member?
- How will Zeta be a stronger organization because of my personal commitment to Service, Scholarship, Sisterhood and Finer Womanhood?

Capture your personal mile-markers in this PASSPORT on your *Journey to Centennial.* It is going to be the trip of a lifetime!

Dr. Jylla Moore Tearte
20th International Grand Basileus
Centennial Commission Chair

CENTENNIAL PASSPORT INSTRUCTIONS

This PASSPORT has been officially licensed by Zeta Phi Beta Sorority, Incorporated's Centennial Commission and should only be used by members of Zeta Phi Beta Sorority. This PASSPORT may be obtained at designated Sorority events through 2020 and online at Amazon. You must be present at the event to receive the stamp.

Members may create and purchase their own stamps to commemorate an event or personal brand through the official *Centennial Passport Project.* For more information on creating or purchasing a stamp for your *Centennial Passport Experience,* contact: centennialpassport2020@gmail.com

Stamp and/or sticker originators, please register all PASSPORT stamps and/or stickers at the official Centennial Website: www.zphib2020.com

ZETA PHI BETA SORORITY, INCORPORATED

OFFICIAL
CENTENNIAL PASSPORT

PERSONAL DATA:

Name..
<<<<<<<<<<<<<<<<<<<<<<<<<<<<<<<<<<<<<<<<

Initiating
Chapter..
<<<<<<<<<<<<<<<<<<<<<<<<<<<<<<<<<<<<<<<<

City/State...
<<<<<<<<<<<<<<<<<<<<<<<<<<<<<<<<<<<<<<<<

Initiating Date/Year ....
<<<<<<<<<<<<<<<<<<<<<<<<<<<<<<<<<<<<<<<<

Grand Basileus
During
Initiating Year ....
<<<<<<<<<<<<<<<<<<<<<<<<<<<<<<<<<<<<<<<<

Current Chapter..
<<<<<<<<<<<<<<<<<<<<<<<<<<<<<<<<<<<<<<<<

City/State...
<<<<<<<<<<<<<<<<<<<<<<<<<<<<<<<<<<<<<<<<

Centennial
Visionaries
Number
<<<<<<<<<<<<<<<<<<<<<<<<<<<<<<<<<<<<<<<<

"Thanks to God for permitting
me to see this day
(40th Anniversary Celebration).
This is a day for rejoicing
for past successes and looking
to the future for higher hills to
climb in service. God give us hills!
And strength for climbing."

Founder Pearl A. Neal, 1960

Sorors and Amicae:

Our incredible journey to celebrate the Founders of Zeta continues as we travel to Centennial in 2020!

Thank you for plotting your course as we celebrate this momentous occasion with this third edition of the Centennial

Passport. It is my hope that this passport will serve not only as a memento of your experiences but also as an example of your passion and commitment to serve and engage as a member of our blue and white family. I trust that every stamp, signature, photograph and/or souvenir will be a marker for how far we've come together and where our journey will take us next.

I am honored to be your leader during this once-in-a-lifetime journey and I look forward to meeting you on the road to "Be Finer in 2020!"

Our Journey Continues with Love,

Valerie Hollingsworth-Baker
25ᵗʰ International Grand Basileus

How fortunate to be a Soror

whose chapter was organized

by one of the "Five Pearls"!

Founder Fannie Pettie Watts, 1949

"In the beginning, the five of us,

Viola Tyler, Myrtle Tyler,

Pearl Neal, Fannie Pettie, and

myself did whatever

our hands found to do."

Founder Arizona Cleaver Stemons, 1920

ZETA PHI BETA SORORITY, INCORPORATED

ESTABLISHED
JANUARY 16, 1920

ZETA PHI BETA SORORITY, INCORPORATED
SCHOLARSHIP – SERVICE – SISTERHOOD – FINER WOMANHOOD

MW006373124

the Journey to Centennial

Passport

CELEBRATING ONE CENTURY · OF SERVICE ·
ZΦB
2020
1920
TM

ZETA PHI BETA SORORITY, INCORPORATED